BRECHT
IN EXILE

BRECHT
IN EXILE

· ·

BRUCE COOK

A New Republic Book
HOLT, RINEHART and WINSTON
New York

First published in January 1983 by Holt, Rinehart and Winston, 383 Madison Avenue, New York, New York 10017.

Published simultaneously in Canada by Holt, Rinehart and Winston of Canada, Limited.

Library of Congress Cataloging in Publication Data
Cook, Bruce, 1932–
Brecht in exile.
Includes bibliographical references and index.
1. Brecht, Bertolt, 1898–1956—Biography—Exile.   2. Authors, German—20th century—Biography.   I. Title
PT2603.R397Z5836   832′.912   82-2926
ISBN: 0-03-060278-5   AACR2

First Edition

Designer: Robert Bull

Printed in the United States of America

10 9 8 7 6 5 4 3 2 1

Grateful acknowledgment is given to the following publishers for permission to reprint portions from:

Bertolt Brecht Poems: 1913–1956, copyright © 1976 by Eyre Methuen, Ltd. Reprinted by permission of the publisher, Methuen, Inc., by arrangement with Suhrkamp Verlag, Frankfurt 1. All rights reserved.

ISBN 0-03-060278-5

ACKNOWLEDGMENTS

Although in the research and writing of this book, I have made use of interviews and a certain amount of unpublished material (principally the incomplete Brecht files made available by the Central Intelligence Agency and the Federal Bureau of Investigation), it is for the most part a book written from other books. Those I have used are cited in the text and in the notes to each chapter. Below, I offer acknowledgment for permission to quote from certain of them. However, I think it only fair to mention a few works that have been far more useful in providing background than might be indicated by the occasional reference or quotation. Those books are: *Bertolt Brecht in America*, by James K. Lyon; *Brecht: A Biography*, by Klaus Völker; *The Brothers Mann*, by Nigel Hamilton; *The Days Grow Short*, by Ronald Sanders; and *Bertolt Brecht: His Life, His Art, and His Times*, by Frederic Ewen. To them and the rest I now give formal acknowledgment.

Citadel Press:
—for excerpts from *Bertolt Brecht: His Life, His Art, and His Times*, by Frederic Ewen. Copyright © 1967 by Frederic Ewen.
Doubleday:
—for excerpts from *Brecht: The Man and His Work*, by Martin Esslin. Copyright © 1960 by Martin Esslin.
Grove Press:
—for excerpts from *Galileo*, by Bertolt Brecht; English version by Charles Laughton; Introduction by Eric Bentley. Copyright © 1966 by Eric Bentley. Reprinted by permission of Grove Press, Inc.

*For Karen Lewis, who suffered through most of this,
and Clifford Ridley, who came through for me*

ONTENTS

PREFACE

Just what we need, you say with an ironic sneer, *another* book on Bertolt Brecht! But before you toss it aside, allow me to argue why this one is different from the rest. Although it covers a period in the playwright's life—his years in exile—that has been treated in other books (much of it with great thoroughness in James K. Lyon's *Bertolt Brecht in America*), it does so from quite a different perspective and with a distinct attitude.

I remember that early in my research on this project I was out in Los Angeles tracking down some of the surviving members of the wartime German émigré community who knew Brecht there. I had been referred to Al Brownmuller of UCLA as someone who might be helpful to me in making contacts—and so he proved to be. After a pleasant lunch in the faculty club on the campus, during which he supplied me with names, addresses, advice, and encouragement, we headed back together toward the building where he had his office. There at the entrance we stood talking a while longer before I was to leave him and head for my car. It was then, as I recall, that Professor Brownmuller asked me where I taught. When I told him, "Nowhere," he seemed slightly astonished. "You mean," he said, "you're a man of letters? You write about whatever pleases you?" I thought about that for a moment. I had been at this for years but had never thought of my work quite like that. Finally, I said, "Well, I wouldn't describe myself as a man of letters, exactly. I'd say I was more of a literary hustler."

If that seems excessively demeaning, then be assured, first of all, that I meant there to be no pejorative connotation. I simply intended that writing about literature these days without the support and dignity lent by an academic position is a not-quite-respectable enterprise at best, one that demands a certain extra energy and craftiness of its practitioners. It's a hustle—a business. I should have used the more polite term and called myself a literary journalist. I certainly don't shrink from *that* label, nor do I feel it necessary to justify it. No less a critic than Edmund Wilson called himself that and nothing more; and if as good and profoundly intelligent a writer as he was saw his work as literary journalism, then why should I pretend to some grander title? Wilson's perspective was always that of the professional writer. His hat was firmly on his head, no matter what or whom he sat down to write about. And I suppose the specific point of view from which this study of Brecht has been written is also that of the professional writer. I have no vested interest in the subject—either political, theatrical, or academic. Not being a committed "Brecht man," I feel no obligation to press the case for him, as some have done, beyond the point where biographical or textual evidence will support it.

So you see that with this point of view comes the distinct attitude to which I referred. This is no exercise in Brechtolatry. A certain skepticism, to put it mildly, should be immediately evident in what follows, and it seems to me that such an approach to Brecht and his work is long overdue. So much has been claimed for him without ever really having been proved that I think a bit of methodological doubt may have the effect of provoking a reexamination of what has now come to be assumed—Brecht's greatness as a writer and his essential humanism.

That conversation with Al Brownmuller took place longer ago than I like to think. This project has stretched on a bit, I'm afraid. Why? To a large extent it is because the more I learned about Brecht the less I liked him. I already knew that I had difficulties with a good deal of his work. That was why I had chosen in the first place to write about his years in exile. I felt that much of what he had written for the theater before he was forced to leave Germany in 1933 was of negligible importance, or in any case was greatly overrated by the hard-core Brechtians. It seemed to me that I could do a fairer job by concentrating on the period in which he wrote those plays—*Mother Courage, Galileo, Herr Puntila and His Man Matti, The Good Woman of Setzuan,* and *The Caucasian Chalk Circle*—on which his reputation truly rests. Any artist deserves to be judged by his best work.

But since the book was conceived as literary biography I could do no less than put those works in the context of his life. And, as I said, the more I found out about that life the less I found to admire in it. Now, it is not absolutely necessary to admire a man to write about him, but it certainly makes the work much easier. I attempted to press on regardless, with not especially satisfying results. The hundred pages or so that I wrote might have covered the territory but they failed in any real way to reflect my misgivings about Brecht, the man and the artist. And so there the project sat until at last I came up with the present approach.

What you have here is a series of connected essays covering Bertolt Brecht's life from 1933 until its end in 1956. Using the essay form has made it possible for me not just to present incidents, events, and attitudes but to comment upon them as well. That is the advantage. The disadvantage of this approach is that because the essays were mostly independently conceived and written, a certain amount of repetition was necessary to set each subject in context. My editor and I have done what we could to eliminate redundance, but in a few cases we have had to retain details that had been given elsewhere in the text in order to make a point more forcefully or tell a story more completely. For these instances I apologize and ask your indulgence.

FIVE DIFFICULTIES IN WRITING ABOUT BRECHT

In 1934, while in his first full year on the lam from the Nazis, Bertolt Brecht wrote a didactic essay intended for secret distribution in which he discussed "Five Difficulties in Writing the Truth." He dealt with them systematically, setting them forth in the first paragraph as follows:

> Whoever wishes to fight against lies and ignorance and write the truth today, has at least five difficulties to overcome. He must *have the courage* to write the truth, even though it is everywhere suppressed; the *intelligence* to recognize it, even though it is everywhere concealed; the *art* to wield it as a weapon; the *judgment* to choose in whose hands it will be effective; the *cunning* to spread it among them. . . .[1]

1   ·

Here, as was usually the case at this time in his life, the "truth" with which Brecht was concerned was political. However, the five difficulties he set forth are of a general kind, and to me at least they suggest certain specific problems in writing the truth about Brecht's own work as an artist.

1. THE COURAGE TO WRITE THE TRUTH

Courage? To write the truth about Brecht? Well, yes—it takes a little. While the Gestapo will certainly not come banging on my door in the middle of the night for what I have to say about him (neither would they on Brecht's, by the way: he advised German writers on truth-telling from the comparative safety of Denmark), there is nevertheless a certain risk involved. Any writer who today treats Brecht as simply another writer invites the wrath of the entire Brecht establishment in all its academic pomp and theatrical glory. Could Brecht, for example, be considered as a playwright whose career followed the usual pattern—whose early work was of negligible value and who only later, during less than a decade, produced the handful of plays for which he is justly famous? Evidently not. Brecht has become one whose most casual plagiarism is exalted by scholars and critics alike as work of lasting importance. He has acquired, according to Martin Esslin's slightly ironic assessment, "the status of an established international classic."[2] Or, as it was put to me in all seriousness by an academic recently, "Brecht is the most important writer since Shakespeare."

In a way, neither Brecht's work nor even the man himself is the problem here. It is his reputation that seems to get in the way—and that is how it has always been. As a young man, he played the *enfant terrible* with such gusto that he managed to shock even Berlin, which in the twenties seemed to have a terrible infant bawling on nearly every street corner. He was especially eager to mock the German literary establishment and the standards of artistic dignity for which it stood. Once established as a poet and playwright, Brecht went so far as to write an advertising jingle for the Steyr Motor Car Company, to which he signed his name, and for which he took a new Steyr as payment. Extolling the sport mystique, he wrote a poem in praise of the middleweight boxing champions ("This is the story of the world middleweight champions/Their fights and careers from the year

1891/To the present day.");[3] and he served the German prizefighter, Paul Samson-Körner, as ghost writer on the latter's autobiography, posing for photographs with him and promising all concerned that Samson-Körner was "a great and significant type." Brecht went out of his way to offend his literary elders in his Berlin days, picking fights he could not then hope to win with the likes of Franz Werfel and Thomas Mann. Werfel, according to Brecht, wrote "kitsch," and Mann's were "artificial, empty and useless books."

When Brecht turned from rowdyism to Marxism during the last years of the Weimar Republic, he was making the sort of choice that most artists of his generation in Germany were making at that time. As the Nazi storm troopers and the Communist Party's *Roter Kampfferband* clashed almost daily, the nation polarized: many who were previously indifferent or moderate began taking one side or the other. The writers, artists, and composers of the Weimar Republic, long the targets of Nazi propaganda, moved almost to a man to the far Left. But Brecht, being Brecht, moved further and faster than the rest; after all, he had a reputation for extremism to uphold. As a result, he left the popular mode in which he had, with Kurt Weill, had his only popular success *(The Threepenny Opera)* and began writing his "didactic plays," of which the most notorious is *The Measures Taken*. Dealing in terms of approval, as it does, with the murder by two Communists of a third who endangers their clandestine mission, it was not in the least popular with Party critics, for it treated openly questions of discipline that Party leaders would just as soon have kept quiet. To this day it repels sympathetic liberal critics. Ronald Gray, for example, in *Brecht: The Dramatist*: "How did Brecht manage to [write such a work]? . . . He may have been playing at politics, putting forward on paper, for the theatre, conclusions he did not expect to see realized in actual life."[4]

But whether he was playing or was in earnest, Brecht was fixed politically by *The Measures Taken* and other works just as extreme, most of which were written when he first embraced Marxism. His reputation as a dogmatic, disciplined Communist activist far exceeded his performance, but that reputation was quite enough to make it necessary for him to flee Germany when the Reichstag burned and Hitler claimed emergency powers. It was also enough to keep him more or less on the run across Europe until at last he left the continent behind him and came, by the longest route possible, to America, only months before Pearl Harbor. Finally, it was that reputation as a Communist activist that brought him under the surveillance of the FBI and, at the end, before the House Committee on Un-American Activities as the eleventh "unfriendly" witness to testify after those who soon became known as the Hollywood Ten. Interestingly, one of the few specific works of Brecht's that he was asked about by his Congressional interrogators was *The Measures Taken*: "Now, Mr. Brecht, will you tell the Committee whether or not one of the characters of this play was murdered by his comrades because it was in the best interests of the party, of the Communist Party; is that true?"[5]

Ultimately, Brecht's appearance before the House Committee on Un-American Activities enhanced his reputation. It made him and his work immediately acceptable in Western Europe and England (not to mention Eastern Europe). Stages were made available; the plays he had written on the run across Europe and in his Hollywood exile (which include all his best work) were performed, most of them for the first time. It was only then—on the strength of these later plays—that the idea of Brecht as a modern classic was born. It was only after he was given a theater company of his own by the German Democratic Republic that he came to be taken seriously as a theorist of stagecraft and acting. Only a few intimates of his knew much about his "alienation effect" and his notions of the Epic Theater before the Berliner Ensemble began touring Europe. Brecht's reintroduction to American audiences took place only gradually during the fifties. Since he left this country in 1947, most presentations of his plays have been university productions. His champion here—in early days his only champion—was Eric Bentley, then as now an academic. Not only did Bentley preach Brecht's gospel at the colleges and universities where he taught, he also translated his plays, and even mounted a production or two himself. Brecht approved of all this. He must have known instinctively that his best chances for survival, for achieving classic status, lay with the noncommercial theater. In any case, that is how it has worked out here in America, where his reputation is in large part a creation of the university community.

A couple of the Brecht productions back in the fifties are worth noting, particularly those of the Playwrights Theatre Club of Chicago. In the long run, their *Caucasian Chalk Circle* (1953) and *The Threepenny Opera* (1954) were the most influential of any in America—certainly more than any university production and even more than the long-running Off Broadway *Threepenny* that starred Lotte Lenya. Why was the Playwrights' Brecht of such importance? Because Playwrights Theatre was one of the early incarnations of the Second City company, the improvisational group that has contributed so many performers to the theater, movies, and television; in fact, Ed Asner, Barbara Harris, and Zohra Lampert were in one or both of those productions. More important, though, was that they were directed by Paul Sills, probably the first conscious Brechtian in American theater. Through his early work with Second City (he has long since left the company, though he was its founding director) and later with his Story Theatre, he has had great and deep, if somewhat covert, influence on American theater—on American acting in particular. That broad, satirical *external* style that we associate with so many actors today—George Segal, Alan Arkin, Valerie Harper, Barbara Harris, Anthony Holland, and the rest—derives directly from their experience in improvisational theater (for many, with Sills), and indirectly from Brecht.

And so to write the truth about Brecht, one must be prepared to take on not only the academic establishment, but also an entrenched faction in show business. All of them, too, have assumed an attitude of embattled loyalty toward their man. Any criticism of him seems to be taken as an attack. They have adopted Brecht as a political position.

2. THE INTELLIGENCE TO RECOGNIZE IT

Bertolt Brecht's personality has always been a puzzle to me. Who was he, anyway? Was he the plaster saint of so many of the essays and studies? Or was he, as at least his most thorough biographer to date, Klaus Völker, presents him in *Brecht: A Biography*, a well-intentioned man who was upon occasion forced to act less than honorably, or was he again something different? His life, and to a certain extent his work as well, has been clouded in myth, a good deal of which was created by Brecht himself. These myths are of a particularly potent kind: they not only tend to obscure a truth but in many cases persuade us to believe its opposite. Some examples?

Brecht always presented himself as a willing collaborator, one who had overcome the bourgeois notion of individual authorship and favored group creation. Indeed, during his career more than fifty people collaborated to one degree or another on various works. These included composers such as Kurt Weill and Hanns Eisler, fellow authors such as Lion Feuchtwanger, and others who simply supplied ideas, like Elisabeth Hauptmann, Margarete Steffin, and Ruth Berlau. How did he work with them? It varied, of course, but one of his collaborators, Bernhard Reich *(A Man's a Man)*, described the process this way:

> When a visitor came Brecht saw in this a lucky occasion for his work—he read him an especially ticklish part, testing the quality of the work on the other or reconsidering it with him. And sitting immediately down to the typewriter, he would hammer out a new version. He understood that the work profits if many take part in it. Brecht gathered around him young people—assistants. They put material together, talked through his plans with him, brought forth proposals, alterations, improvements. They were listed in the printed edition of his work as collaborators.[6]

In fine print, that is, on the reverse side of the title page, tucked into the copyright material. The impolite term for this sort of "collaboration" is brain-picking, and Brecht seems to have done a good deal of it. Even his publisher, Siegfried Unseld, remarks in his book *The Author and His Publisher*, "Whoever didn't qualify as [a collaborator] was soon dropped from his circle of acquaintances."[7]

Many, if not most, of these "collaborators" were women. In fact one of them, Elisabeth Hauptmann, had the distinction of taking the rap for Brecht on one occasion when a play on which he was working was doomed to certain failure. *Happy End*, which was to succeed *The Threepenny Opera* as the next Brecht-Weill collaboration, simply could not be whipped into shape, because Brecht, having undergone a conversion, was giving all his attention to his Marxist "didactic plays." A production was set and songs had been written by Weill, but the play was going to be a disaster, and Brecht knew it. Indeed, it turned out to be, but it was assigned at the last minute to Elisabeth Hauptmann, his secretary and "collaborator." She became nominally the author of *Happy End*. Brecht took credit only for the lyrics to Weill's excellent songs.

This was fairly typical of Brecht's treatment of Hauptmann—and of women in general. He used them professionally, sexually, and any damned way it pleased him—and a few of them he used up. Hauptmann attempted suicide when he married his second wife, Helene Weigel. When he set out for America from Finland with Weigel and their children, he had not one but two mistresses in tow. He left one of them, Margarete Steffin, to die along the way in Moscow. The other, Ruth Berlau, died an alcoholic some years after bearing him an illegitimate child, one of at least two he is known to have fathered. He was no Don Juan. He had no need to be: from the time he began writing until his death, women simply flocked to him, attracted (mesmerized!) by what they perceived as his genius—and he availed himself of whatever they had to offer.

With all this, the irony is that Brecht is widely held to be a champion of women because he wrote such excellent roles for them— *Mother Courage, The Good Woman of Setzuan, St. Joan of the Stockyards*, and *The Visions of Simone Machard*, among others. The fact that he shared leadership of the Berliner Ensemble with Helene Weigel is also cited in his favor, but actually Brecht treated her no better than any of the rest of his women; he was simply wise enough to make use of her abilities as an actress and as an executive.

What kind of man was he? It would be easy and perhaps even just to write him off as an opportunist—a bad man, simply put. God knows he acted badly often enough. There are instances of cowardice, greed, cruelty, and dishonesty in his life. And if that is how he was, then that is how he was. Often, after all, I think we expect too much of our artists—of our writers, in particular. As though it were not enough for them to write well, we also expect them to behave well, to be nothing less than moral exemplars. Hence the reaction against Robert Frost and Ernest Hemingway following their deaths, as it has gradually been revealed what rats they really were. What relation have ability and morality? None. We have only to reflect on Céline and Solzhenitsyn to realize that: Céline—fascist, anti-Semite, in some ways a vicious sort—wrote like an angel (a dark one); Solzhenitsyn, a difficult man perhaps, but withal a kind of modern saint, writes so crudely and clumsily that if he had not had to *smuggle* his manuscripts out to the West they would probably never have been translated and published here at all.

Strictly speaking, all that should be asked of Bertolt Brecht was whether he wrote well. Part of the time he did; he had great talent as a young writer, and it developed to maturity under the most difficult conditions, some of them self-imposed. Did he have genius? He showed it in his best work, so he must have had. It was just that as an artist he kept himself under such firm intellectual and political control that his genius seems almost to have "escaped" into such plays as *Mother Courage, Puntila and Matti, The Caucasian Chalk Circle*, and *Galileo*.

Yes, into *Galileo* especially. It is the most autobiographical drama of this least autobiographical of playwrights. Written in Denmark, rewritten for the Charles Laughton production in America in 1947, and rewritten again for the Berliner Ensemble production that was in preparation at the time of Brecht's death, *Galileo* was revised in each successive version apparently to make the scientist seem less sympathetic, less conventionally heroic. The crux, of course, was Galileo's conflict with the Church hierarchy over his theories regarding the revolution of the planets around the sun. What began in Brecht's mind as a classic confrontation between the individual and authority became in rewriting more deceptive and ambiguous. At various times the Church must have presented itself to him alternatively as the Nazi state, as the U.S. House Committee on Un-American Activities, and as the Communist leadership of the German Democratic Republic. Brecht dealt with the latter two as he had Galileo deal with the Church—squirming, weaseling, willing to make any compromise. As Brecht sold himself out, parcel by parcel and pound by pound, his Galileo does the same until he seems a scoundrel at worst and an antihero at best. They made their deals: Galileo kept his life and was able to write his *Discorsi*, smuggling them out of Italy in pieces; Brecht did better, getting a company and a theater from the East German government, so that he was able to see into production practically every play in that trunk full of manuscripts he had brought back with him from his prolific exile. Brecht offers his own confession through Galileo, characterizing him as far worse than he really was in the process.

Bertolt Brecht himself continues to elude us. Did he foresee this? Is this what he meant when shortly before his death he answered a German Protestant clergyman: "Don't write that you admire me! Write that I was an uncomfortable person, and that I intend to remain so after my death"?[8] Perhaps. Yet he was and is far less trouble to those in authority in the East and West than to those who are left with the job of tracing an honorable course through his shifts and turns, who feel obliged to explain away his faults, to those who must justify his shabby behavior.

Yet why should it be necessary to clean up after him at all? Why must Brecht always be presented as the sort of hero he himself purported to despise? Perhaps with regard to this second "difficulty" in writing the truth about Brecht, having the "intelligence to recognize it" may also mean having the good sense to set what we know about him aside and not let our opinion of the man (good *or* bad) get in our way as we look at his work.

3. THE ART TO WIELD IT AS A WEAPON

Some good may come of this exercise in applied skepticism. Bertolt Brecht has probably received less *literary* criticism than any major writer of the twentieth century (if indeed he qualifies as such; for so far that has been assumed rather than proven). Even critics such as Martin Esslin, Eric Bentley, and John Willett, who are more or less the accepted commentators on his work, have approached it from a biographical or historical angle and have then been caught up in explaining his works almost purely in relation to his life and times.

He has received political attacks from both the Left and the Right. On the Left, Georg Lukács, who reigned for years as the chief spokesman of literary Marxism, was Brecht's sharpest critic. He refused to be taken in by Brecht's conversion to communism. He continued to see him in the role of the decadent that Brecht had played with such style in the twenties—and Lukács attacked him again and again. Klaus Völker tells of a 1941 meeting in Moscow between writer and critic, in which Brecht proposed that the two of them bury the hatchet: "Look, a lot of people are continually inciting me against you," he is alleged to have said (Lukács is the source of the story). "There are sure to be a lot of people inciting you against me. It would be better if neither of us paid any attention to them."[9] Whether or not this appeal actually served some purpose, Lukács's later treatment of Brecht was somewhat gentler. Actually, Lukács, a strong theorist of socialist realism, saw Brecht's later work as much closer to the European classical tradition (which it was) and praised it in passing as such. For, at least according to Lukács, the closer one

approached European classical ideals, the nearer one came to socialist realism.

From the Right, Brecht caught it from the ex-Communist Ruth
Fischer, who pilloried him as "the minstrel of the GPU" in her book
Stalin and German Communism.[10] Hers is pretty crude stuff, using
as its chief texts Brecht's didactic play *The Measures Taken* and a
couple of odes written by him to Stalin. But it is of real interest
because she probably provided Brecht's House Un-American Activities Committee interrogators with whatever background they had on
his life and work. She is also the only writer to have stated that Brecht
was actually a member of the Communist Party, a claim that, coming
from her, cannot be lightly dismissed. Fischer, the sister of Marxist
composer Hanns Eisler and Communist theoretician Gerhard Eisler,
was herself an official of the German Communist Party in 1930, the
year she claimed Brecht joined.

Brecht has also received more than enough attention for his theories of the theater, both from academic drama departments and
from some in the professional theater. At least one critic, however,
Gerhard Szczesny, in a short but fairly devastating attack entitled *The
Case Against Bertolt Brecht*, has given it that these theories were
shaped after the fact to conform to his practice as a playwright.
"What Brecht called his theories were on the whole very superficial
and mechanical attempts to apply a simplistic Marxism to the dramatic structure of the pre-exisitng vaudeville theater of types."[11] It's
true that as Brecht left this "theater of types" (as he certainly did in
the writing of the major plays of his exile), he found it increasingly
difficult to reconcile theory with practice. When it came time for him
to mount productions himself with his Berliner Ensemble, he began
to play down his theories: "These descriptions and many of the judg-
ments do not apply to the theater that I practice, but rather to the
theater that my critics derive from the reading of my treatises. . . .
All my theories are much more naïve than people think and than my
means of expression permit one to imagine."[12] Finally, in *A Short
Organum for the Theater*, which Brecht wrote in Zurich in 1948 as
a summary of his theories, he cites Laughton's playing of Galileo as
a perfect example of Epic Theater acting; and if Laughton's playing
of *anything* qualifies as Epic Theater acting, then it is certainly no
different from acting of a very old-fashioned kind. I think Brecht's
theories may safely be set aside.

And so as a man, and as a political figure, and even as a theoretician of the stage, we have come to know Bertolt Brecht perhaps all too well. It is purely as a writer that he has been neglected. The case for Brecht as a writer has never been proven because it has never seriously been tried. Certainly the critic who has come closest to Brecht in this way is Eric Bentley, yet he has been an active advocate of Brecht for so long that he is disinclined to dismiss that considerable amount of the playwright's work that is of negligible importance or is simply bad. It is only when some friendly but reasonably objective critic comes along and calls the crap crap, and tells us why it is, that we will ever be able to trust someone to assess the worth of the rest.

What will such a critic need to do this? With all that has been written about Brecht so far, surely sufficient documentation has been assembled for any thorough study. But that, perhaps, is just the trouble: maybe too much has already been written. Although the territory in which he will be traveling will be familiar, it is poorly mapped and has become badly overgrown. He may need a guide, someone to precede him a little, one familiar enough with the territory to be unintimidated by it, willing to tramp down trails that lead nowhere and mark those that will take the critic where he needs to go. In short, he may need someone like me.

But will he need a weapon? Should the man who would write the truth about Brecht carry a cudgel to subdue his subject? A sword to cut Brecht down to size? Perhaps a high-powered rifle to bag him at a safe distance, so that he may plant that tonsured head up on the wall of the trophy room? No, an implement of another sort is called for — as well as a less violent metaphor. Let the critic use a flail on Brecht's whole crop of work; let him beat down upon it unmercifully and keep only what survives such tough treatment. I'm convinced that a rich yield will remain.

4. THE JUDGMENT TO CHOOSE IN WHOSE HANDS IT WILL BE EFFECTIVE

Have I revealed myself as a sexual chauvinist? I suddenly realize that throughout my charge to this ideal critic, I have referred to the critic as a *him* — and this actually goes somewhat against my intentions. Such a critic may well be a woman. No male critic so far, for instance, has dealt completely successfully with the women — call them heroines, for that is what they are—of Brecht's later plays. Since these include Courage of *Mother Courage*, Shen Teh of *The Good Woman of Setzuan*, and Grusha of *The Caucasian Chalk Circle*, you can see that a considerable job is left to be done and it is one that it seems likely a woman might do best. But in her thinking, if not necessarily in her writing, she must be prepared to deal with the realities of Brecht's personal relations with women, which were exploitative to say the least. At the same time she must not let this blind her to the strength and excellence of the female characters that he created, particularly in those later plays.

No matter what the sex of the critic, he or she should be politically neutral—or at least be capable of suspending political bias while treating the playwright's work. Far too much of a politically partisan nature has been written about Brecht already. Many critics seem to have been at least initially drawn to him because he was by his own proclamation the playwright of the Left *par excellence*. If Brecht's best work sometimes did not fit quite so narrow a notion, well—no matter; by quoting liberally from his pronouncements it could be made to fit. As Eric Bentley has remarked, "By this time [1960], there are many people who approve of Brecht on the grounds that he is a Communist, but is that why they are attracted to his work? Rather, he is approved for one reason and enjoyed for another."[13]

Whether Left or Right, most of his critics make the mistake of assuming he was far more politically astute and clever than he really was. His political education and conversion to Marxism in the late twenties is usually thought of as having ushered in the major phase of his work. This is true only if we accept *St. Joan of the Stockyards*, *The Measures Taken*, and a monstrosity like *The Round Heads and the Pointed Heads* as belonging to that major phase. No, he wrote his best work in exile for the trunk, far removed from the watchful eyes of Party critics and well out of the reach of the cultural commissars. Whatever inspiration and peace of mind his political faith may have provided him, it made him no more astute about things political. He simply followed the Party line. In some ways he seemed almost embarrassingly ignorant of anything beyond it. Reading through the daily entries in his *Work Journal* during his California years, one is constantly dismayed at his comments on American politics; they show little grasp of the workings of the democratic system and even less of the personalities involved.

In the same vein, both Martin Esslin and Eric Bentley have pushed the view that during Brecht's appearance before the House Committee on Un-American Activities in 1947, he was in control from first to last, that he tossed out red herrings, threw up smoke screens, and so on—and in this way generally made monkeys of the Committee. Quoting Esslin in *Brecht: The Man and His Work:*

> While some of the members of his circle were terrified by the prospect [of an appearance before the Committee] and suggested ways and means to avoid his having to face the ordeal, Brecht himself was only too eager to pit his impertinence and Schweikian servility against what he considered the darkest and most evil forces in the country. He had always enjoyed such encounters and delighted in misleading pompous representatives of authority by "sticking strictly to the untruth," as he had done when summoned before the censor of his film, *Kuhle Wampe.*[14]

It is in this tone that Esslin proceeds to summarize and report Brecht's interrogation by Robert Stripling, counsel for HCUA. But if you read carefully through Brecht's complete testimony, either in Eric Bentley's *Thirty Years of Treason* or in the *Congressional Record*, from which it is excerpted, I think you will have a much different view of Brecht's "impertinence and Schweikian servility." He seems scared. He weasels, equivocates, and on a couple of occasions tells outright lies. Listening to the tape recording of Brecht before the Committee reinforces this impression: he *sounds* scared.

There is every reason why he, an alien who was largely ignorant of his rights, should have been scared there in open session before photographers and reporters and an assemblage of U.S. Congressmen. In the same position, anyone else would have been too. What I object to is having Brecht characterized as totally in control of the situation simply because this fits some *ex post facto* conception of him as the sort of sly, politically sophisticated individual who could handle the Committee with no difficulty whatsoever. For the record, Brecht himself felt that he had conducted himself badly. Lester Cole, one of the Hollywood Ten who preceded him in the witness chair, told me that when he had shared a cab back to the hotel with him after their testimony (or, in Cole's case, refusal to testify), Brecht

broke into tears and apologized for not taking the hard line that the
Ten had taken before him, explaining that as an alien, and a German
at that, he felt he could not.

5. THE CUNNING TO SPREAD IT AMONG THEM

Even to bring up Brecht's appearance before the House Committee on Un-American Activities reminds us rudely of a time when it
was not easy to speak of a Marxist writer except in condemnation. It
also reminds us of the debt we owe Eric Bentley and the others who
translated Brecht, produced his plays, and promoted his reputation
during the forties and fifties. They did so at some professional risk.
If Brecht has become, unchallenged, a modern "classic" due to their
efforts, it does not mean that they did badly but rather that they did
their work too well. It is time for the challenge to be made.

Yet there persists among some a sense of unease about the present
situation. Although the atmosphere of threat and intimidation that
was the domestic fallout of the Cold War is now substantially in the
past, the suspicion remains that with only a slight alteration in circumstances it could all return. Such a fear isn't without foundation.
Those that hold it view the increasingly conservative temper of American voters and candidates as a foreboding of hard political times
ahead. They find perhaps even more alarming the new intellectual
respectability of conservatism provided by its neoconservative contingent—old, former liberal, hard-line anti-Communists. There is a certain drawing-in, a hint of the siege mentality creeping into the thinking of even some of the most open-minded on the Left: they don't
want to lose what they have gained. And as the elevation of Brecht
to his present eminence might be counted by some as such a gain,
there may be a feeling of protectiveness toward him. Even those with
no political stake in his reputation might feel that because of the
general cultural climate today the time is not right for the sort of
reexamination of his work that I have called for here.

Well, if they feel that, they are wrong. There is no wrong time to
do such a job if it needs to be done, and no better time to do it than
right now. Brecht is presently held by some to be more than just a
writer—even a major writer; to them he is a culture hero, even (God
help us) a sage. But heroes exist to be tested, and the wisdom of sages

must always be questioned. That is the price they must pay for their status. It goes with the territory.

And so, no matter what the difficulties, the time has come to write the truth about Brecht and spread it among the many. Since he has become, if not exactly a popular favorite, at least a writer intensely admired by a highly influential minority, then it follows that the reexamination of his work should be conducted as publicly as possible. There is no point in hiding such a discussion inside the pages of academic journals, or in seeking the shelter of the Brecht Society. Brecht, after all, has become the most public of playwrights. His work is performed here in America more frequently than that of any other European, and it has become assigned reading at universities where he is discussed and quoted as though he were infallible. *Is* he as great as he is assumed to be? We will never have the answer until the question is asked loud and often, skeptically and demandingly.

1

ARRIVALS AND DEPARTURES

Bertolt Brecht's years of exile began immediately following the burning of the Reichstag on the night of February 27, 1933. Hitler had come to power only a month before, having been appointed chancellor by Hindenburg in an attempt to restore order to a Germany that had fallen into outright street warfare between parties. Elections were scheduled for March 5, and the Nazis then threw off all restraints in hopes of provoking the Communists and Socialists into a revolution that they might crush with the legitimate power of the state. Communist meetings were banned and the Party's press was shut down. Social Democrat rallies were broken up by Brownshirts; speakers were beaten. During the thirty-three days of the election campaign, fifty-one prominent anti-Nazis were murdered. Still, the uprising that Hitler and Goebbels had counted on simply never materialized. As the election grew near, the

Nazis were driven to try another tactic. Goering planned and executed the burning of the Reichstag and on the very night it was done, in the light of the flames, he declared it to be the beginning of the Communist revolution. The next day, Hitler persuaded Hindenburg to sign an emergency decree "for the protection of the people and the state." It suspended individual and civil liberties and gave legal sanction to the mass arrests that began immediately. In all, more than four thousand Communists, Socialists, and leading independent Leftists, including deputies of the Reichstag, were arrested in that single sweep.

Brecht would certainly have been one of them had he not departed on February 28, the day the decree was signed and the arrests began. Brecht and his family journeyed first to Prague and from there to Vienna, where he sought out an old friend, the novelist Gina Kaus. He had first met her some years before in Berlin; the two had been introduced at a coffeehouse by Carola Neher, who was then Brecht's mistress. Brecht liked Kaus. She was strongly to the Left in her own political orientation and could argue nearly as fiercely as he could. "When we met that time in Vienna," Gina Kaus remembered in an interview, "we talked about his books being burned by the Nazis, and of course we discussed the situation in Germany, if and when he could return, and so on. I urged him to get to work on something that could be published outside Germany. I had published in Holland, and so I sat down and wrote a letter to that publisher for Brecht. And that was how the publication of the *Dreigroschenroman* [*Threepenny Novel*] was arranged."[1]

The story of the creation of the *Threepenny Novel*—which had not then, of course, even been written—reveals a lot about the way Brecht thought about his work and the way he accomplished it, particularly in his exile years. That fact that an Amsterdam publisher, Verlag Allert de Lange, could be interested enough in such a project to offer an advance on it is proof not so much of Brecht's reputation but of the magic of *The Threepenny Opera*. Inside Germany, Brecht might have been known as a leading playwright of the avant-garde stage, or as a gifted, mordantly ironic lyric poet, or as the tendentious Marxist dramatist he subsequently became, but outside Germany he was known chiefly as the author of *The Threepenny Opera*. His 1928 collaboration with Kurt Weill had been a frank effort by both to achieve a commercial stage success—and as such it succeeded gloriously. *The Threepenny Opera* established them internationally. It was the capital on which they borrowed on occasions all through their years in exile. It made possible Weill's lucrative career in America as a composer for the Broadway theater, and it continued to open doors for Brecht in Hollywood and New York.

Following the run at Berlin's Theater am Schiffbauerdamm in the fall of 1928, there were productions of *The Threepenny Opera* all around Europe and even in New York (in 1933). Sheet music was sold. Recordings were made. It was an international hit, one of Europe's biggest between the wars. What made all this official was the announcement that a talking and singing film was to be made of it by G. W. Pabst for Nerofilmgesellschaft. It was to be shot simultaneously in a French-language as well as a German-language version for worldwide distribution. Brecht was to do the screenplay with another writer, but in the course of writing it, he introduced new material into the plot that followed a strong Marxist line. Nero and Pabst rejected Brecht's new version—although subsequent use was made of some of the material in it in the finished picture. A suit by Nerofilmgesellschaft led to a countersuit by Brecht.

When Brecht proposed to write the *Threepenny Novel* for Verlag Allert de Lange, what he had in mind was presenting in narrative form the film outline that the producers had rejected. This, fundamentally, is what he did. In the novel, there are digressions, amplifications of character, and many incidents added—chiefly at the end where Brecht has his way with the plot and tacks on the whole new, complicated ending in which bank president Polly Peachum becomes the biggest bandit of them all. When the novel was published in 1934, it was not a great success.

The fault lies in large part with Brecht himself, for he was no novelist, and *Threepenny* was not much of a novel. He had written many short stories and eventually became quite skilled at the shorter form (some of those in his postwar collection, *Kalendergeschichten*, are very good indeed), yet somehow he never managed to write a truly successful longer work of fiction. *Threepenny Novel* was, in fact, the only one he finished. The others—*The Tui-Novel* and *The Business Deals of Julius Caesar*—are only long fragments. Why should he have had difficulty with the form? After all, by the time he wrote *Threepenny Novel* he had developed this theory of narrative realism in drama and had successfully put it to practice, notably in his dramatic adaptation of Maxim Gorky's novel *The Mother* (he reduced the novel to a revolutionary chronicle in fifteen episodic scenes). It might seem that a playwright who had adopted such an approach would be able to translate it back again for use in the novel. Had he been able to turn to fiction, the difficulties he experienced in earning a living in exile would have been greatly relieved. Yet he could not. Why? Partly because the structure of the novel eluded him: situations and events that he saw merely as episodes a real novelist would have used as plot elements or at least have incorporated into a general sort of story line (the proof of this is in the *Threepenny Novel*).

There was also something antipathetic in his style of working, perhaps in his very nature, to the writing of novels. Of all forms, after all, it is the most time-consuming. To write a novel requires what the Germans call *Sitzfleisch*, the ability to settle down and concentrate hour after hour, day after day, until the job is done. That wasn't the way that Bertolt Brecht worked. He liked to gather people around him, pick their brains, and use what he could of what they gave him. He preferred to have an audience when he wrote, trying out scenes and even lines for their effect as he pulled them from the typewriter. For the playwright, this may have been practical; for the novelist, it was impossible.

The *Threepenny Novel* was written hastily in 1933. In August of that year, with Hitler obviously in firm control of Germany, Brecht reconciled himself to an extended stay in exile and took a house for himself and his family near Svendborg on the Danish island of Funen. Why Denmark? Austria or the German-speaking section of Switzerland might have seemed a more practical choice. Brecht was looking, above all, for a place to work, and in Denmark, he knew he had that. And besides, he was about as close to Germany as it was possible for him to be. He could keep his ear to the ground, question travelers, and, should the situation in Berlin suddenly change, he could be in Germany in less than an hour. As exiles are wont to do, he chose a station near the border.

Through his father, Berthold Friedrich Brecht, he made arrangements to have his belongings shipped from his flat in Berlin to his new home at Svendborg. Brecht was especially anxious to have his books sent to him there, and these were all shipped off in cartons to his father in Augsburg, who, it was agreed, would then transship them to Denmark. When they arrived in Augsburg, however, they were followed closely by a man from the Gestapo. Brecht's father was a successful bourgeois businessman (the managing director of a large paper mill), and was the sort of man the Nazis treated with some care at the time. The Gestapo man was quite polite. "Herr Brecht," he said, "we quite understand that you are not associated with your son politically, but these books of his you have been sent, we must ask you to burn them." The matter was left in Herr Brecht's hands. In a few days the Gestapo man returned and asked if the matter had been attended to. "No, I couldn't burn them," explained Herr Brecht quite innocently. "I looked at those books, and the bindings on them were quite good. They were things of worth, you see, so I sent them on to my son."[2] His appeal was quite apolitical and addressed strictly to middle-class standards of value; the Nazis could not—or would not—argue with that.

Before settling in at Svendborg, Brecht went to Paris to see to the publication of his poetry collection, *Lieder Gedichte Chöre*, which was to be brought out by the master propagandist of the Popular Front Era, Willi Muenzenberg, in his Editions du Carrefour. Arrangements were made for various translations, and Margarete Steffin was to see the book through publication. Steffin was to become one of Brecht's most frequent collaborators and one of the women closest to him during his period of exile. He invited her to come and visit him at Svendborg. If they were not then already, the two were about to become lovers. Steffin would soon visit him at Svendborg, where she served as his collaborator on a number of projects.

Brecht did not feel himself greatly impeded by the bonds of marriage. Helene Weigel, who was his second wife, had borne him two children, but she was willing in most cases to look the other way when Brecht took up with an actress or one of his collaborators. It had happened before; it would happen again.

And it did, soon. In the fall of 1933, another woman, Ruth Berlau, came to visit him, and he was immediately taken with her. She was a Danish actress married to a Copenhagen physician and was, as her photographs reveal, a strikingly beautiful woman. Even then an ardent Leftist, Berlau had played the role of Anna in the Copenhagen production of Brecht's *Drums in the Night* and had come to him at Svendborg to seek his permission to translate *The Mother* for production with a workers' theater group. He was delighted to give it, and at her invitation went to Copenhagen, where she introduced him to a number of Danish theater people; with them he discussed the possibility of a production of *St. Joan of the Stockyards* at the Royal Theater. Berlau even managed to scrounge up a secondhand Ford for Brecht, so that he might commute to Copenhagen and assist her in her work on the translation, which continued for a year or more. Even after the production of *The Mother* by the Revolutionary Theater in Copenhagen in 1935, Brecht's visits continued. Berlau quite willingly accompanied him when he emigrated later to the United States.

As he expected, the house near Svendborg proved a good place to work—almost too good for Brecht, who missed the turmoil of "collaboration" he had known in Berlin. He was soon referring to Svendborg as his "Danish Siberia." Even so, he accomplished a great deal there. He not only completed the *Threepenny Novel*, but also, with Steffin as his collaborator (she was installed in a house nearby), he revised *The Round Heads and the Pointed Heads* and wrote *The Horatii and the Curatii;* and then he did the series of one-act plays and scenes that he assembled under the title *Fear and Misery in the Third Reich*, and his Spanish Civil War play *Señora Carrar's Rifles*, and the original version of *Galileo*. In addition, there were articles, essays, open letters, declarations, and, as always, a steady stream of verse. Of these last the most impressive are the political parables, many of them in the Chinese style, that were collected and published under the title *Die Svendborger Gedichte*. From the standpoint of Brecht's personal life, the most interesting from this period are the two simple love poems, "Buying an Orange" and "The Eleventh Sonnet," which he wrote to Margarete Steffin. The latter is a charming and simple poem that begins:

> As I sent you off to foreign parts
> Reckoning on a very cold winter, I looked to find
> The thickest pants for your (beloved) behind
> And well-woven stockings for your lower parts![3]

He continues in this vein, attending to the details of her departure, and telling her, in effect, to button up her overcoat when the wind is free. It is the sort of sentiment that one seldom gets from Brecht.

He was sending Steffin off to Moscow in 1934. He himself traveled to Russia the following year at the invitation of Sergei Tretyakov, the Soviet playwright who had translated three of Brecht's plays that were published in a volume entitled *Epic Drama*. None of those translated by Tretyakov had been produced there; indeed Brecht has rarely been produced in the Soviet Union. Nevertheless in 1935 he was extended an official welcome, invited to give an address on Moscow radio, and afforded ample opportunity to meet with Germans who had emigrated to Russia following the Nazi takeover. These included Wilhelm Pieck and Johannes Becher, who later became high officials of the German Democratic Republic, and a number of old Berlin theater friends such as Erwin Piscator and Carola Neher.

Except for a few perfunctorily enthusiastic expostulations in verse (e.g., "How the Workers of Moscow Took Possession of the Great Moscow Subway on April 27, 1935"), he was rather tight-lipped regarding his impressions from his visit to the workers' paradise. A good deal, however, can be perceived from this third-person account of Brecht in Moscow by the English editor, poet, and literary historian John Lehmann in *The Whispering Gallery*.

> I was taken one evening to the House of Writers in Moscow, where a celebration was being held to honour Berthold [*sic*] Brecht. After the speeches of welcome, a young Russian poet got up, to read a translation he had made of one of Brecht's famous longer poems; it was a fiery declamation: the young Russian lashed himself into a passion, gesticulating dramatically and turning purple in the face with the effort, and then sank back to his seat with bowed head. There were storms of applause. Then Brecht himself was asked to recite the same poem in his original German. He read it sitting down, with dead-pan face, in the totally flat, antirhetorical manner he had intended it. A look of bewilderment came into the young Russian poet's eyes; and embarrassed glances were exchanged among the other Russian writers there. At the end the applause was respectful rather than enthusiastic. I had a suspicion that Brecht was secretly deriving immense enjoyment from the episode.[4]

What Lehmann witnessed and noted so accurately was a fundamental conflict of styles. Brecht, ironic and understated, was never very happy with the sort of religious fervor, much less the conformity, required of artists in the Soviet Union. If he went there to scout the territory, he must have come back convinced that, attractive as it may have seemed to others, the climate there in Moscow would eventually prove inhospitable to him. How right he was.

The same year, 1935, he also traveled to the United States. That solidly and respectably left-wing enterprise, the Theatre Union, had been negotiating for rights to produce *The Mother* as the opening play of its 1935–36 season. Paul Peters's adaptation was sent to him, and Brecht rejected it out of hand. In a number of subtle and not-so-subtle ways Peters had attempted to shape this epic drama to fit the mold of social realism. Quite naturally Brecht objected and withheld his permission. A member of the Theatre Union's board, Manuel Gomez, was dispatched to Denmark to win over Brecht but he only managed to do so by extending the board's offer to bring the playwright to America so that he might argue text changes in person and sit in on rehearsals. Brecht signed the contract, and was given a ticket on a Danish freighter to New York.

Both Brecht and the Theatre Union people had deluded themselves in supposing that the other could be dominated. In the end, both lost. Brecht arrived in New York at the end of October 1935, attended his first rehearsal, and immediately fell into conflict with the young director of the production, Victor Wolfson, and with the cast, and with the members of the Theatre Union board. The battling continued unabated for days and days, Brecht objecting both to the changes in his original text and in the interpretation put on the work by the director and cast. The fundamental problem, of course, was that the Theatre Union was utterly ignorant of Brecht's theatrical intentions. They knew nothing about Epic drama and were hostile to what he tried to teach them of it. The Theatre Union, with its preference for Stanislavski and their strict social realist orientation, was giving Brecht the Moscow production he had never had. If he was having problems with them, he would have had double the trouble in Russia.

Things came to such a pass that the matter was placed for arbitration before V. J. Jerome, the unofficial cultural commissar of the American Communist Party. Brecht liked and trusted the man, but that did not prevent him from continuing to fight on even after Jerome had struck what was thought to be an equitable bargain on textual changes, allowing a few for the Theatre Union and restoring some for Brecht.

The whole thing came to a head at a dress rehearsal to which a couple of hundred of the Theatre Union's backers had been invited. Brecht, of course, was there as well. He sat there through the performance, taking it as long as he could, until at last, in the middle of it, he jumped up and started screaming, "That is shit! That is garbage! I will not have it!" Then he stormed out. When he returned to rehearsals two days before the play was to open, he was thrown out of the theater.[5]

The word then was that Brecht would seek a court order to prevent the production from opening. But that he would actually seek legal recourse in a foreign country was extremely doubtful; in any case, no court order was forthcoming, and *The Mother* opened on schedule on November 19, 1935, to absolutely terrible reviews in the New York press. The bourgeois press dismissed it out of hand, and on the Left they were sympathetic but confused. Those who were in on the battle behind the scenes noted the unfortunate mixture of styles and hoped timidly that next time things might turn out better. Vain hope!

More than anything else, Brecht seems to have offended the Theatre Union people personally. Many years later, Albert Maltz, who was then a member of the board, looked back on the protagonist of the whole sorry episode and declared in an interview, "The man stank! It was disgusting. I don't believe he ever took a bath, and the way he surrounded himself with that harem of women. I never saw anything like it."[6] It was more than likely a harem of one, for Elisabeth Hauptmann had come to New York from St. Louis, where she had emigrated, to be with Brecht during this difficult time, and while she was there she was constantly at his side.

If Brecht offended some personally, he nevertheless got along with others very well indeed. He spent evenings discussing art and politics with V. J. Jerome, and on one visit to the admiring Marc Blitzstein he presented the American playwright with the germ of the idea for *The Cradle Will Rock*. According to George Sklar of the Theatre Union, Brecht saw every gangster movie playing in New York during his visit; Sklar speculates that they provided the inspiration for *The Resistible Rise of Arturo Ui*, written just a few years later. And when he wasn't studying the flickering image of Jimmy Cagney on the silver screen? "His big luxury and dissipation was a seat in the balcony at Minsky's burlesque on 42nd Street," wrote Hy Kraft, who met the playwright during his visit. "He said this was the only honest Broadway theater in New York." Kraft reports that when he first met Brecht he asked him what he was doing in America, and Brecht "said he'd come here *'zu überwintern'* (to spend the winter); the United States was, so to speak, a political Palm Springs or Palm Beach."[7] Perhaps so, but he also found it an artistic Siberia. He left New York when the winter had barely begun on December 29, 1935.

When he got back to Denmark he wrote a regretful letter to V. J. Jerome. Brecht was sincerely sorry that his contacts with American writers had been so limited and that he had returned from New York still largely ignorant of American writing. Of the plays he had seen he had very much liked Clifford Odets's *Waiting for Lefty*, but the same author's middle-class psychological drama, *Paradise Lost*, not nearly as well: the work gave him problems. Later, when he met Odets in Hollywood, Brecht would write his poem, "Letter to the Playwright Odets," in which he set forth his objections:

> You, comrade, who showed compassion towards the man
> Who has nothing to eat, do you now feel compassion
> For the man who has stuffed himself sick?[8]

Except for a sojourn in London that involved a little work on the motion picture *Pagliacci* and a bit of Popular Front politicking at a Writers' Congress, Brecht stayed close to Denmark during the year 1936. It was a fairly productive writing year for him, but he had not much to show for it in publications and nothing at all in theatrical productions.

He went the following year, 1937, to the Writers' Congress in Paris. No matter what he may have felt personally about such affairs he was obliged to attend them. He was one of the more important German writers in exile and perhaps the most important of the Marxists. He was also coeditor, with novelists Lion Feuchtwanger and Willi Bredel, of the exile literary journal *Das Wort*, which was issued from Moscow.

Brecht traveled to Paris with Ruth Berlau. When, however, the Congress voted to adjourn and reconvene days later in Madrid so that the writers might demonstrate their support for the Spanish Republican cause, Brecht thought it a bad idea and refused to go. It seemed excessively risky to him to travel to a city that was then under artillery fire and subject to daily air raids. He remained in Paris, sending an address and a poem to be read at the Madrid Congress. Berlau was not to be intimidated by a mere Civil War. She continued on to Spain, perhaps inspired and encouraged in the undertaking by her recent reading of *Señora Carrar's Rifles*, Brecht's reworking of Synge's *Riders to the Sea* to a Spanish Civil War setting, which he had finished only a little earlier that year. For his part, Brecht admitted to being "one of the cowards."

Later that same year, Brecht's wife, Helene Weigel, went out on what amounted to a tour, taking *Señora Carrar's Rifles* to Prague, Paris, Zurich, and Vienna, all in a little over a month. He made an effort to ease the rigors of the road with three poems written to her, each one a separate tribute to her skill and power as an actress. "The Actress in Exile," "Description of the Performance of H. W.," and "Helene Weigel as Señora Carrar" reveal not only the deep professional respect he held for her as the leading interpreter of his own Epic Theater but also the strong personal feelings he had for her. One can only speculate on the complexity of their relationship, for at the same time Brecht was working ever more closely with Steffin on various projects, he was becoming more deeply involved personally with Berlau.

The year 1938 brought Brecht news of the arrest of Sergei Tretyakov, Brecht's sponsor and translator in the Soviet Union. Tretyakov, an ex-futurist and a free spirit of the Soviet theater, was a victim of the general crackdown ordered by Stalin on artists and intellectuals during the period of the purge trials. Brecht was greatly troubled by what was going on inside Russia. Tretyakov was not just a colleague but a personal friend as well. He disappeared into the Soviet prison system and is presumed to have died not long afterward.

Through the summer of 1938, the critic Walter Benjamin was staying with Brecht as his guest at the place near Svendborg. Such extended visits were common there, and Brecht welcomed them. Karl Korsch had written most of his book on Karl Marx at Svendborg in 1936. Benjamin himself had been there before for a summer-long stay in 1934 and then again in 1936. He and Brecht, though in many ways very different, were quite important to one another. An intellectual of the first order, Benjamin possessed the sort of strong, analytical mind that Brecht, who delighted in dialectical debate, wished to have close by to use as a sounding board (not having such companions about was what he missed most about Berlin). To Benjamin, Brecht was more important as a creator.

The two had met in 1929, introduced by a Soviet film director, then visiting Berlin, named Asja Lacis. Neither was then a member of the Communist Party, nor evidently did they become members. Walter Benjamin had, in fact, for years maintained an intellectual interest and a limited commitment to Zionism, although when it came to the decision to emigrate he found himself too attached to the intellectual and artistic tradition of Western Europe to uproot himself and travel to Israel. He never felt himself any less a Jew for it, however, and his brilliance as a critic and philosopher of language reflects the years he spent interpreting the mysteries of the Cabala under the guidance and encouragement of the Jewish scholar Gershon Scholem. Benjamin's essay on Kafka, one of the keenest and earliest appreciations of Kafka's work, is the sort of study that benefits richly from the fact that both critic and subject were Jews; it is informed by the spirit and literature of Judaism, yet seems not in the least parochial.

As early as 1924, however, Walter Benjamin had begun to turn toward Marxism. That year, he began reading the work of the Communist critic Georg Lukács, which greatly impressed him, and he met Asja Lacis on the Isle of Capri. A committed Marxist artist, she sang the success of the Soviet experiment and urged him to visit Russia and see it for himself. Two years later, he did. Having declared himself a "thoroughgoing Marxist," he left for Moscow in 1926, commissioned to write the article on Goethe for the Soviet encyclopedia. He stayed the winter and departed in the spring of 1927 with rather ambivalent feelings regarding his commitment to communism; although he considered himself no less a Marxist than before, his exposure to Stalinism was sufficient to convince him that Russia might have seemed to some a workers' paradise but it was certainly no heaven for intellectuals. Having at first been offered a free hand in the writing of the Goethe article, he was forced to rewrite it in order to make it conform to the preconceptions and requirements of Soviet cultural policy. For Benjamin, that was a rather chastening experience.

By the time he met Brecht he had come to think of himself as an "independent Marxist." He had by then also begun an association with Theodor W. Adorno and the Marxist-oriented Institute for Social Research, then part of the University of Frankfurt; it was an association that was to last into his years of exile.

Bertolt Brecht was six years Walter Benjamin's junior. He had enjoyed considerable success as a playwright in Berlin during the twenties and early thirties, but his had been in part at least a *succès de scandale*. Benjamin, while not as well known, had a much more solid reputation. In a sense, the respect of such a critic tended to legitimate Brecht as a serious artist—and Brecht must have known that. What is more, Benjamin was also the first to take the playwright completely seriously as a theorist of the drama. His essay "What Is Epic Theater?," which was published in the émigré journal *Mass und Wert* in 1939, set forth Brecht's dramatic categories and prescriptions quite clearly, though in much less provocative fashion than the playwright himself had ever done. As presented by Benjamin, there seems an ingenuously appealing and almost amiable quality to Epic Theater—perhaps more so than there ever really was in practice.

"What Is Epic Theater?" is only one of a number of essays related to Brecht and his work and to Brechtian aesthetics that Benjamin wrote between 1930 and 1939. (There were enough, in fact, that a small book was recently made of them, titled in its English translation *Understanding Brecht.*) Since most were written during the years that the playwright and critic were in exile, it should be apparent just how important the two really were to each other during this period—artist and interpreter, author and ideal reader. Brecht's relations with his collaborators aside—and the contributions of most of them are questionable—his literary friendship with Benjamin was probably the most beneficial and sustaining of any he maintained during the period of exile. They saw a good deal of one another: there were not only Benjamin's visits to Svendborg, but Brecht's more frequent trips to Paris, where Benjamin had settled to pursue his studies of nineteenth-century French culture.

It was, in fact, to work on a book on Baudelaire that Benjamin came to Svendborg in 1938. As was the case with a number of his projects, this one was never completed. About all that survives of it is contained in a forty-odd-page essay in the collection *Illuminations*, entitled "On Some Motifs in Baudelaire," a brilliant exploration of the effect of Paris street life on the poet and his work. It suggests just how good the finished book might have been. In Brecht's *Work*

Journal he notes that Benjamin is staying with him and briefly describes his project. Except for a passing reference to something said by Benjamin, this is the only mention of him, even though he was there as a houseguest from June until October. Benjamin, on the other hand, kept copious notes of his conversations with Brecht. They appear in *Understanding Brecht* and offer a fascinating insight into Brecht's feelings during these days of exile. There is in them, for instance, open dismay expressed by Brecht at what was happening in the Soviet Union. Benjamin writes:

1 July. Whenever I refer to conditions in Russia, Brecht's comments are highly sceptical. When I inquired the other day whether Ottwald was still in gaol (in colloquial German: whether he was "still sitting"), the answer was: "If he can still sit, he's sitting." Yesterday Gretl Steffin expressed the opinion that Tretyakov was no longer alive.[9]

25 July. . . . He is following the developments in Russia and also the writings of Trotsky. These prove that there exists a suspicion—a justifiable one—demanding a sceptical appraisal of Russian affairs. Such scepticism is in the spirit of the Marxist classics. Should the suspicion prove correct one day, then it will become necessary to fight the regime, and *publicly.* But "unfortunately or God be praised, whichever you prefer," the suspicion is at present not yet a certainty. There is no justification for constructing upon it a policy such as Trotsky's. "And then there's no doubt that certain criminal cliques really are at work in Russia itself. One can see it, from time to time, by the harm they do."[10]

Yet Brecht had far harsher things to say about the Nazis and what they had done to him and were doing to Germany. He was never for a moment confused as to the real and present danger:

3 August. . . . "We must neglect nothing in our struggle against that lot. What they're planning is nothing small, make no mistake about it. They're planning for thirty thousand years ahead. Colossal things. Colossal crimes. They stop at nothing. They're out to destroy everything. Every living cell contracts under their blows. . . . They're planning devastations on an icy scale. That's why they can't reach agreement with the Church, which is also geared to thousands of years. And they've pro- letarianized me too. It isn't just that they've taken my house, my fish-pond and my car from me; they've also robbed me of my stage and my audience. From where I stand today I can't, as a matter of principle, admit that Shakespeare's talent was greater than mine. But Shakespeare couldn't have written just for his desk drawer, any more than I can."[11]

And Brecht's program as a politically committed artist?

25 August. A Brechtian maxim: "Don't start from the good old days but the bad new ones."[12]

These were certainly the bad new days for Brecht. Forced as he was to write for the desk drawer, it is remarkable that he was able to produce at all—and altogether astonishing that under such circum- stances he was able to do some of his best work. For example, 1938: with war a certainty, with pressure on him from the Danish govern- ment to leave, with continuing financial stress, and torn by doubts as to what was really going on inside the Soviet Union, he wrote the first version of *Galileo*, as well as *Fear and Misery in the Third Reich*. The first *Galileo* was written with a New York production in mind, and toward that end was immediately handed over to Desmond Vesey, the English translator of Brecht's *Threepenny Novel*. *Fear and Misery* went into production in Paris immediately. In addition, Brecht prepared his volume, *Poems from Exile*, for publication, dashed off the usual number of individual poems, and continued work on the novel *The Business Deals of Julius Caesar*, which he had begun that same year as a play. The following year, 1939, brought the long-expected outbreak of war, in September. Brecht and his fam- ily, anticipating it, packed up and left Denmark for temporary quar- ters in Sweden. In 1939 he wrote *Mother Courage and Her Chil- dren* in a matter of weeks, the first version of *The Trial of Lucullus* in a matter of days, and began work on *The Good Woman of Setzuan*.

The Brechts were forced to move from neutral Sweden to still- neutral Finland early in 1940. It was a rather awkward place for a refugee German playwright who was notoriously sympathetic to the Soviet Union. After all, the Russo-Finnish winter war had just ended in a standoff, and Finland's secret alliance with Germany against Russia was only a little over a year in the future. In his *Work Journal* entries during the Russo-Finnish war, Brecht had been consistently critical of the Soviet Union. It made no sense to him. Here, for instance, is what he had to say, still in Sweden, on New Year's Day, 1940:

> The foreign policy of the USSR is indeed the foreign policy of a state in which a structure of socialist elements is taking shape, but it is no socialist foreign policy. The Finnish campaign, directed toward military goals, may be aimed at a liberation of the Finnish proletariat from the rule of the bourgeoisie, but the socialist goals are only aspired to in the interests of the military goals and are regulated by them. The USSR would probably be glad if it could achieve its military goals without social measures. Because of the war the Finnish working class, in great measure, will be driven to the side of the bourgeoisie.[13]

Less than four months later, Brecht, his family, and Margarete Steffin were in Helsinki. Just how extreme was their situation is evidenced by the fact that they sought an avenue of escape in the direction of Finland. It also says something of the Finns' democratic hospitality that such an avenue was not closed to Brecht.

From the start, the reason for going to Finland was to secure American visas. Brecht set about obtaining them immediately; and it looked in the beginning as though they would be quickly forthcoming. Helene Weigel went so far as to reserve steamer tickets for their expected departure from the Finnish port of Petsamo on August 5, 1940. But they did not finally leave Finland until more than eight months after that date, held fast as they were in Helsinki by yards of American red tape. Their way out to the west was barred by the success of Hitler's war machine. The Brecht party was in Sweden when the war had at last begun. There is evidence in the few journal entries made during the early months of World War II that Brecht, along with the rest of the world, fully expected the armies of France and Great Britain to contain the Wehrmacht at the Maginot Line, and believed that the conflict might grind on for years there. That, of course, was not what happened. Brecht looked on in consternation from his vantage point high up in the northeast corner of Europe as, in a few short weeks in May and June 1940, Hitler's mechanized divisions swept through Holland and Belgium and into the heart of France behind the main body of the Allied forces. And yet Brecht continued to work. It was not easy, as he himself attests in this journal entry dated June 11, 1940:

> I go now for the tenth time through *The Good Woman of Set-zuan* word by word with Grete. I guard my mornings jealously in recent days, since the news reports have become so bad, and I consider whether I should switch off the early morning news broadcast. The little box stands next to the bed, and my last move at night is to turn it off; my first in the morning to turn it on.[14]

A draft of *The Good Woman* completed, he returned to *The Messingkauf Dialogues*, which has survived as a fragment of near book length and is the most detailed statement of his Epic Theater ideas. With his dramatic works barred from production, he turned—as he did again and again—to theory.

Unexpectedly, however, there came a possibility for a production of some sort through his Finnish hostess, the writer Hella Wuolijoki. She told him of a play competition in Helsinki. If he could only write a *Finnish* play in German, then she would translate it and it could be entered. Well, why not? Taking Wuolijoki's tales and her play, *The Sawdust Princess*, as his sources, he began work on what was to become *Herr Puntila and His Man Matti*. Again Brecht commented tellingly in his *Work Journal* on his odd situation:

> It would be unbelievably difficult to express the emotional circumstances in which I follow the battle for Britain on the radio and in the bad Finnish-Swedish newspapers and at the same time write *Puntila*. This spiritual phenomenon makes clear that such a war can be and that literary work can always be carried on. *Puntila* concerns me almost not at all, the war completely; about Puntila I can write almost everything, about the war nothing. I don't mean "may," I really mean "can."

It is interesting how far literature, in practice, is removed from the center of all decisive events.[15]

Thus the play was finished in short order. Although she was not at first completely happy with the use Brecht had made of her materials, Hella Wuolijoki dutifully translated it. However, before *Herr Puntila and His Man Matti* was or could be produced in Finland, the American visas at last came through, and the Brecht party was free to emigrate to the United States. By that time Ruth Berlau had also joined them.

But when they made ready to leave—Brecht, his family, and his two mistress-collaborators—they found that for all practical purposes their way out to the west was closed off. In preparation for the coming war with Russia, the Finns had turned over the operation of the main seaport of Petsamo to their prospective allies, the Germans, eliminating the possibility of the departure by sea they had planned months before. However, the border to Soviet Russia was not yet sealed off and that was to become their exit. Brecht arranged their interminably long and somewhat bizarre route to America, which would see them traveling across the entire length of Russia on the Trans-Siberian railway to Vladivostok, where they would catch a steamer for California. They planned only to interrupt their journey in Moscow for a few days. That stop proved fateful.[16]

They departed Helsinki on May 13, 1941, passed through Leningrad, and a few days later arrived in Moscow, where they put up at the Hotel Metropol. There Brecht kept a rather low profile, no doubt sensing just how precarious his position really was. The Soviet Union, after all, stood on the brink of war with Germany. Though a professed Marxist, Brecht was also a German, one who had entered the country from Finland, which would also soon be at war with Russia. It is significant, though hardly surprising, that apparently at no time did Brecht consider taking refuge in Russia. He had been given a hint of the possible destiny that awaited him in the disappearance of his friend Sergei Tretyakov. In this case his instinct for survival proved absolutely correct: shortly after Russia was invaded by Germany, Stalin ordered a general roundup of German nationals in the Soviet Union, with the exception of only those who were highly placed in the Comintern. First they were relocated in camps in Soviet Asia, then most were shipped off to Siberia, where all but a few perished.

Brecht's onetime mistress, Carola Neher, who had starred in the film version of *The Threepenny Opera*, was one of those who died anonymously and without record during the war. Margarete Steffin collapsed in Moscow. She had been ill before they left Helsinki, brought low by the poor diet on which they had all existed there. Thus weakened she fell victim to an infection, which quickly advanced to pneumonia. When she entered the hospital in Moscow, a lobe of one of her lungs had filled completely with fluid. Upon their arrival in the city, Brecht had proceeded to book passage on a Swedish freighter out of Vladivostok, but it now appeared that it would be necessary to leave her behind. He was assured by no less than Alexander Fedayev, a Soviet novelist who was a great power in the Writers' Union, that she would be sent on as soon as she was well and that her passage from Vladivostok was assured.

Having no other choice, Brecht made plans to leave Moscow by train with his family and Berlau on May 30, 1941. They boarded the train for Vladivostok without Steffin. Along the way, Brecht sent telegrams to her and received them in reply. Then, after two days, her answers ceased. Finally on June 4, 1941, in Ulan-Ude, just beyond Lake Baikal in Siberia, he received a telegram informing him that Margarete Steffin had died. On June 5, 1941, the Brecht party boarded the Swedish freighter *Annie Johnson* and sailed for America.

The circumstances of Walter Benjamin's death serve as a counterpoint to Brecht's escape. Benjamin had died on September 27, 1940, but word of his death came to Brecht only in August 1941. It was duly recorded in the *Work Journal*. The circumstances surrounding Benjamin's death are so pitiful and so characteristic of the personal tragedies of refugee life during that period that they are worth recounting in some detail here.

When the German army occupied Paris, Benjamin departed the city, taking with him only what books and manuscripts he could carry, and headed south for unoccupied France. There he managed to gather all the visas and documents necessary for emigration to the United States through Portugal—all except one: an exit visa from the Vichy government. This meant that he would have to make his entry into Spain by stealth, traveling on foot with a party of refugees like himself, led through the Pyrenees by a Basque guide. The climb on the steep mountain trail was almost too much for Benjamin, a hunchback who was never physically vigorous and had been considerably weakened during the preceding months by poor diet and the prolonged emotional stress put on him by his precarious situation. Moreover, when at last he arrived with his party at Port Bou, their entry to Spain, he found that although the border was unguarded by the French police, it had been closed by the Spanish that very day. The party of refugees was told to turn around the next morning and start back the way they had come. This, finally, overwhelmed Benjamin. Physically depleted, fearing deportation to Germany and a lingering death in a concentration camp, he gave in to despair and committed suicide by taking poison. In the account of his death contained in her long essay introducing Benjamin's collection, *Illuminations*, Hannah Arendt suggests that the Spanish authorities were so moved by his desperate act that they threw open the border. Perhaps. In any case, the party of refugees with which Benjamin was traveling was allowed to pass through the next day. Weeks later the Vichy government lifted its ban on exit visas for refugees. By such reckoning, Walter Benjamin becomes the victim of nothing more nor less than the bad luck that had hounded him throughout his life.

Brecht, of course, saw it differently. He remarked, upon hearing of his friend's death, that it was the first real loss Hitler had inflicted upon German literature. As we see in the gloomy poem that he wrote shortly afterward, he held the Nazis directly responsible:

I'm told you raised your hand yourself
Anticipating the butcher.
After eight years in exile, observing the rise of the enemy
That at last, brought up against an impassable frontier
You passed, they say, a passable one.

Empires collapse. Gang leaders
Are strutting about like statesmen. The peoples
Can no longer be seen under all those armaments.

So the future lies in darkness and the forces of right
Are weak. All this was plain to you
When you destroyed a torturable body.[17]

2

WHY HOLLYWOOD?

When the Swedish freighter *Annie Johnson* docked in San Pedro on July 21, 1941, Bertolt Brecht descended the gangplank with his wife, Helene Weigel, and their two children, Stefan and Barbara, and his mistress Ruth Berlau. Theirs had been a long voyage from Vladivostok—thirty-eight days that included a five-day layover in Manila. There were rumors of Nazi submarines operating in the Pacific during that summer, and although the *Annie Johnson* flew a neutral flag the German passengers were in constant fear that their unarmed ship would be stopped and searched and their identities discovered. But they made it across the Pacific without incident.

When at last they emerged from customs and immigration they found a small reception committee awaiting them. Marthe Feuchtwanger was there, wife of the novelist Lion Feuchtwanger, who had preceded Brecht to California by less than a year and had been instrumental in bringing him over. Also on hand was Alexander Granach, an actor whom Brecht had known since he had appeared in the 1922 production of *Drums in the Night*. He had left Germany in 1933 and made his way more or less directly to Hollywood. By the time Brecht arrived, Granach, known for his work in *Ninotchka* and other films, was well established. Seeing how Granach had prospered, Brecht may well have taken heart.

From across the continent, Elisabeth Hauptmann, his old secretary, collaborator, mistress, and factotum, had prepared the way for him and his party. She had rented a house for them through a friend in Los Angeles. Their bags were packed into the car and Granach drove them there. The place was at 1958 Argyle, not far from Gower and near Columbia and Paramount studios. Efforts had been made to make him feel at home. Did they satisfy Brecht? Was he pleased? Not in the least. He wrote in his *Work Journal* a few days after the five of them had settled: "In practically no other place was life harder for me than here in this showplace of *easy going*, the house is far too pretty. . . ."[1]

During those first few months in America, Brecht puttered about the city, unable to work, visiting other émigrés in the movie colony, some newly settled like him, others well established and prospering. But for months after his arrival he was unable to undertake any serious new work or return to any of several projects he had begun and set aside. It was partly because of Walter Benjamin's death. It may have also been simply that he felt that the theatrical climate was all wrong for him in America, for as he remarks in one brief entry in his *Work Journal*: "Writing for the theater is nowhere more difficult than here, where only theatrical naturalism is practiced."[2] Or it may more likely have been that he was simply unprepared for America. It was all too different, too strange, even for Brecht, who had managed to work in every refugee way station across Europe, even to begin to feel at home. It took considerable effort for him to come to terms with America—and especially with California.

When I used to tell people that except for some extended trips to New York Brecht spent his years in America in Hollywood, I often got a curious reaction: they would laugh. For a while I wondered why, but gradually I understood. Brecht, the austere political playwright, seems so far removed from the style and spirit of life in the movie colony, so perfectly the antithesis of the Hollywood writer, that there .

is something almost surrealistic about the picture we get when we try to imagine him spinning out his days beneath the palm trees. He didn't belong there, and he knew it. The question presents itself: Why did he stay?

There is a direct answer given to this in the entry Brecht made in his *Work Journal* the day after he arrived in America. He had been to see the novelist Lion Feuchtwanger and had found his old collaborator unchanged, "only a little older in appearance." They had discussed Brecht's prospects in America, and Feuchtwanger had proved to be his usual practical self. "His advice," wrote Brecht, "is to remain here, where it is cheaper than N[ew] Y[ork] and where there are more possibilities to earn money."[3]

Feuchtwanger meant, of course, that there was a greater chance to earn it in the movie industry—and there was good reason for him to say so. Ever since Hitler had come to power—and even somewhat before—the American movie industry had had its arms open to the best that Europe, and particularly Germany, had to offer. This infusion of Middle European talent during the thirties and early forties contributed immeasurably to the rise of American film during this period. In front of the camera were Peter Lorre, Oscar Homolka, Marlene Dietrich, the Austrians Luise Rainer and Paul Henreid, and the Hungarian S. Z. Sakall, among a good many others. Directors who emigrated from Germany and Austria during Hitler's rise to power included Josef von Sternberg, William Dieterle, Curt and Robert Siodmak, Fred Zinnemann, Edgar Ulmer, and, of course, Fritz Lang. There were even a few screenwriters who managed to overcome the language barrier and work in American films: Salka Viertel achieved some eminence in the thirties as a writer on Greta Garbo's films; director Billy Wilder broke into American pictures as a screenwriter; and Brecht's friend, the Austrian novelist Gina Kaus, worked with some success, if somewhat irregularly, as a writer in Hollywood.

Brecht could afford to be optimistic. He knew many of those who were already well established. His reputation as a dramatist would open some doors for him in Hollywood. Besides he had at that time what few others in his position could claim—a potential American collaborator, Ferdinand Reyher. Reyher was a playwright, novelist, and screenwriter born of German-American parents in 1891. Fluent in German, he had spent the twenties in Europe and had met Brecht in Berlin in 1927. The two formed a friendship—or the closest thing to it Brecht was capable of—and kept up a steady correspondence, especially during Brecht's years of exile in Europe. The discovery of this correspondence and their long-standing relationship by Professor James K. Lyon of the University of California at San Diego is one of the important finds in Brecht scholarship. It led eventually to the writing of Lyon's book, *Bertolt Brecht in America*.[4]

On one important occasion during Brecht's European exile they met—in Copenhagen in October 1938. There they discussed Brecht's plans for doing the life of Galileo. Significantly, it was first thought of as an appropriate subject for a screenplay. Yet as they talked it through, Brecht saw that it might better be done in his epic style with a series of long, movielike sequences—and that of course is how he wrote *Galileo*. The first version was completed in a few weeks after their meeting, and Reyher was given the important job of adapting it for the American stage and seeking a New York production (he had already translated and adapted scenes from *Fear and Misery in the Third Reich*). Although nothing came of it at that time and in that version, it brought Reyher in as collaborator on the later Laughton version that was eventually produced in America and has become more or less the standard text for the play.

By 1938, Ferdinand Reyher had been working in American films for a number of years. Always at least facile, Reyher could produce on demand, and he piled up a number of original story and screenplay credits during the thirties—movies with titles like *Fugitive Lovers, You May Be Next, Special Investigator*, and *Ride a Crooked Mile*—B-pictures. He did no work at all in films for a decade and half. In fact, Reyher left Hollywood in 1943 and returned to New York to write fiction—although he did return in the fifties to work on his two biggest pictures, *Wait Till the Sun Shines, Nellie* and *The World, the Flesh and the Devil*.

It was during this period, when Reyher was more or less permanently between movie assignments, that Brecht made his appearance. Reyher had been a regular contributor to a fund started in 1939 to help support Brecht and his family and to bring them to America. After they arrived, he was with them on numerous social occasions, often at refugee gatherings when he was the only American present. Given their mutual circumstances, it was no doubt inevitable that they would collaborate on freelance film projects, and they did on two. The first, barely more than an idea (and not a very good one at that), came out of a couple of hours of conversation the two had on October 4, 1941, as recorded by Brecht in his *Work Journal*:

> I narrate to Reyher from film materials the plan for *Joe Fleisch-hacker in Chicago*, and in a couple of hours we develop a film story, *The Bread King Learns Bread Baking*. There is no real bread in the States, and I really like to eat bread; my main meal is at night, and it is bread with butter. R[eyher] thinks the Americans have always been nomads, and nomads understand nothing about eating. Since one must study what the ground yields, etc. they have no need of real bread because it can't be sold in slices, and it must be sliced so that you can eat it quickly, standing or on the go. They really are nomads— they change their jobs like boots, build houses to last 20 years and don't live in them even that long, so that their home towns are no real places at all. Not for nothing has the great disorder here developed so luxuriously.[5]

The story they came up with wasn't much, and as Hollywood material it was quite impossible. Nevertheless Reyher thought enough of it to register their outline for protection at the Screen Writers Guild. Nothing came of it, however. *The Bread King Learns Bread Baking*, which is very much in the style of Brecht's old Chicago plays of the twenties, is distinguished only as the first of a number of Hollywood film projects on which Brecht would work, only one of which was finally ever produced. At least he was off to a start.

· ● ·

Film writing was not a new direction for Brecht but rather an old one that he began earnestly pursuing partly out of necessity but perhaps partly also out of a desire to achieve a degree of success where it had always earlier eluded him. The history of his involvement with motion pictures is a very long one yet is remarkable (for him) in its singular lack of real accomplishment. The East German critic Werner Hecht speaks persuasively of the "unhappy love affair" that the playwright had with film from the start.[6] In a very real sense the wonder is not, as some of the more straitlaced theatrical purists among his critics maintain, that Brecht chose to work in film—but that he did it with so little success.

His interest in the medium was real, natural, and, according to Margot Resch, quite inevitable: "By its very nature, cinema represents an ideal medium for his theatrical concept of the epic form. . . . Movies provide extensive exposure and could serve Brecht's didactic purposes far more effectively than the stage. And last but not least, they entail reputation and money, both of which Brecht was fond of."[7]

To these very good reasons I would add another: film was then *the* modern medium, and no writer in postwar Germany was as strenuously modern in his interests and attitudes as Bertolt Brecht. He had the showman's sure sense of what was in the air at any given moment. His early success in the theater—right up to his Marxist conversion—stemmed at least in part from his willingness to act upon this keen intuition. He gave the public not so much what it wanted as what it deserved. It was not lost on Brecht, the young drama critic in Augsburg, that while there was only one ill-attended legitimate theater in the city, there were eight movie houses doing thriving business. The public obviously wanted movies.

Brecht was a passionate picturegoer. He used his theater column in the Augsburger *Volkswille* to give occasional attention to movies as early as 1919 and wrote most enthusiastically about the work of Charlie Chaplin, who would continue to fascinate him as a filmmaker and as a performer. But Brecht's interest in film was not just critical and aesthetic. He went to the movies during this period in Augsburg as often as any young man in his twenties might—with this or that girl three or four times a week. His diaries at the time are filled with entries noting his visits:

Been to the cinema a lot. Specially detective dramas. . . .[8]

To the cinema with Orge in the evening. . . .[9]

In the evening Hedda and I went to the cinema. Scenes at sea. Why aren't there any pirate films? One day I'll write some. . . .[10]

And so on. In this way it was in the natural course of things that the young movie fan—as he also happened to be a provincial drama critic, a poet of growing national reputation, and a playwright of great promise—should soon write movies himself.

In the beginning, he turned to films for the same reason that he would return to them again and again in the coming years: in the hope of making money. He wanted it, and he needed it to get married to the singer Marianne Zoff. ("But now I write films, trying to do it just to put a roof over her head.") His first effort was evidently that pirate film he had declared he would write. Titled *Hanna Cash*, it dealt with the adventures of a female buccaneer, and though not even an outline of the plot survives, it may well have been the source of the fanciful "Pirate Jenny" song that fits so ill in *The Threepenny Opera*. Brecht had also planned a bizarre story that he notes in his diaries under the title *The Mormon Pope*. This one, it seems, had to do with a Latter-Day Icarus who, in order to astound his earthbound coreligionists, attempts a balloon flight higher than he really ought to go. Whatever their merits, these early efforts had no real prospects for production when he wrote them.

Production, however, was soon to come. Through his friend, subsequent collaborator, and fellow Augsburger, Caspar Neher, Brecht was put in contact with the Stuart Webbs Film Company in Munich. Stuart Webbs was not the producer or principal stockholder, but was rather the name of a fictitious English detective who was portrayed by actor-producer Ernst Reicher in a series of mystery-adventure films. The series, which had originated in 1913, had been quite popular but by 1921 was on its last legs. Brecht had no way of knowing this when, with Neher, he agreed to write a scenario for a new Stuart Webbs film.

What the two came up with was a complicated and rather hokey thriller, *The Mystery of the Jamaica Bar*, involving the disappearance of a number of beautiful women on the island and a bar owned by a sinister planter who is secretly running a white-slave operation on the side. Webbs rescues the women, foils the plot, and captures the villain. Except for the exotic locales and the white-slave racket situation, there is little of Brecht in the scenario. It was intended merely as a Stuart Webbs vehicle and might have served as well as any of the rest but, according to producer Reicher, the company was unable to raise enough to finance the production. In any case, Brecht and Neher were never paid for their efforts.

Once begun, however, the two kept at it. An intensive collaboration during three days in July 1921 brought forth *Three in the Tower*, a melodramatic love story involving a captain, his wife, and her lover, a young lieutenant. In a fit of jealous anguish, the captain commits suicide, but, mysteriously, his body is not to be found. He haunts the two lovers until at last—just as mysteriously—his corpse is discovered, and the lieutenant and the captain's widow are left free at last to consummate their illicit passion. In his study *Film bei Brecht*, the East German critic Wolfgang Gersch suggests the influence of Strindberg on *Three in the Tower*—and that, to put it bluntly, is just the trouble with it.[11] With both *The Mystery of the Jamaica Bar* and *Three in the Tower* Brecht and Neher were trying to do things that could not really be done in silent movies. The plot complications of the first were far too intricate to be managed in purely visual terms; and what little action there is in the second is psychological, largely internal, and quite beyond the limited narrative resources of the silent cinema.

Something of the same difficulty mars *The Diamond Eater*, a much more interesting piece of work from the same period and quite the most successful of Brecht's silent movie scenarios. He wrote this one without Neher's assistance, and what sets it most apart from the rest is how remarkably Brechtian it is in both style and substance. The setting is a waterfront dive, the cast a gang of thieves, and the action revolves around an ambitious larceny. A priceless diamond is stolen and hidden away in an orange. Because the gang doesn't know which orange it might be in, they are obliged, in one memorable scene, to eat their way through a great pile of them. Unknown to them, however, their leader, Latte, has palmed the diamond, and makes off with it himself, along with the lady from whom it was stolen. There is an amoral tone to the story that anticipates *Happy End* and *The Threepenny Opera*, and Latte, who wields a knife menacingly on occasion, seems an early version of Mack the Knife.

Brecht managed to make some money with only one of his silent film scenarios—and that came about more or less by accident. In 1922, the magazine *Tagebuch* together with the Richard-Oswald-Gesellschaft film company offered a prize competition for a film scenario to be produced by the Oswald company. Brecht, who happened to be in Berlin at the time, got together with his newfound friend (and Nazi-to-be) Arnolt Bronnen, and the two brainstormed a story that they titled *Robinsonade on Asuncion*. It owed something to *Three in the Tower*, so the original idea was probably Brecht's. They elaborated upon it considerably, however, switching the setting to the Pacific island of Asuncion in the Marianas, and isolating the trio—two men and a woman—from civilization by means of a devastating volcanic eruption. The trio of survivors are left to shift for themselves, and immediately the men begin to compete for the only prize left on the island worth possessing—the woman. She passes from one to the other as competition for her grows fiercer. Finally, they kill one another over her, and when at last the rescuers arrive to pick up survivors of the volcanic blast, they find only one: a woman gone mad. The story, which might be read as a kind of anti-Nietzschean fable, was sketched out only in bare outline by Brecht and Bronnen, but it was sufficient to win the *Tagebuch* prize for them.

According to Bronnen, who reported the episode in his autobiography, *Arnolt Bronnen gibt zu Protokoll*,[12] it was all a put-up job: first prize was practically assured them because he knew somebody on the jury. The two shared the award of 100,000 paper marks (not nearly so grand a sum in those inflation days as it might seem), and they looked forward to having their melodrama produced. In fact it was—though not in the form in which they conceived it. Bronnen wrote a script for the Oswald company and had that rewritten in turn. When at last *S.O.S. Island of Tears* was released, neither writer claimed it.

• • •

None of his early attempts at film writing came to matter very much to Brecht, however, for between the time that he collaborated on the story with Bronnen and the time the film was released, his play *Drums in the Night* had its premiere in Munich, and he was awarded the Kleist prize for it. Suddenly he became the most important young playwright in Germany. He married Marianne Zoff and began a spectacular career as a celebrity-dramatist that culminated with the popular success of *The Threepenny Opera*. As Wolfgang Gersch says of him, "A choice between theater and film was probably never even considered."[13] Brecht showed no further interest in writing for movies until they started to talk.

The advent of sound coincided neatly with the international success of *The Threepenny Opera*. Nerofilmgesellschaft bought film rights to work on a production by one of the leading directors in the German film industry, G. W. Pabst, and Brecht was commissioned to do the screenplay (see p. 19). If there were to be changes, Brecht wanted to make them. In fact, he wanted to make quite a few. His intention was to reorder the original work so that it might better express the Marxist philosophy he had recently embraced. Toward this end, he wrote a treatment of moderate length that was so different in approach and content that he went so far as to retitle it *The Boil: A Threepenny Film.*

The Boil is the sort of extravagant story that might seem like a terrific idea when told to friends over drinks but evaporates when you try to get it down on paper the next day. Deficient in incident and without much real plot, the only real conflict in it is the underlying one of the class struggle. The elements of John Gay's eighteenth-century work *The Beggar's Opera,* which originally inspired Brecht, have been dropped almost completely from *The Boil.* Only the characters remain and they—MacHeath, Peachum, and Brown—are now all too plainly cast in roles personifying separate forces of repression. They patch up their differences and form hasty alliances just to keep a lid on the lumpen. The beggars have rallied around Filch, the man with the boil in the title (plainly also a revolutionary symbol for a sick society—a boil to be lanced), and they now threaten to shake loose from Peachum's firm grasp. When he plans the beggars' demonstration, his wife warns him: "You're a genius, Peachum, but don't go too far: You wish to make a show of misery, but just remember that misery is very great."[14] Even thus couched in negative terms, Brecht's revolutionary message comes through loud and clear.

It was far too plain, in any case, for Nerofilmgesellschaft, which declared in the trial that followed that Brecht had attempted to give the film "an outspoken political tendency"—which was nothing more or less than the truth. In fact, Brecht had been given a "right of codecision" on the screenplay in his contract but had no right to veto the film itself. On such apparent contradictions lawsuits are based. From the beginning he had done all that he possibly could to maintain control over the adaptation of his work to film. He was to write the treatment, which was Nero's way of honoring its contractual obligation of "codecision," but his contribution was to end there. Yet before he had even begun it, he managed to get Leo Lania signed to do the screenplay. Lania, politically and professionally sympathetic to

Brecht, was a writer Brecht felt he could influence. The two worked together fairly closely in the beginning, but when Nero saw where Brecht and Lania were headed, they demanded that Lania proceed on his own and that Brecht indemnify them for having exceeded the role extended him by contract and in this way having slowed down Lania's work on the screenplay. There was no real basis for such a suit, for Brecht had done nothing to hinder Lania, but had, rather, simply urged him in a direction not to Nero's liking. Brecht was not required to pay damages to Nero and had, in the meantime, filed a suit of his own.

The suit was brought by Brecht and Kurt Weill. Weill joined the suit as a gesture of solidarity, complaining that his score had been altered on the basis of a trumpet fanfare that had been added to the wedding music for MacHeath and Polly Peachum. Their joint action, which came to be known as the *Threepenny* trial, was really, therefore, undertaken more or less as a countersuit. When Nero failed in its effort to wring damages from Brecht, Brecht might reasonably have been expected to drop his own action—and he was urged to do so, even by his friends on the Left. He was, however, out to prove a point, and a very big one it was. He intended nothing less than to wrest artistic control of the film industry from its capitalist proprietors and deliver it to the filmmakers. His suit asserted the right of the writer to control his own material.

He lost. Custom prevailed: although Brecht's contract with Nero clearly gave him a voice in the preparation of the screenplay, it was customary then—as of course it is still now—that the producer have the final word on story decisions and changes. Brecht, it had been argued, knew this when he entered into the contract with the film company. Furthermore, the verdict maintained that he could not withhold his consent to changes made in his original work since he himself had contributed to the adaptation.

While it might have been far more satisfying to see Brecht's idealistic bid for artistic control upheld, there was certainly some justice in the court's verdict in this case, for, as it turned out, a good deal of *The Boil* found its way into G. W. Pabst's finished film, *The Threepenny Opera*. We may assume that Leo Lania's first-draft screenplay followed Brecht's treatment fairly closely, for it was to this Nero had objected in the first place. It is interesting how much of it was retained in later versions by Bela Belasz and Ladislaus Vajda. The first third of the film—right through the wedding of MacHeath and Polly—follows Brecht's outline closely. The one major new story element suggested by Brecht—the acquisition of a bank by Polly and MacHeath's gang in his absence—was also left in, though pushed back in the plot a bit and de-emphasized somewhat. The demonstration of misery by the beggars, with which Peachum threatens to disrupt the coronation in the original play, is depicted graphically in a dream sequence by Brecht in *The Boil* but actually takes place at the conclusion of the *Threepenny Opera* film. It offered a potential for visual spectacle that director Pabst found simply irresistible. It should be underlined that Pabst's governing intention throughout was to make a good film and not necessarily one faithful either to the original or to the author's new intentions. He was his own man, and considering the quality of the movies he had already made (*The Love of Jeanne Ney, Westfront 1918*), he had every right to be. He oversaw the rewriting of the script and, apparently indifferent as to the outcome of the *Threepenny* trial, made preparations for the production even as it proceeded.

Pabst's confidence was more than vindicated by the finished film. Released in 1931, it is among the three or four finest to have been produced in pre-Hitler Germany and one that indelibly bears Pabst's signature of authorship. In story it represents a compromise between the original stage play and the radical departure from it proposed by Brecht in *The Boil*. Politically, there is nothing to it at all: Pabst's underworld is as amoral as the one first presented by Brecht and lacks even the behaviorist apologia offered in the original. What it does have, however, is remarkable style, Pabst's own, and the absolute integrity of style with content. It all fits together; not a frame, not a gesture is out of place. Pabst managed to create a microcosm in the *Threepenny Opera* film, a brooding shadow-world of his own, and within that environment all is consistent. A large part of the credit for this must go to designer Andrei Andreiev, who created the huge, mostly three-dimensional set in and around which the action takes place. It is part Soho, part German backstreet, part never-never land, but at the same time pure Pabst. The dark and misty look of the film—it is never quite daylight—fits the action exactly. What is perhaps most remarkable is that within such a visual context the film's humor and its songs work as well as they do. All of this is to say that Brecht's worst fears regarding the adaptation of *The Threepenny*

Opera to the screen were realized—spectacularly and beautifully. The film is not a work of Bertolt Brecht's but of G. W. Pabst's—and that, remembering what Brecht showed us of his intentions in *The Boil*, may be just as well.

With regard to Brecht's development, probably the most important result of the entire episode was that it provoked him to write the long essay, "The Threepenny Trial." The piece is more than a record of the trial—and more, too, than a justification of his intentions in it. In "The Threepenny Trial," he sets forth nothing less than a theory of popular culture, with particular reference to film. It is, perhaps inevitably, a Marxist theory. In fact, there is evidence that his renewed interest in the motion-picture medium came not so much as a consequence of the advent of sound as because of his conversion to Marxism. Film seemed then the medium *par excellence* for communicating the revolutionary message to the masses. Hadn't Lenin himself said as much, after all, when he emerged from a screening of D. W. Griffith's *Intolerance?* Weren't the films of Eisenstein, Dovzhenko, and Pudovkin proving that art and propaganda might be mixed to achieve stirring results? If Brecht had not been previously interested in film—and of course he had been—then a commitment to it would practically have been thrust upon him along with his new political commitment. Thus the new concern with the medium that he shows in "The Threepenny Trial" is more theoretical and programmatic than it is practical. He seems less interested in film for what it was or could be than for what it could do.

The heavy emphasis in his essay on "capitalism" and its relation to film, as well as the whole thrust of his argument during the *Threepenny* trial, should make it clear that Brecht saw it as a necessity to move film production outside the marketplace. Could movies be made outside the established framework of capital financing? Could they be distributed outside regular channels? Filmmakers—especially those on the Left—had been trying to solve these problems for years and are still trying today. Brecht himself was involved in one such effort beginning in 1931, the year "The Threepenny Trial" was published and the Pabst film was released. It was the only film production on which he worked from first to last. If Brecht's work in film is to be judged, it should probably be on the basis of his contribution to *Kuhle Wampe.*

That the picture came to be made at all was due almost wholly to the tenacity of the four creative personalities who worked together on the production. All were committed Marxists and were determined that the film they set out to make should reflect their commitment. Ernst Ottwalt, Brecht's collaborator on the script, had been a miner and a metalworker before becoming a novelist and joining the Communist Party; his novels reflected both his working-class origins and his political point of view. Ottwalt was to be another of the unlucky German refugees in the Soviet Union. There, in 1936, he was swept away in the wave of arrests accompanying the Moscow trials. Executed in 1943, he was "rehabilitated" in 1953. Director Slatan Dudow, a Bulgarian, had emigrated to Germany in 1922 where he had worked in the theater first with Erwin Piscator and later with Brecht; *Kuhle Wampe* was his first film. Hanns Eisler, the composer, was the brother of Communist Party functionary Gerhard Eisler; he had become and would remain Brecht's chief musical collaborator after Kurt Weill.

Dudow went to Brecht with the idea for the film. He had come across an article in the newspaper on the suicide of a young man, one of millions of unemployed in Germany in that Depression year of 1931. From this, he had put together a brief treatment that put the young man in the context of his family—the unemployed father holding forth testily on the need for each to pull his own weight; the mother seconding him loyally; the employed sister defending her brother. The son commits suicide. The family, much in arrears in its rent, is evicted and must take refuge in the summer tent colony in Kuhle Wampe (a district of Berlin). That was as far as Dudow's treatment went, yet for Brecht that was quite enough. He was greatly intrigued with the possibilities of doing a film on the current economic crisis in Germany. The two turned immediately to Ottwalt for his ideas for such a story. As possibilities for music in the production began to suggest themselves, Eisler's aid was enlisted.

With a finished script in hand, the collaborators went to Prometheus-Film GmbH, which had served as distributor for Soviet films in Europe and had on its own produced a few left-wing films in Germany. Given the go-ahead, Brecht and the others went into production on *Kuhle Wampe* and were well begun when Prometheus went bankrupt. Praesens-Film GmbH then agreed to take over the production but only on condition that the actors and filmmakers involved in it forgo their fees. Because by that time they knew they were working on something special, all the "above the line" talent agreed to do just that. Production continued—but troubles were far from over. When shooting was all but finished, the company that supplied the sound equipment—a monopoly—informed the filmmakers that it was withdrawing its equipment essentially for political reasons; threat of a lawsuit, however, forced the company to honor its contract. The courts later proved no threat at all when the government took action.

Kuhle Wampe was described with considerable accuracy by the government censor in the document banning the finished film as "no pure dramatic feature. It is a mixture of dramatic feature, propaganda film and reportage. . . ." So it is indeed, and so it was meant to be. The film is, to a remarkable degree, a realization in fact of the theory that Brecht put forth on film in "The Threepenny Trial." You see it especially in the first and final sections in the heavy use of documentary techniques that Brecht advocated in his essay. Used as they are in the film, they accomplish precisely what he hoped they would—abstracting the characters who emerge from the mass, depersonalizing them to a certain extent, but above all making them representatives of a certain class, a certain age group, people in a certain situation. There is not—and some may legitimately object to this—much opportunity offered for empathy, for we are offered only surfaces to scrutinize. The young man who commits suicide in the first section, for example, says nothing and is not even given so much as a Christian name. He is identified only as "the Bönike son" and is personified only by his action. Yet somehow—for his suicide is the most moving moment in the film—this is quite enough. When a neighbor views his body and comments cynically, "One less unemployed," it seems like a verdict read upon an entire generation.

Just when we may be getting personally involved with one or more of them, our interest is diverted to others previously on the periphery of the action. The young man commits suicide in the first section; there is not a word mentioned of it in the second. As we become interested in the problems of the sister, Anni, when she becomes pregnant by her young auto mechanic, Fritz, the focus of the action is shifted to Anni's workmate Gerda and her Kurt. In the final section the separate strands of the story, such as it is, are tied together in only the most makeshift sort of knot, and the real action here is provided by the mass sport meet of Communist youth. Gerda and Kurt participate as contestants, and Anni and Fritz as spectators, but the event—the singing, the athletics, all those anonymous happy faces who seem curiously quite like Hitler Youth—is itself in the foreground and is not merely used as background to the personal stories. The approach, which keeps all "human interests" to a minimum, is distinctly and designedly antidramatic—and in this way uniquely Brechtian.

Does it work? Emotionally, no. But I suppose it does intellectually. We are interested in the young people of *Kuhle Wampe* not so much for who they are as for what they represent—a whole generation of young people in Germany who have been dispossessed by the economics of their elders, a generation on whom a fateful decision is now being pressed. (*Kuhle Wampe* was released in America as *Whither Germany?*) Even here, however, something is wrong, for the choice presented in the picture is not one between communism and national socialism, as it had become in those last couple of years before Hitler's rise to power, but rather one between communism and the vulgarity and political ignorances of the older generation. The Nazis are not even hinted at. Using the older members of the Bönike family and their friends as the whipping boys of Hitler, Goebbels, and company (as Brecht and his collaborators did in *Kuhle Wampe*) seems, under the circumstances, if not cowardly at least not terribly brave. Admittedly, if a bolder line had been pursued the picture might not have gotten released at all.

Eventually, of course, it was released—though not without a fight. The action halting the distribution of *Kuhle Wampe* was taken by the government office of film censorship on March 31, 1932. The government was in an awkward position. With demonstrations leading to mass brawls between Nazi Brownshirts and Red Guard street fighters an almost weekly occurrence, it seemed fairly certain that the release of a film with such a pronounced political point of view would only add fuel to a fire already burning out of control. Accordingly, the film was banned. A great roar of protest rose from journals of the Left and Center. It was useless trying to fight the ban in the courts, but because the case had gained such publicity, the office of film censorship agreed to hear an appeal.

Brecht's ironic record of the proceedings, a short piece that he titled "A Small Contribution to the Theme of Realism," proved that the censor they were dealing with was no fool. At issue was the suicide of young Bönike. In the film it takes place immediately after he hears news of the "emergency decree" of President Hindenburg that ended unemployment benefits for the Bönikes and thousands of others. Cause and effect are clearly implied, the censor argued. Beyond that, he declared, he objected to the scene on *artistic* grounds. Taken somewhat aback at that, Brecht and his collaborators asked the censor to explain:

> He went on: "Yes, it may astound you that I object to your portrayal on the grounds that it doesn't seem *human* enough to me. You haven't portrayed a human, but rather—yes, let's admit it—a type. Your unemployed worker is no real individual, no man of flesh and blood, distinct from all other men, with particular worries, with particular joys, and finally with a specific fate of his own. He is presented in a completely superficial way—if you, as artists, will pardon me for this strong expression—so that *we learn too little about him*, but the consequences are of a *political* nature and force me to raise a protest against the release of your film. Your film has the tendency to present the suicide as typical, as something not just appropriate to this or that (morbidly inclined) individual but rather as the fate of an entire class! It is your position that society encourages young people to suicide by denying them the possibility of employment. And you really don't concern yourself either with giving further advice to the unemployed so that they can change their situation. No, gentlemen, you haven't behaved as artists, not here. It wasn't your intention to present a single, shocking case—that nobody would have objected to.[15]

After listening to the censor's interpretation of their work (which was, after all, very close to what they themselves had intended), Brecht wrote, "We had the uncomfortable impression that we had been seen through." Not to be discouraged, however, Brecht launched into a specious argument to the effect that indeed young Bönike *was* an individual with all sorts of personal characteristics. Why, just consider, he urged, the telling detail that had inspired the suicide scene—Bönike carefully removing his watch before jumping out the tenement window. The censor argued details with them and matters of artistic intention. The lawyers present were baffled. At last they hammered out a compromise by which certain specific cuts were agreed to by the filmmakers, and in return the censor reluctantly permitted the film's release. The meeting ended and Brecht concludes: "Leaving the building, we did not withhold our admiration for the sharp-witted censor. He went much deeper in understanding our artistic intentions than our friendliest critics did. He had read us a short course in realism. From the point of view of the police."

Kuhle Wampe opened in Berlin on May 30, 1932. There were some demonstrations outside the theaters but nothing of the size and sort that the police had feared. The film was a great commercial success. There were fourteen thousand paid admissions the first week alone, and the next week they opened it in fifteen more Berlin theaters. As a postscript to the affair, when the movie played at about the same time in Moscow, it did well enough, but the suicide scene puzzled the audience. Nobody could figure out why a worker (unemployed or not) who was sufficiently well off to own a wristwatch should wish to commit suicide.

• • •

Less than a year later Hitler had come to power and Brecht had gone into exile. Remarkably enough, along with all the other writing he did as he jumped from Denmark to Sweden to Finland, Brecht managed also to do some work on film projects. All of it was very tentative— proposals, outlines, treatments—and none of it even got to the script stage. Yet it proves that the interest was there. Brecht kept looking for the main chance, a financial opportunity that would lift him from the permanent state of penury in which he lived as a refugee and into a life with some degree of security. Entry into the movie industry would have provided that. Having had some success with *Kuhle Wampe*, he must have wanted nothing better than a chance to show that he could repeat it.

While Scandinavia was right for him as a writer's retreat, it placed him far from any movie action. He must have guessed that early on, for the first serious interest in any of his film proposals came from London. Leo Lania, who as early as 1934 had made contacts in the British film industry, was there. He let Brecht know that he was in a position to put a project before Alexander Korda, and Brecht and Lania began immediately to cast about for a suitable subject. They came up with quite a promising one—a film biography of Ignaz Semmelweis, the nineteenth-century Viennese physician (actually, he was born a Hungarian, as was Alexander Korda) who was responsible for identifying the cause and cure of childbed fever. In the proposal, they suggested that Semmelweis's scientific investigations could be presented with the same sort of excitement and suspense as a criminal investigation, that his story was essentially a detective story. It could have been done just that way, too—if Korda had only taken on the project. But, after giving it serious consideration, he turned it down. He was convinced the public couldn't be interested in medical subjects—this in a ten-year span that saw Paul Muni as Pasteur, Edward G. Robinson as Ehrlich, and Greer Garson as Madame Curie.

Although more film ideas passed between Brecht and various other collaborators, the next real event in his episodic screenwriting career came in 1936 with the work he did on *Pagliacci*. London again was the scene of the action. Brecht was brought into the production by Fritz Kortner, an old friend from the Berlin theater (he played Shlink in the first Berlin production of *In the Jungle of Cities*). Hanns Eisler also became involved. When Brecht came to London to work on the film, which had been tagged for production right from the start, he found himself working on the script while Eisler worked on the score. "The man was industrious," Eisler remembered. "He really wanted to do a job. That is to say, in his hands the *Pagliacci* script took on the most remarkable shape. Great poetic beauties emerged intolerable for the producer but most of all for [Richard] Tauber."[16] (The German tenor Tauber was to be the star of the film.) Brecht was fired from the film in a matter of days and, although paid off in full, received no screen credit when *Pagliacci* was released in 1937.

Not long afterward, there was the possibility of a project with Erwin Piscator. Brecht submitted an idea for a film dealing with the blockade of Bilbao during the still-continuing Spanish Civil War, which he titled *Potato Jones*, after its hero, an American blockade-runner. Yet Piscator's prospects for production proved ephemeral, and no copy of the story survives. Others do, however. There is a story in Swedish, *We Want to Fly* (on which he collaborated in Stockholm with one Henry Peter Matthis), about a working-class boy whose ambition it is to be a pilot. There are notes and plans for the adaptation of nearly all his plays to film. There are ideas—paragraphs, sentences from his notebooks—that show that even during this, his most productive period as a playwright, he had certainly not abandoned his interest in the motion-picture medium. Had he, as he later insisted, looked upon it purely as a means to make money, he would not have written so much on his own initiative. True hack work is done only on demand.

Perhaps just as important for the Hollywood experience that was to follow was the fact that even though he was tucked away through this period in the northern corner of Europe, he managed to maintain relations with the scattered left-wing refugees of the German theater, many of whom found their way eventually into American films. He also managed to make American acquaintances during his Theatre Union misadventure in New York that he would later renew in Hollywood. And, during his European years of exile, he made a friend of Jean Renoir. He visited the French director a number of times at the latter's home in Meudon. In Renoir's autobiography, *My Life and My Films*, Renoir speaks warmly of one occasion in particular on which Brecht came accompanied by Margarete Steffin, who brought along her concertina accordion. They sang songs, German and French, late into the night. Renoir preceded Brecht to Hollywood by only a few months. These and other such relations, partly social and partly professional, proved essential to his continued survival in America. More than most, the movie industry is one that thrives on friendship and its counterfeits.

It wasn't long until Brecht was involved with one of his Hollywood friends in a paying movie project. His collaboration with Fritz Lang on *Hangmen Also Die*, which provided him with his single Hollywood credit, is a story in itself, a long and complicated one that is told in Chapter 4. Ultimately its importance lay in the fact that it provided him with the wherewithal to pursue theater projects in New York. He had, after all, come to America with a whole suitcase full of unproduced plays, which included his best work, and his first obligation was always to the theater. Other movie money came his way, and it's true that whenever he found himself in financial straits he attempted to write screen stories on speculation, as he had done with Ferdinand Reyher. But such attempts always met with the same negative results. Better than anyone else, Brecht knew the nature of his talent. He was a playwright, and essentially would remain one for the rest of his life.

3

WHICH WAY TO
DOHENY?

I t is very likely that when the history of
American civilization during this century comes to be written, the
single most important event in it will prove to be one that took place
thousands of miles away from here: the rise to power of Adolf Hitler
in Germany. That, and the consequent *Anschluss* of Austria to Germany, drove thousands and thousands of German-speaking refugees
out of Europe. Most of them were Jews and many were those who
had actively opposed the Nazis on their way to power and were therefore considered political enemies of the new regime. The overwhelming majority of the refugees, whether political or religious, came
eventually to the United States.

Yet it is not the quantity but the quality of this wave of immigrants
from Germany and Austria that concerns us here, because it included
the cream of the intellectual life of what was perhaps Europe's most

advanced culture. For example, with Freud in England, and Otto
Fenichel, Erik Erikson, Karen Horney, Theodor Reik, and Wilhelm
Reich in the United States, the locus of significant thought and activ-
ity in psychoanalysis shifted from the German-speaking world to the
English; and it has never shifted back again. In science and physics
there were many who came here, but certainly the most illustrious of
them all was Albert Einstein, probably the greatest scientific mind of
our age. In music, there were Arnold Schönberg, Kurt Weill, and
Otto Klemperer; in literature, Thomas and Heinrich Mann, Hermann
Broch, Alfred Döblin, Bruno Frank, and Franz Werfel; in the theater,
Max Reinhardt, Erwin Piscator, Carl Zuckmayer, and of course Bertolt Brecht.

Brecht was one of a considerable number of German-speaking
intellectuals who settled, at least for the period of the war, in California. Of course the movie industry had long been open to European—
and particularly German—talent. Even before Hitler, directors such
as Erich von Stroheim, William Dieterle, Josef von Sternberg, and
Ernst Lubitsch had found their way to Hollywood and made their
mark. As refugees from the Nazis came Fritz Lang, Curt and Robert
Siodmak, Fred Zinnemann, and Billy Wilder. There were many
actors on the German stage and in films who became well known to
American moviegoers—among them Peter Lorre, Conrad Veidt,
Oscar Homolka, and Luise Rainer. Various movie companies (most
prominently M-G-M and Warner Brothers) had offered writing contracts to German novelists such as Heinrich Mann and Alfred Döblin,
making emigration easier for them because they had employers of
record, and easing the way for them during their first year or so. Yet
not all of those who arrived in Los Angeles had anything at all to do
with the movie industry. Thomas Mann moved there simply for the
climate, perhaps seeing himself as a latter-day Goethe in search of
"the land where the lemons grow." Franz Werfel must have come
for just about the same reason. Max Horkheimer, the social philosopher who had founded the Frankfurt Institute for Social Research,
went there for his health—and was followed by his friend and second
in command, Theodor Adorno, and for a time their associates, Herbert and Ludwig Marcuse. The assemblage of German-speaking intellectuals there in the Los Angeles area was such that Thomas Mann
hazarded that not even Weimar in its Goethe-Schiller heyday could
have boasted such an array. Not long ago the American novelist

Bruce Jay Friedman commented in bewilderment on this period in Hollywood when he might have pulled up in a car beside Thomas Mann on foot (it is difficult to imagine him any other way) and asked, "Which way to Doheny?"

Bertolt Brecht apparently knew them all. He had remained in Santa Monica in hopes of getting movie work, but his circle of acquaintances stretched wide to include many who were not involved in movies or the arts, many with whom he disagreed, and many for whom he felt a certain intellectual contempt. Brecht fancied himself a Marxist philosopher. As a defender of the true faith, he felt called upon to involve himself in debate at every opportunity with those who opposed it or deviated from it in order to set them right. Friendship had nothing to do with it. As a matter of fact, Brecht had no talent for friendship. His intellectual arrogance was such that those who did not bow to his opinions on any question were simply considered stupid or malicious. His attitude may have made him insufferable to others, but even by his own accounts in his *Work Journal* it made for some very lively evenings of conversation.

He did have a few whom *he* counted as friends, however. Among them was the composer Hanns Eisler. Eisler and Paul Dessau were the two musical collaborators with whom Brecht worked following Brecht's break with Kurt Weill. A far more talented musician than Dessau, Eisler was nevertheless completely willing to subordinate his own ideas to Brecht's. In fact, he was quite facile and adaptable as a composer; it was his strength as a craftsman and his weakness as an artist. He started out as a student of Schönberg, yet never undertook many ambitious works in the twelve-tone scale or any other. His reason for coming to Hollywood was to find employment writing music for the movies. Given his chance, he proved quite capable—as his former teacher, who was also on the scene, did not (Schönberg was ludicrously unwilling to compromise with studio requirements). Because Eisler was profoundly convinced of Brecht's genius and made that plain, there was never any conflict between them. He, like Brecht, was a dedicated and quite orthodox Marxist (his brother was Gerhard Eisler, the Comintern functionary, and his sister was Ruth Fischer, the apostate Communist who later aided the House Committee on Un-American Activities), so there were no arguments about politics.

In spite of his radical politics, Eisler was a man who liked to please people. Possessed of considerable personal charm, he mixed well with those whose outlook was quite unlike his own—with Thomas Mann, for instance, whose home he visited frequently. Mann's wife, Katia, recalls in her book, *Unwritten Memories*: "My husband found him quite entertaining, especially his critical remarks about Wagner. He always said, 'Just listen—that passage, for example, it's—all I can say is, that old rascal!' "[1]

Not only did Eisler collect celebrities, he also made it a practice, as Boswell had before him, to bring them together just to see what sort of fireworks might occur. He did that once with Brecht and Schönberg. Yet even Eisler felt some trepidation in this case: "I did not want my respected and ailing teacher Arnold Schönberg to be upset by some remark of Brecht's which Brecht could not anticipate; and I also did not want Arnold Schönberg to make one of his stupid remarks against socialism, which I was used to taking in silence, since he was sick and must not be excited."[2] He knew that if any such remark was made Brecht would certainly not take it in silence. But in the event, things went relatively well. Although it became clear early on that Schönberg had no idea whatever who Brecht might be, the two sat and exchanged pleasantries for nearly an hour until Schönberg told an anecdote that made things much easier between them:

> Schönberg related: "Once I climbed a hill, and since I have a weak heart the steep path was very difficult for me. But in front of me there walked a donkey. He did not walk up the steep path, but always in a zigzag left and right of the path, thus compensating for the steepness. So I imitated him, and now I can say that I have learned something from a donkey."[3]

Brecht was charmed by the story—in fact he later made use of it in a poem. He, too, may have learned something from Schönberg's donkey. Later in his life, as his way in politics grew steep and wearying, he made frequent recourse to the zigzag path.

Brecht's Boswell presented him to a number of people he might not otherwise have met—often, one suspects, with the intention of sitting back to watch the ensuing explosion. It was through Eisler that Brecht met the entire West Coast complement of the Frankfurt Institute for Social Research. Theodor Adorno was the contact here.

Besides his expertise in philosophy and the social sciences, Adorno was an accomplished musicologist who had studied in Vienna with Alban Berg. Eisler had known Adorno for years, and through him had met his colleagues Max Horkheimer and Herbert Marcuse in Germany and in America. He was sure that Brecht would find their company . . . stimulating.

Brecht already knew what he thought of the Frankfurt Institute for Social Research. He had become acquainted with it and its principals at a remove through Walter Benjamin, who in the thirties was himself a member of the Institute. Benjamin operated its Paris branch after their expulsion from Germany. Why were the members of the Frankfurt Institute for Social Research expelled? Why did they feel it necessary to flee as a group from Germany? Because the Institute, which was loosely affiliated with that city's university, was dedicated to the modification of Marxism to practical, democratic ends, and because most of the members of the Institute—certainly Max Horkheimer, Theodor Adorno, and Herbert Marcuse—were greatly interested and stirred by the teachings of Sigmund Freud and were attempting a reconciliation of the revelations of psychoanalysis regarding the individual with the social and political philosophy of Karl Marx. Freud and Marx, of course, were both on the Nazis' ideological hit list: *deutsche Kultur* was to be purged of all traces of their influence. When the Nazi rise to power seemed imminent, the Institute managed to shift a share of its considerable endowment out of Germany to banks in America. Horkheimer and Adorno, both Jews, followed their funds to New York where for a while the Institute enjoyed the same sort of loose affiliation with Columbia University that it had had with Frankfurt. Branches were set up in Zurich, with Herbert Marcuse in charge, and in Paris with Walter Benjamin; Marcuse and Benjamin were also Jews.

Brecht and Benjamin argued frequently about the Institute, with Brecht taking the orthodox Communist position against the Institute's brand of revisionism. Benjamin usually deferred. Out of these arguments and earlier ones in Berlin came Brecht's uncompleted *Tui* novel, a 138-page fragment of text and notes in his collected works. He began it in 1934 and made a speech that drew on the novel material at the Writers' Congress for the Defense of Culture in 1935. Taking off from *Turandot*, he posited a Chinese republic (meant to suggest Weimar) that is ruled by a well-intentioned but rather silly society of sages, the Tellekt-Ual-Ins (a crude anagram of the word "intellectuals," of course, which provides the acronym Tui, which he used throughout). He meant to suggest the mess that the Frankfurt Institute principals and their Social Democratic allies had made of things by adulterating Marxism. There is not much plot development in the fragments. For the most part the material consists of jottings on the curious history and contradictory customs of the Tuis. He may have decided that in satirizing the Weimar Republic he was beating a dead horse; in any case, he discontinued work on the *Tui* novel in 1935, only to begin thinking about it again in 1943 when, in Hollywood, he found himself face to face with some of its leading characters.

By the time Brecht met Horkheimer, Adorno, and Marcuse for the first time, they had given up their first freehold in the New World at Columbia and had found their way out to the land of palms and orange blossoms. The first meeting with Adorno and Horkheimer is recorded by Brecht on March 19, 1942, less than a year after his arrival in America. He notes a rather heavy discussion of the theories of the physicist Hans Reichenbach. It was more or less typical. He does later describe a lighter evening spent at Adorno's listening to recordings of music by Hanns Eisler. Afterward, however, he could not deny himself the pleasure of launching into an attack on Arnold Schönberg. (No wonder Eisler was a bit fearful of bringing the two together.) In general he seems to have been on better terms with Adorno because at least with him he could discuss music, a subject on which he also considered himself an expert. (Eisler was nevertheless there to act as a buffer between them.)

When Brecht met with the entire Frankfurt Institute, though, he always became quite contemptuous in his journal jottings. There were, for instance, full-scale seminars—one of them called for a discussion of a pronouncement by Vice President Henry A. Wallace to the effect that the war was a revolution of the people and that the century of the common man was on its way (according to Brecht, the Institute members thought this dangerously intemperate). Another called for a debate over Aldous Huxley's novel of the future, *Brave New World*, at which Huxley himself and Reichenbach, the physicist, were also present. It was after these that Brecht began talking about returning to his story of the "Tellekt-Ual-Ins." "Adorno here. This Frankfurt Institute is a mine for the *Tui* novel. . . ." The last and longest jotting—also the most important—was entered in Brecht's *Work Journal* on December 18, 1944, although it was actually an excerpt from a letter to his son, Stefan:

> The Frankfurt Sociological Institute (which inspired my *Tui* novel) has now consolidated its fragile financial foundation: the New York Jews are financing them on an all-embracing project of research on anti-Semitism. Horkheimer and Adorno have already worked out questionnaires by which *the fascist type* is supposed to be ascertained, methodically and on strict scientific grounds. It is the type who is the potential anti-Semite, and from now on he can be diagnosed (and perhaps treated) in a nonvirulent stage. Only a few questions: "Do you believe that the world war closes off natural catastrophes, epidemics, earthquakes, etc.? Do you hold syphilis to be unhealthy?" I brought the conversation around to the short essay on the Jewish question by K[arl] M[arx] and heard once again that it is obsolete (and chiefly because it came from the *young* M[arx]). M[arx] is supposed to have fallen into Goebbels' distinction between creative and grabbed capital. . . . M[arx] took the Jews as a historical "paradigm" shaped by historical persecution and resistance into an economic specialization dependent upon liquid assets (the necessity to buy and sell freely), their cultivation of age-old suspicions, etc., etc., and Marx advised them to emancipate themselves (and showed how this could be done). . . .

Brecht reveals a good deal of himself here. There is, first of all, a strong indication of his own anti-Semitism, which was of a rather peculiar sort. It was, of course, not religious: although baptized a Catholic, he had had no use for religion of any sort since he was a boy, and by the time he was a man he was a thoroughgoing atheist. It was also not personal: Helene Weigel, his wife, was half-Jewish, and many of those he worked with in the theater—Kurt Weill, Peter Lorre, and Lion Feuchtwanger among them—were Jews; for that matter, Marx himself was a Jew of sorts. No, Brecht's anti-Semitism was of an economic and political sort. Economic because of what he perceived as the Jews' intimate involvement with capitalism, the system he hated. Political because he was profoundly annoyed that Hitler's campaign against the Jews had diverted attention from what he felt was the real issue—the Nazis' ideological and military war against Marxism. He had even written a terrible and muddled play, *The Round Heads and the Pointed Heads*, to "prove" that Hitler's anti-Semitism was a phony issue. It is important and interesting to note in the passage just quoted how uncritically and completely Brecht evidently accepted Marx's pronouncements on any subject. He was more than an orthodox Marxist; he was a true believer. If an opinion or theory on any subject differed from that of Marx (or of his acceptable commentators, Lenin and Stalin), Brecht rejected it as rank revisionism.

No matter how skeptically Brecht regarded the Horkheimer-Adorno study of "the fascist type," it proved to be quite an important one. When it was finally published in 1950 as *The Authoritarian Personality*, this psychosociological study, altogether new to America and the English-speaking world in its intentions, brought the two principals of the Frankfurt Institute a degree of professional and public renown that later made it possible for them to reestablish themselves in Germany. "What was new about *The Authoritarian Personality*," writes H. Stuart Hughes in *The Sea Change*,

> was its juxtaposition of American and émigré authorship and of empirical and speculative method. While Horkheimer had been its original moving spirit, he did not participate in the actual research and writing; this devolved, for the quantitative analysis of test and interview material, on a team of native-born psychologists based in Berkeley, California, and, for the "qualitative" interpretation, on Adorno himself. Adorno was later to recall that the "cooperation in a democratic spirit" which characterized the work, "in contrast to the academic tradition in Europe," had been "the most fruitful thing" he had experienced in America....[4]

To paraphrase Hughes, the study rested on the assumption that in any Western democracy there existed a "fascist potential." *The Authoritarian Personality* sought to isolate that potential in specific traits of personality. It searched out and described an "authoritarian syndrome" that derived from a "sadomasochistic resolution of the Oedipus complex"—an individual felt hatred for his father that was transformed into admiration for those he perceived as strong (father figures) and an equivalent contempt for those whom he saw as weak. Among the weak was the Jew who, to the authoritarian personality, was often "a substitute for the hated father." So anti-Semitism was an important component of the syndrome. But so, also, were a tendency to think in stereotypes and a weakness for exhortation and high rhetoric, whether in politics, advertising, or professional life.

If this sounds familiar, it may be because the authoritarian personality has a good deal in common with Herbert Marcuse's *One-Dimensional Man*. The Marcuse book, written a decade and a half later, went so far as to suggest that a type recognizably similar (except for the emphasis on anti-Semitism) to the one defined by Horkheimer, Adorno, and their researchers was the dominant one in mass democratic society—particularly in America. If not actually Fascist, Marcuse's mass man was easily and frequently manipulated to achieve ends that were essentially Fascist.

Herbert Marcuse did not take part in those wartime researches on the authoritarian personality. By the time the project was under way, he was settled in Washington, D.C., at the U.S. Department of State, where he had come at the invitation and arrangement of Franz Newmann, another pro-tem member of the Frankfurt Institute for Social Research, to work as an expert on German affairs. Originally Marcuse was attached to the Office of Strategic Services, but during his decade of service he made the transition without qualms (one assumes) from the OSS to its peacetime incarnation, the Central Intelligence Agency. He left only when academic posts became available to him—first at Columbia University's Russian Institute, then, in 1954, at Brandeis University.

· ● ·

Another of Brecht's Los Angeles "friends" was the novelist Lion Feuchtwanger. Although not as docile as Hanns Eisler, he was Brecht's oldest professional collaborator (in age and duration). He had given Brecht his first theatrical production at the Kammerspiele in Munich. There he had also collaborated with him on one of his early plays, *The Life of Edward the Second of England*. The two got on remarkably well, considering the difference in their ages—Feuchtwanger was born in 1884 and Brecht in 1898.

Brecht fascinated Feuchtwanger—so much so that he made him

a character in his novel *Success*, which was published in 1930. Here, as presented by Feuchtwanger, is the Brechtian character, "rude and awkward" Kaspar Pröckl:

> He was steeped in the theories of that time which found an economic interpretation for every historical event, and he was convinced that the first duty of aesthetics was to discover the function of art in a socialistic state. Marxism had omitted to define this function, quite excusably, for it had more important work to do. But the science of aesthetics had the chance of freeing itself for the first time since its inception from dry-as-dust abstractions, and of coming to life by joining with political science in making fruitful the soil for art in the new proletarian State: therein lay its sole significance. . . .[5]

It is perhaps unusual that Pröckl concerned himself with aesthetics at all, for in *Success* he is an engineer in the Bavarian Motor Works plant in Munich, in which city the novel is set. Yet Pröckl is an engineer who composes ballads and sings them to the accompaniment of a guitar—as Brecht also did in his younger days. Pröckl and Brecht also share a number of physical characteristics. Feuchtwanger makes frequent reference to Pröckl's eyes, like Brecht's "deep-set and passionate" or "watery blue" and sometimes "superciliously half-closed." Pröckl's "lean, sullen face was badly shaven"; Brecht managed always to appear with a day's growth of beard on his face. He also affects a black leather jacket, which was an important piece of Brecht's uniform in the twenties. Mere details? Of course, but they added up to a portrait of Bertolt Brecht that was recognizable both to him and to the German public.

Success was perhaps the least successful of Feuchtwanger's novels. A few of them—notably *Jud Süss* (published in English as *Power*) and his *Josephus* trilogy—became international best-sellers. When he went into exile, translations and foreign editions of his works made it possible for him to enjoy a much more comfortable style of life than all but a couple of the German refugee artists. He lived with his wife in a villa on the French Riviera through most of the thirties. An extremely prolific writer, he turned out novel after novel, most of them thick, historical romances (he boasted that he could write steadily at the rate of seven typewritten pages an hour) that sold quite well. Like many others, Feuchtwanger was caught completely off guard by the swift fall of France in 1940. Trapped there, he was interned for a while by the Vichy authorities but finally managed to get free and make his way through Spain and Portugal to the United States with his wife, Marthe.

Again, due to his wide readership in America, he was able to establish himself in comfort in this country. The Feuchtwangers moved to a house near the ocean in California, where the Thomas Manns and the Franz Werfels were their neighbors. The novelist aided materially in bringing Brecht and his family to the United States. When at last they arrived, Feuchtwanger sent his car, driven by his wife Marthe, to welcome them and pick them up at dockside in San Pedro. Always industrious, he stayed at home to work. The playwright and the novelist met the next day. Brecht's entry in his *Work Journal* for July 22, 1941:

> Feuchtwanger lives in Santa Monica in a big house in the Mexican style. He is in manner unchanged, nevertheless appears aged. He is working on a piece about a German astrologer and charlatan for the theater in his country. . . .[6]

Given his predilection for collaboration, it was only a matter of time until Brecht proposed to Feuchtwanger that they get together on a project. After all, they had worked successfully once before, and now Feuchtwanger was well known in this country. His name on a play might make possible a Broadway production—which was Brecht's goal from first to last. He proposed that they work on an idea that the playwright had been carrying around in his notebook since July 1940. It was to be a variation of the Joan of Arc legend translated to the time of the collapse of France before the German army. Feuchtwanger had been there at the time. Surely he could add a great deal? More, perhaps, than Brecht might have wished.

On October 30, 1942, when they began to work together on the play that was to become *The Visions of Simone Machard*, Brecht was still somewhat involved with Fritz Lang on *Hangmen Also Die*. Perhaps because his attention was then divided, or more likely because Feuchtwanger proved a strong and independent-minded collaborator, the play got a little out of Brecht's normally tight control. As the two met regularly at Feuchtwanger's new home in Pacific

Palisades, there were sharp disagreements between them on details of plot and character. And these disagreements were never completely resolved, for Feuchtwanger finally insisted that he write his own version of the story as a novel, and in fact he did just that. There are some specific but rather superficial differences. For instance, the title of the novel, which was written afterward and published in 1944, is simply *Simone*; there is no direct reference to her "visions," and although they are there in the novel, there are only two, and they do not occupy quite the same central position that they do in the play. Simone Machard in the play becomes Simone Planchard in the novel. But the essential difference between the two is in the ages of the two Simones. Although in the play her age is not specifically given, Brecht clearly intends her to be taken as not yet having reached the age of puberty: there are no male-female complications to divert her from the rather straightforward action of the play. Feuchtwanger's Simone Planchard is fifteen and almost a woman. After she has committed an act of sabotage but before she has been apprehended, she is nearly dissuaded from her course of open defiance of the Germans and the collaborationist French by Maurice, a bus driver who pleads with her to come with him to the unoccupied zone. There is certainly a sexual attraction between them.

Yet even though Feuchtwanger eventually wrote his own *Simone*, he seems to have exerted more than the usual influence over Brecht in the writing of the play. The tone of it is quite different from the rest of the playwright's works. Gentler and sweeter in style, *The Visions of Simone Machard* stands out as about the only play in the Brecht canon that might possibly be described as charming. It *does* have a certain charm: anachronisms abound; there is a good deal of childish confusion in Simone's mind as to what she is actually supposed to *do*; her naïveté is altogether disarming. In this it is possible to read the specific influence of Feuchtwanger, who often tended toward sentimentality in his novels. If this was so, it was all to the good, for although the play is not often performed (most Brechtians certainly sense the difference and seem to regard it with suspicion), *Simone Machard* is a fine piece of work, the most underrated of all Brecht's "American" plays—perhaps of all his works.

Marthe Feuchtwanger throws some interesting light on the colony of German exiles. I interviewed her at the house in Pacific Palisades, which lies just west of the city of Los Angeles, off Sunset Boulevard and up a hill. My appointment was for six o'clock. Frau Feuchtwanger had made it clear that she could not offer much time: she had an appointment in the city at 7:30, and she had no intention of being late. Because traffic was unexpectedly favorable, I arrived ten minutes early, found my way to the front door (so overgrown with palms and shrubbery that it was like a secluded grotto), and rang the doorbell. I waited and rang again. At last there were footsteps, and then a strong female voice spoke from the other side: "Who is there, please?"

I gave my name and reminded her of our appointment.

There was no sound from inside for a moment and certainly no move to open the door. Finally: "You're early."

I allowed that this was so.

"Wait until six." I listened to the steady, receding click-click-click of heels as she walked away from the door, which remained tightly shut. I had no choice but to sit down on a worn concrete garden bench next to the door—had it been put there for just such occasions?—and wait what was now eight minutes until the appointed hour.

Lion Feuchtwanger had died in 1959. He and Marthe had married in 1912, at a time when he was just beginning to establish himself in the Munich literary world. They were together through it all—his rise to prominence, their flight from the Nazis to France, and their subsequent escape to America. Lion and Marthe Feuchtwanger were very prominent in the exile community: he a novelist well established and commercially successful in America, and she his tall, Teutonic, and rather aristocratic wife—the perfect hostess for Feuchtwanger, the German Jew. They did a good deal of entertaining in Pacific Palisades, though at another house, nearer town on Sunset. They bought this villa on the hill with its view of the Pacific not long before Feuchtwanger's death.

Precisely at six there were sounds on the other side of the door. I rose and was admitted by Frau Feuchtwanger—gray-haired, erect, somewhat aloof. Without much more than a handshake she led me upstairs to a large room that may or may not once have been her husband's study. Yet whatever it had been during his life, in his death it had become a kind of shrine to him. Photographs of him and literary mementos covered the walls. His books, in a variety of editions and translations, were exhibited face up on a long table in the center of the room. She pointed to a straight chair near the wall, and sat down on the one opposite mine. Here we talked.

"Brecht?" she echoed my inquiry. "He was a little irrational, illogical. When we lived on Sunset he would come every day to work with my husband on *Simone*—and we would go to his house in the evenings sometimes, too.

"The collaboration went very well. For both of them it was a great time. Brecht did a lot of shouting while they worked together. He defended his views fanatically. But he always called my husband 'doctor' and was full of respect. If my husband would look skeptical at him, Brecht would drop his objection and go on to the next thing."

I asked what they disagreed about.

"They were not of the same opinion on the age of the girl. My husband said she had to be fifteen or more. Brecht said, 'She must be thirteen! She should be actually thirteen!' And he more or less had his own way in that. When it was done on the stage in Germany, the actress who played Simone was just a child. If she was thirteen, she looked younger. Did you know that the idea for the play was Ruth Berlau's?"

I told her I had no idea of that. She went on to assure that it was so, that it all came about while Brecht's Danish mistress was with him in Finland, and they were listening daily to reports of the imminent collapse of France before the Wehrmacht. It was then that Berlau suggested that he do a modern Joan of Arc drama set in the France of that moment. He made the entry in his *Work Journal* and did a bit of outlining on it in Hollywood before approaching Feuchtwanger on the project in the fall of 1942. Supporting Marthe Feuchtwanger's claim that the original idea for Simone came from Ruth Berlau is a report that in the agreement drawn up between playwright and novelist, she was named to share in the profits from the play and the novel. And they were considerable: according to Marthe Feuchtwanger, the novel *Simone* "had a great success." It was, in any case, bought for the movies by Sam Goldwyn, though it was never brought to the screen.

I asked about the early relations between the two writers; there was, after all, a considerable difference in their ages.

"My husband discovered Brecht in Munich," Frau Feuchtwanger

said flatly. "He was with the Kammerspiele there then doing his own plays and producing the works of others. Brecht called him up about a play he had written about the Spartakists, and my husband said, 'Yes, of course, bring your play.' Brecht came and said, 'You must understand I wrote this only to make money. It's not a good play.' He said he had another play that was much better but would be difficult to produce. That was *Baal*, which was really not as good. Well, my husband decided to produce the second play, which was originally titled *Spartakus*. I thought of the new title, which of course was *Drums in the Night*. Did you know that my husband almost went to jail over that play?"

She explained that during the counterrevolution, when the Freikorps troops marched into Munich and began standing Leftists up against the wall and shooting them, the soldiers came into the Feuchtwanger home and began searching it—for guns, they said. They looked in Lion's desk and found a copy of *Spartakus*, which was being prepared for production. "They looked at it and decided it was quite revolutionary. They took it with them and said they would be back. People were killed then for less." Not long afterward, in 1925, the Feuchtwangers moved to Berlin. "Because," said Frau Feuchtwanger, "you couldn't live in Munich after what had happened there. It was so Nazi. They told us, 'We could put you in jail in a minute.'"

What about Brecht and Kaspar Pröckl?

"It's true that my husband used a part of Brecht for that character in his novel *Success*. Mostly it was the outside of him—his habits and mannerisms. But Brecht was unhappy about it. He read the manuscript and asked my husband to change it. But my husband told him he couldn't because it was already in print.

"You know, Bruno Frank and Thomas Mann were quite indignant about that book. Mann said, 'How ungrateful of you to write this way about this beautiful city, Munich!'" Feuchtwanger, a native of Munich, had gone to school with Thomas Mann's wife, Katia, and in general the two families were on very good terms. In California, their homes only a mile and a half apart, they saw a good deal of each other. Katia Mann handed down her verdict in *Unwritten Memories*: "At Christmas and on other occasions, they . . . often visited us in our house in Pacific Palisades. Feuchtwanger was very intelligent and most amusing. He was quite vain, but in a completely disarming way. . . . Thomas Mann liked his books. They were written with great knowledge of the subject matter, and several were excellent in their way, especially the later ones, *Goya* and *The Jewess of Toledo.*"[7]

Marthe Feuchtwanger talked at some length about the exile community there in Los Angeles: "There were really two groups—the Austrian and the German. There were many more Austrians than Germans, most of them actors and movie people. Billy Wilder, for instance, was Austrian, though he had worked in Berlin. Josef von Sternberg was also an Austrian. Brecht was familiar with both groups—probably because of Eisler, who was very Austrian, very *küss die Hand.* Brecht's lawyer here was the husband of Gina Kaus, an Austrian writer and good friend of mine today. Schönberg lived in Rockingham in an old Spanish house just beyond Mandeville Canyon.

"The novelists? We got on well with Thomas Mann and saw him and his wife often. But Brecht couldn't stand him. He hated Mann's solemn manner. It would be no exaggeration to say that Brecht hated Thomas Mann. All of us really liked his brother, Heinrich, better. He [Heinrich] had a very difficult time of it here. He was only known in Hollywood for *The Blue Angel,* and he made nothing from it. He used to say, 'My only fame in America consists of the legs of Marlene Dietrich.' He was supported by my husband and his brother through the European Film Fund without him knowing it. About Franz Werfel—well, he wrote *The Song of Bernadette,* you know. He was very much captivated by Catholicism, although he was a Jew. He *believed* he was a Catholic, but he didn't want to turn his back on the Jews. His wife [Alma Mahler Werfel, Gustav Mahler's widow] was very witty."

No matter how illustrious, the German-speaking exiles were all given close surveillance by the FBI. If they were not naturalized citizens, they were subject to a ten o'clock curfew during the early years of the war. Spot checks were made to be sure that it was observed. Many of the exiles had good reason to believe that their homes were bugged.

"I think ours was," said Frau Feuchtwanger. "I remember one day I found two people working outside the house on our telephone line. I asked them what they were doing and they said our telephone was out of order. I said that it certainly wasn't, that I had just phoned somebody. Since I didn't know who they were, and I was suspicious, I sent them away. The next day it did go out of order and then suddenly came back. Then they came back and said the whole house had to be rewired. At first I didn't think about that. I let them do it. I joked with them and said they were bugging the house. Then America got into the war, the curfew was started, and the Japanese were relocated. We stopped joking then.

"We had to go every month to some office downtown and report our activities and answer questions. Naturally when we came to this country we took out citizenship papers. My husband never became a citizen, but I became one after he died. He was called down to the Federal Building and interrogated and once they came here to ask questions—though he was never brought to Washington, as Brecht was. They said to my husband, you wrote a revolutionary poem in 1915. He said, 'No. That was an antiwar poem.' "

The basis for suspicion, of course, was not that these "enemy aliens" might be sympathetic to the Nazi cause—all of them were confirmed anti-Nazis—but that they were "premature anti-Fascists." Most of them were Leftists and were therefore suspect for their sympathies and associations. Marthe Feuchtwanger recalled only one contact with a "real" Communist. That came one night when Hanns Eisler was invited to dinner: "He called beforehand and asked, 'May I bring somebody?' We said sure, and he brought his brother Gerhard, who was up from Mexico. After the introductions, Gerhard didn't say a word. He just listened."

Bertolt Brecht was a little too far to the Left for most of the members of the exile community, especially since most felt that they were under FBI surveillance.

"Bruno Frank, the novelist, was once my husband's best friend. But they broke up over Brecht. It was usually not Brecht's personality that put people off. He was much more abrasive in his writing than in person. I was amazed to find what he said about some people in his *Arbeitsjournal.* I think a lot of it was just a mood. He was really not so bad with us. Brecht joked, and he could laugh, and when he would laugh, he would always hit his thigh. He always had to have an audience. He would be inspired in his work when people would express other opinions and give him new lines and new outlooks. He was a very original man."[8]

• • •

When Bertolt Brecht was called before the House Committee on Un-American Activities in 1947, it threw the entire exile community into fearful disarray. It seemed to them that what they had left behind them in Germany was beginning all over again in America. Katia Mann, who had no use for Brecht, nevertheless wrote sympathetically of his conduct before the Congressmen:

> Brecht's speech in his own defense before the Committee on Un-American Activities was broadcast on the radio, and I heard it. Brecht was very sly indeed: he pretended to be stupid, and the others *were* stupid. The whole business of loyalty checks was a great disaster, and today it's almost as bad again. We experienced the whole so-called McCarthy era; during it my husband was continually attacked as a Communist, which he never was in his life.[9]

And if Thomas Mann, who had on a number of occasions been invited to the White House by President Roosevelt, was open to such accusations, then it must have seemed to the exiles that none of them were safe.

Thomas Mann's response to the years of the witch-hunt in America was influenced more than a little by his own sense of his important position in German literature. He had become an American citizen. He had made propaganda broadcasts for the United States beamed at Germany in which he chastised his people eloquently for allowing Nazism to take root and flower in their native soil. He had even written his last major novel, *Doctor Faustus*, as an examination of that presumed sickness in the German soul that made it subject to demonic possessions such as the one that seized it in 1933. And if he had diagnosed the malady, he seemed also to feel called upon to treat it. During the decade between the end of World War II and his death, Thomas Mann seemed to see his role more and more clearly as personal physician to the German people. Even though he had declared he would never again live in Germany, he began making fairly frequent trips to his native land, speaking at centennials and cultural occasions, reminding Germans of the humanist tradition in their literature and philosophy, prescribing the kind of medicine he felt they must have to effect a complete recovery. A couple of these appearances brought him to East Germany. When he was strongly criticized in America for lending his dignity and support to events sponsored by a Communist regime, he responded by moving to Zurich, in the German-speaking section of Switzerland. While he could not bring himself to return permanently to Germany, he could and did set up residence nearby, the better to treat his patient. He died there in 1955.

As early as 1948 Max Horkheimer received an invitation to return to Frankfurt and bring with him the Frankfurt Institute for Social Research. The following year the university offered him the post he had held there earlier. In 1950 he came, and in 1951 he was made rector of Frankfurt University. Again, Theodor Adorno followed him there. Together they introduced to the German intellectual world the practices of American social science they had learned during the research for *The Authoritarian Personality*; statistical analysis and profiling would ever afterward dominate sociology as they do here. Adorno published an important book of philosophical essays, *Negative Dialectics*, in 1966. Yet their triumph was purely professional. Horkheimer and Adorno were regarded by the new postwar generation as relics of the past. Although they were Jews who had actively opposed the Nazis and had been forced into exile in America, their brand of Marxism was entirely too weak and revisionist in its tendencies to suit the young Leftist militants who came to dominate German university life during the sixties. Having retired in 1958, Horkheimer escaped the brunt of their contempt. However, it fell full force on Adorno. To quote H. Stuart Hughes on the curious fate that befell Adorno:

> After repeatedly occupying the building of the Institute, in April 1969 the young militants invaded Adorno's classroom; three girl students bared their breasts and mockingly overwhelmed him with flowers and kisses. Thereupon, with characteristic cruelty, they declared him dead "as an institution." For one so vulnerable, the experience must have come as a fearful shock; apparently he never fully recovered. Five months later he died of heart failure.[10]

And in 1973, Max Horkheimer died in retirement at his villa in Italian Switzerland.

Ironically, the intellectual hero of the international Leftist student movement on which Theodor Adorno's death has been blamed was his old colleague from the Institute for Social Research, Herbert Marcuse. After the decade (that he successfully lived down) as a cold warrior in the State Department and at Columbia's Russian Institute, Marcuse moved on to Brandeis University, where Angela Davis was among his students. The two books that he published while at Brandeis did a lot to determine the intellectual direction of the student revolt of the sixties. *Eros and Civilization* (1955) was, as might have been expected from a veteran of the Frankfurt Institute, an effort at a synthesis between Marx and Freud; yet in it he was far bolder and more extreme in his conclusions than Horkheimer and Adorno had ever been. *One-Dimensional Man* (1964) is far more specifically Marxist in its approach, offering, as it does, a criticism of mass society in the Western democracies, using theoretical socialism as its standard for judgment.

He moved on to the University of California at San Diego, and it was while there that he quite suddenly achieved fame as the guru of the young Left. In the spring of 1968 he made international headlines in a barnstorming tour across Europe as he addressed student groups in riot-torn Berlin and then in Frankfurt, and went on to Paris where he appeared at a mass rally at the barricades. I recall encountering Marcuse at UCSD upon his return from that apocalyptic spring junket. During an hour-long interview he kept returning again and again to what he termed the "crisis at hand" and showed little inclination to discuss his books and the larger intellectual questions with which they dealt: he was every inch the political intellectual. However, sitting in on one of his classes, where I was just one of more than a hundred in a large lecture hall that was packed to overflowing, I found him, remarkably, to be a teacher of the traditional sort, very much in the German university mold. He delivered a dense lecture from detailed notes on the French philosopher, Pierre Joseph Proudhon, that made no intellectual concessions whatever to his students. I couldn't help but note the contrast between the man in the headlines and the philosopher in the classroom. His students must have noticed and wondered at it, too.

In a way, Brecht had the last word. Even though he died in 1956, before any of the Tuis whom he so despised, he took his revenge upon them before he did. The novel that began as a reworking of *Turandot* went back into dramatic form. The last play completed before his death was *Turandot, or The Congress of Whitewashers*, with music by Hanns Eisler. And, like the uncompleted novel, it tells of the futile carryings-on of the Tellekt-Ual-Ins, who held their power by selling their opinions to the Emperor. To date it has not been produced in the West.

4

BRECHT AND
FRITZ LANG

Juxtapose three words—Brecht and
film—and you have an instant symposium, perhaps a book, at the
very least an article for *Sight and Sound*. What is it about this con-
junction of maker and métier that so inspires critics and scholars?
After all, Brecht worked extensively on only two films in his lifetime—although it's true that he had an abiding interest in the
medium and, during his stay in Hollywood from 1941 to 1947, managed to make a precarious living working on the fringe of the movie
industry. Even so, the bare *idea* of Bertolt Brecht and the film
medium is one that exists, for the most part, in the potential rather
than the actual: It's not so much what he did in film as what he could
have done.

Brecht seemed first of all to have the instincts of a screenwriter:
his approach to playwriting was generally cinematic. He seldom wrote

in acts and long scenes the way that his contemporaries did; his plays, especially the best of the later ones, were written in quick, episodic sequences, a series of coolly modern antidramatic moments tied together by jumpcuts. With the addition of camera direction, *Herr Puntila and His Man Matti*, *The Caucasian Chalk Circle*, and *Mother Courage* could have been shot as movies just about as Brecht wrote them—and in fact these three plays were.

But merely to breathe the words "Brecht and film" evokes something more. It suggests an approach to cinematic art that is at once noncommercial, didactic, and revolutionary. It reminds us that from the time that Lenin saw Griffith's *Intolerance* and proclaimed this to be *the* medium with which to propagandize the revolution, film has been suspected (usually wrongly) of being an instrumentality of the Left. It seemed to many, and evidently seems to many still, that Brecht himself and Brechtian dramatic principles offered special promise to the cause of revolutionary cinema. And in fact he has had direct influence on such diverse filmmakers as Jean-Luc Godard, Lindsay Anderson, and Rainer Werner Fassbinder. Yet revolutionary cinema is no more a reality today than it was when Brecht came to Hollywood in 1941. He failed to transform the medium, as in retrospect he might have been expected to do. The reason for this failure is always understood to be the commercial nature of moviemaking in general and of American moviemaking in particular. (Hollywood, after all—what can you expect?) And certainly Bertolt Brecht himself did all that he could to foster this notion, making his excuses in advance, as it were, with a series of poems he wrote in his first years there. The bitterest of them is the one most often quoted:

Every day, to earn my daily bread
I go to the market where lies are bought
Hopefully
I take up my place among the sellers.[1]

By the time he arrived in Hollywood, as we saw in chapter 3, Brecht had had some experience as a screenwriter. And, also as we have seen, only weeks after his arrival in California he was at work on screen stories of a remarkably unsuitable sort with his American writer friend, Ferdinand Reyher.

There were others done with various collaborators: something

called "Bermuda Troubles," written together with a German actor
named Robert Thoren, who had managed to get on as a screenwriter
at M-G-M; two film ideas intended for Charles Boyer, which he
worked out with another German actor, Fritz Kortner; and so on. It
is worth noting that Brecht had access to established producers, directors, and actors in Hollywood, directly or through others. He wrote
a couple of screen stories intended for Peter Lorre, who had played
the leading role in the Berlin production of his play *A Man's a Man.*
For Oscar Homolka, who had played the title role in the brief 1926
production of Brecht's *Baal,* he did a treatment for a biographical
film based on the life of Henri Dunant, founder of the International
Red Cross; in this project he also hoped to interest producer William
Dieterle, another old friend from Berlin. Yes, he had contacts—a
network of friends and fans who were able and willing to boost his
work and front his projects. Yet with a single exception, none of these
plans and projects came to production—for the most part because of
Brecht's unwillingness to work within the naturalistic conventions of
the Hollywood film.

Brecht's circle of movie acquaintances was not restricted to exiles
and émigrés. There are accounts in his *Work Journal* of evenings
spent with Herman Mankiewicz, Ben Hecht, Clifford Odets, and
Charlie Chaplin. There is a little episode involving the radio writer
(Lights Out) and screenwriter *(Escape)* Arch Oboler, who evidently came to Brecht seeking material for a home-front propaganda
series that he was producing on a small budget for ABC. The episode
reveals a little of Brecht's nascent attitude toward Hollywood screenwriters. In his journal Brecht describes Oboler as "smart, not unin-
teresting whenever he talks about technical matters."[2] In an interview after nearly forty years, Oboler remembered Brecht more
effusively: "I was a little in awe of him, shall we say. I was at the top
of the heap in radio. Still, I had a sense of inadequacy—I wanted to
write for the theater. So when I met a man whose work I respected,
who had no dollar signs on him, well, I was in awe."[3] Later, however,
the two fell out when Brecht accused Oboler of stealing a radio play
written by Brecht's secretary and mistress, Ruth Berlau: "[Oboler]
gets no money for it, since it is for defense, but rather the credit. He
wonders why Ruth wants to do nothing for defense, as he puts it when
she protests over the theft. Difference between making sacrifices and
taking them."[4]

There was also that infamous business with Billy Wilder. Brecht met the then Paramount screenwriter through Paul Czinner, the director, who was married to the Viennese stage actress Elisabeth Bergner. What did he think of Wilder? This entry from his *Work Journal*, dated April 11, 1942, tells us:

> Months ago Czinner told me a film beginning (about hypnosis) and asked me if I might want to think through a continuation [of the story]. I worked with him for some weeks, also with Bergner. In the end I had my story. Bergner told it to some Americans, in order, as she said, to get their opinion. After that she began to have doubts and lost interest, even though she's up against it financially [and] has debts. Czinner began to work with Billy Wilder (filmwriter, German) on the screenplay, but then had no time. Now Bergner tells me that my film may already have been sold by someone else, a friend of Wilder's, in all details the plot, only in another setting—but without the hypnosis introduction. $35,000. . . . Bergner found him charming. She read the story. . . .[5]

Wilder, for his part, has no memory of this. "I met him two or three times at parties during the war," he said of Brecht in a brief interview. "That's all I can tell you." Nor is it necessarily true, or even very likely, that there is anything to remember. The fact that Brecht entered this in his *Work Journal* does not really mean that it was a personal note, one intended primarily for his own eyes. He had a keen sense of his own potential position in German literature and was often quite clearly writing for posterity in his *Journal* as he defended himself and accused others. He set out avidly collecting injustices almost as soon as he arrived in Hollywood, evidently determined to cast himself as a victim of movie capitalism. As in this instance he goes to some trouble to reconstruct the history of his involvement with the project in order to establish the supposedly stolen story as his own, yet at the same time gives no other information—neither the name of Wilder's friend, nor details of the plot—this indictment seems a little questionable. It is as though he wished to imply more than he was willing to state.

In any case, it should be clear that Brecht, who himself had held such a casual view of the sacredness of literary property, was con-

But were they? In many ways, Lang was the most unlikely collaborator possible for Brecht. The two were altogether different in style—if not in outlook. Vienna-born, the son of an architect, Lang was every inch the aristocratic artist. The two had seen a little of one another in Berlin (they had been introduced in Munich by Peter Lorre), and although there was considerable mutual respect between them, they had evidently maintained a wary distance even then. However, by the time Brecht arrived in America, he owed a great deal to Lang: the director had started a fund for the support of the playwright and his family in Europe, and he and Lion Feuchtwanger had also sworn affidavits that made it possible for Brecht, his family, and a mistress to enter this country.

For his part, Lang greatly admired Brecht as an artist. At the time of *M*'s release many remarked on the similarity of Lang's underworld to the gangster society portrayed in *The Threepenny Opera*. Questioned about this as late as 1963, he responded to a German interviewer, Gero Gandert: "Did Brecht influence me? Of course he did. Nobody who tried to come to grips with the time could escape his influence."[9] To Peter Bogdanovich in 1967, Lang conceded that he had even done one film directly under Brecht's inspiration—although not with especially happy results. In the long interview that comprises most of Bogdanovich's short book *Fritz Lang in America*, the director declared that "there's no question that Brecht was most responsible for *You and Me*, and for a very peculiar reason. In my opinion, Brecht is, up to now, the greatest talent of this century in Germany. He invented the epic theater and something else—the *Lehrstück*—a play that teaches something. . . . And I wanted to make a play that teaches something in an entertaining way, with songs."[10] Lang was so anxious to re-create something in the style of the *Lehrstück* that he went to the only one of the old team then in America, Kurt Weill, and asked him to collaborate on the film. Weill did the music for one song but then walked out on the production; perhaps he saw how far wide of the mark Lang's shot would land. At any rate, it was successful neither on Brechtian terms nor as the gangster comedy it ultimately became. Even Lotte Eisner, friendliest of all critics to Lang, dismisses *You and Me* with "*Lehrstück* as parody, a kind of *Robber Symphony*."[11]

As late as the year before Fritz Lang's death (1975) his assistant and secretary, Lily Laté, went to great pains to assure me of her chief's unstinting devotion to Brecht. "Mr. Lang admired him very much and still admires him very much. It was only his manner of working he didn't like." She talked of the collaboration of Brecht and the director on *Hangmen Also Die* and of all that had been written about it since. She concluded sternly: "I hope there doesn't come another book that idolizes Brecht and puts Mr. Lang down."[12]

She would have been referring then to Brecht's own *Work Journal*, which was published in 1973 in West Germany, and to *Film bei Brecht* ("Film and Brecht"), by Wolfgang Gersch, published in 1975 in East Germany, and to a third book, of which Miss Laté probably also had some notice, James K. Lyon's *Bertolt Brecht in America*, which was then in preparation and was published in 1980. All three of these find against Fritz Lang. Lyon's book simply develops in detail the indictment presented by Brecht in his *Journal*. Wolfgang Gersch, who was apparently influenced in his account by John Wexley, the American screenwriter called in on the project, was slightly less censorious of Lang but went to great pains to demonstrate that *Hangmen Also Die* was "no Brecht film."[13]

It is Brecht, as usual, who is angriest and most bitter. Reading through his *Journal*, we see him jump from mild hope as he speculates on all that movie money might bring him ("assured work time, a better place to live, music lessons for Steff [his son], no more dependence on charity") to this angry, cynical outburst against Lang that he entered on June 29, 1942:

> I work with Lang usually from nine in the morning until seven in the evening on the hostage story. A remarkable period during which it emerges that the logic of a process or a development under discussion is: "The public will accept that." The mastermind of the underground movement hides himself behind a curtain when the Gestapo searches the house—the public will accept that. Also the commissar's corpse falling out of the closet. Also "secret" mass meetings at the time of the Nazi terror. Lang "buys" things of that sort. Interesting also that he is far more interested in surprises than in tension.[14]

His opinion of Lang darkened considerably more as they became more deeply involved in the project. They came into conflict over casting. Brecht strongly urged Lang to consider his friend Oscar

Homolka for the part of Czaka, the Czech traitor, and his wife Helene Weigel for a smaller speaking role. Lang refused both for the same reason: he had already decided that all Nazi roles would be played by refugee German actors but that all the Czechs in the cast should be played by Americans in order to increase audience identification ("The public will accept that").

The fact that Brecht took it upon himself to give advice on casting indicates how closely the two were collaborating—at least in the beginning. Between them they worked out the entire story in broad outline during eight weeks of day-long conferences of the kind described by Brecht. There were problems built into the arrangement, however, that were never really worked out, at least not to Brecht's satisfaction. Lang had been drawn to the subject originally because he saw the possibility of working out the escape and pursuit of Heydrich's assassins along lines he had established in *M*. Brecht was brought into the project—at least according to what Lang told the producer, Pressburger—because he was an expert on the anti-Nazi underground in Europe. While Brecht's expertise in this line at the time is certainly questionable, he seems to have taken it all very seriously. He did some research into wartime conditions in Czechoslovakia and other Nazi-occupied European nations. He looked into methods of sabotage practiced by Czech workers in the huge Skoda works outside Prague. He sought the grisly details of the retribution exacted by the Nazis against the hostages they had taken (it only later came out that the entire village of Lidice had been wiped out as an example to the Czech underground and to those who supported it). What is more, Brecht meant to make use of all this: he wanted the movie to focus on the mass resistance to the Nazi occupation (his title for it, for a while, was *Trust the People*). Lang, on the other hand, intended to make it a tale of pursuit—and escape. There were almost certainly daily arguments as to treatment and emphasis. Because it was Lang's picture, you can be sure he won most of them—and Brecht hated not having his own way.

At the beginning of August, a new element was added to the equation. "We finished an exact outline and then," Lang told Peter Bogdanovich, "because Brecht didn't speak English, we tried to find a writer. We settled on [John] Wexley, who spoke perfect German, so they could really work together."[15] The choice of Wexley was clearly also intended in another way as an accommodation to Brecht. Lang,

the monocle-wearing aristocrat, was barely even liberal in his politics—yet he was anti-Fascist and he wanted the film to stand as a
strong, direct statement against Nazism. John Wexley was, if anything, even further to the Left than Brecht. In bringing him in, Lang
must have been aware that he was supplying Brecht with at least a
potential ally. According to Wexley, however, more often than not
he was forced to mediate between writer and director.

It seems that Brecht was suspicious of Wexley to some degree at
the start. The size of the American writer's salary, which was considerable ($1,500 a week), annoyed Brecht greatly. Wexley's work
methods also left him skeptical: "First I take him through a sequence,
he dictates the English to the secretary, she makes four copies, and
because I want one, he makes the most childish excuses." All copies
carried Wexley's name on top. Brecht records one incident involving
the German translation of some material in one scene: "So he trans-
lates what has to be done in one handwritten copy. I take the scrap
of paper with me; afterward he telephones around after me—it seems
I may have taken a sheet with me that he may need, and he can't
go on working without it. It appears that these tricks are highly
paid."[16] It is evident that Wexley, by then a veteran of the Hollywood
game, was collecting as much paper on the project as he possibly
could. It also seems from this, however, that although Brecht was
providing oral input, talking through scenes suggested in the outline
he had worked out with Lang, Wexley was doing most of the actual
writing on the screenplay.

Yet the two at least had their politics in common, and their politics
encouraged a certain agreement between them on the approach to
the story. Apparently Brecht brought Wexley around to his view that
this should be the story of resistance by an entire people. By mid-
September he commented in his *Journal* that work on the film was
going better because he was now working more directly with the
screenwriter and had the opportunity to "correct" his work. Also:
"Above all I have won [Wexley] over to writing with me at my house
in the evenings a completely new ideal-script that will be submitted
to Lang. Naturally I lay the heaviest weight upon those scenes that
involve the people."[17]

It was evidently Brecht's thinking that if he and Wexley actually
got this approach into screenplay form, Lang and presumably also
Pressburger could be won over. Less than a month later, however,

the "ideal-script" experiment had ended incomplete with only seventy pages done. At about that time Brecht reports that Lang had pulled Wexley into his office and reminded him angrily that it was a *Hollywood* picture he wanted to make and to hell with "scenes involving the people, etc." By this time, it seemed all of Brecht's resentment was directed at Lang: "He sits with the bearing of a dictator ... behind his executive desk, full of drugs and prejudice against every good idea, gathering 'surprises,' little tensions, dirty sentimentalities and inauthenticities, and taking 'licenses' for the box office."[18]

Then came the incident that Lang later felt was ultimately responsible for the break in their relations: he was suddenly handed a start date by Pressburger that was three weeks earlier than anticipated. The script was completed, after a fashion, but was far too long—280 pages, according to Lang. He had about a week to cut it down to size, and he did it himself—that is, without Brecht or Wexley, but with the aid of a third writer brought in especially for the job. The screenplay was cut to 192 pages. Naturally, since Lang did the editing, the hostage scenes were those that were deleted; the manhunt story remained intact.

Production began. By this time the playwright was involved with novelist Lion Feuchtwanger in writing *The Visions of Simone Machard*. But since he had been allowed access to the set, he would check in from time to time with *Hangmen Also Die* (the new title, for which a secretary was awarded one hundred dollars in a name-that-movie contest held in the United Artists office). On one of these visits he watched Lang filming an action sequence and was impressed in spite of himself. In commenting later, he was willing to grant that what the director did on the set was "something close to art," that it had the "dignity and respectability of craftwork."[19]

Yet Brecht was in for still another rude surprise before the film was released. As soon as the credits were posted by United Artists, he found himself involved in an action by John Wexley, who was convinced that he should receive sole screenplay credit on the film. The matter was brought before the Screen Writers Guild in a credit arbitration. As Brecht noted in his *Journal*, Wexley had been diligently collecting paper right from the beginning of their collaboration, and so he had an imposing pile of material—scenes, notes, memos, and all with his name on them—to back up his claim in the arbitration procedure. Evidently it was enough to do the job.

"He got it despite the fact that [Hanns] Eisler, the composer, and I both went in front of the Screen Writers Guild and swore that many, many scenes—obviously—were written by Brecht," Fritz Lang told Peter Bogdanovich, "and that nobody else in the whole world, certainly not Mr. Wexley, could have done them. But they said, 'Well, Mr. Brecht will go back to Germany but Mr. Wexley will stay here. Mr. Wexley will need the credit much more than Mr. Brecht.' "[20]

Because of this and because of the general esteem in which both Brecht and Lang are held, John Wexley has come to be considered the villain of this entire episode. But was he truly the heavy? Or was he simply a fall guy, even a scapegoat? It is a question worth considering, for as often as the case has been discussed in academic circles and by film scholars, very little has been heard from or about John Wexley.

That in itself is remarkable, for only recently could he have been considered an obscure figure. He had established himself as a playwright at the age of twenty-eight with *The Last Mile*, the prison melodrama that was produced on Broadway in 1930 and shot Spencer Tracy into stardom in the role of Killer Mears, the leader of a prison revolt. He wrote a number of other plays, including the very well-received *They Shall Not Die* (which was based roughly on the Scottsboro Boys case), before beginning an overlapping career as a screenwriter. By the time he received Fritz Lang's call at his farm in Bucks County, Pennsylvania, and journeyed across the country with his Viennese wife to work on *Hangmen Also Die*, he had done a number of fairly distinguished screenplays, among them *City for Conquest*, *Angels with Dirty Faces*, *Confessions of a Nazi Spy*, and *The Amazing Dr. Clitterhouse*.

Even to name Wexley's plays and films one must surely notice a certain political and social bias evidenced in his work. He was in the thirties and forties one of the most militant and committed of Hollywood's left-leaning writers. In fact, during the making of *Cornered* in 1945, he brought such pressure to bear on the film's producer, Adrian Scott, and director, Edward Dmytryk, in an effort to get his anti-Fascist message across in undiluted form that the two became disenchanted and left the Communist Party. Dmytryk reported this to the House Committee on Un-American Activities in 1952, and with that, Wexley's then-unofficial blacklisting within the motion picture industry became very official indeed. During his years on the blacklist, he wrote and had published *The Judgment of Julius and Ethel Rosenberg*, a long and exhaustive study of the atomic spy case that finds (naturally) in favor of the Rosenbergs. In the last years, although he has gone unpublished and unproduced, he has not been inactive. He has continued to write, if only for the drawer—just as Brecht had done during all those years he spent in exile. He and his wife still live in Bucks County, in the same old farmhouse in which they were living during the war. "We've had this place since 1934," he told me. "We used to commute back and forth from here to the Coast. I made it a rule not to be back there more than eleven months at a time. We used to drive back and forth. Those years I had more energy and I could do that sort of thing."

Even so, he now seems a tough, vigorous man for his age. Bald and bullet-headed, barrel-chested, strong and vigorous in his movements and gestures, Wexley, born in New York City, seems almost a country man at heart today. We sat together in the big kitchen of the old farmhouse and sipped the tea his wife replenished from time to time. I listened to him recall the details of his association with Brecht so many years ago.

"You see," said Wexley, "my contact with Brecht while I was writing the screenplay was all after working hours. I would work on it during the day and then visit him at night. He was more or less 'interned' in his house in Santa Monica. All aliens in his position were more or less restricted to their houses after dark by a curfew. So I would keep him up to date on what I had done, more or less as a courtesy. And of course we were both very interested in the project. But that was only one of a number of things we would talk about.

"We talked a lot about plays and playwriting. There was a lot of discussion between us on the problem of saying something and at the same time being entertaining so people would go and see it. We both agreed that you can know too much, that it can get in the way of the writing."[21]

Was it in this way that Brecht's plan for the "ideal-script" got under way?

"Oh, that. I guess you could say that that got going because of all these scenes I was doing about the Czech people. For instance, I had gotten from the Czech government in exile official replicas of the leaflets handed out to factory workers with the aim to get them to do sabotage. The underground passed out these leaflets to get them to slow down production. It was just a tortoise. I loved it. I had written a scene where the leaflets are found in surprising places—in a lunch box, wrapped around a cup of soup, and so on. These scenes developed the character of the Czech people. Brecht loved them. But Lang said to me, 'John, don't try to politicize this.' Whenever anything had to do with anti-Semitism or the Czech resistance, he would say, 'Take it easy.' Part of his fear, I think, was the fear of being taken as a Communist. The Czech resistance, after all, had ninety-five percent Communist leadership. Lang, knowing Hollywood, saw that everybody who was anybody for a certain period was on the Left. It was quite fashionable. In the period before that, however, to have that brand was the mark of Cain. So at this time he was very apprehensive."

But about the ideal-script?

"Yes, I'm getting to that. You see, the very thing Lang wanted to get out was what Brecht and I wanted to get in. And in a joking way I said to Bert, 'Wouldn't it be wonderful if we could do as we like in this film and not be wretched writers at all?' And this idea became the source of the ideal-script. We would take scenes I had written and had removed and then restore them. We would add others. Then there were other things, matters of emphasis and so on. Fritz leaned a lot toward sentiment, and we wanted to alter this emphasis. So parts of this ideal-script were written and others were simply compiled from what had been rejected. We put in some scenes and took out others, so that it would have looked for the most part like a substitute script of scenes that had fallen by the wayside. Then came the big day. We made some kind of speech. Fritz may have invited it, said something like, 'Well, let's see how your idea stacks up with what we have.' That may have been the invitation. Anyway, we started to read it, and he said 'Stop! Stop! Let's get back to where we were.' He made a big show of indignation, and that was the end of it. But there was a point earlier when he said, 'You can talk, and we'll listen, then we'll decide.' Well, he decided."

Obviously, there are discrepancies, even contradictions in John

Wexley's account of the writing of *Hangmen Also Die*. The area of closest agreement with Brecht's entries in the *Work Journal* is of course Wexley's portrait of Fritz Lang: by 1942, the aristocratic artist of the Berlin days had evidently metamorphosed into the thoroughgoing Hollywood professional. Even Lang's fear that he might be taken for a Communist, mentioned by Wexley, was confirmed by the director himself in the heated denial he made to Peter Bogdanovich in the latter's book-length interview of him. In 1967, some years after the McCarthy period had passed, he told of having been put on a kind of graylist because of his support of Henry Wallace in the 1948 election, and of how he had been made to pay the price of his wartime associations: "I was never a Communist. I was never a member of the Communist Party. I had many, many Communist friends. It was very chic during the Roosevelt time to belong to the Party. When I came to this country, the Big Powers—England, France too—tried to appease Hitler, and what actually happened? No one really gave a damn about what was going on in Germany. . . . That was one of the reasons why so many people here in Hollywood turned to the Communists—because they *believed* that the Communist Party was the only group really fighting the Nazis."[22]

But back to John Wexley on *Hangmen Also Die*. His story of the credit arbitration is just as instructive as what he had to say about the writing of it. "This is how it came up in the first place," says Wexley. "Brecht and Lang had a common agent—Sam Jaffe. I say this in passing because while Fritz Lang and I kicked around the story plenty, I only talked to Brecht about it. Their idea was very schematic. The story was to take somebody—later Brian Donlevy—who was a professional, a doctor or a dentist, and have him seek refuge at the home of a professor, later played by Walter Brennan. And that the professor would have a daughter, later played by Anna Lee. And the Gestapo would be after the professional, and the professor's family helps him. Well, it went as far as for them to say, 'Let's make him a doctor. We'll do certain things in a doctor's office.' But there were none of the details or the interweaving of the plot there. Having admired *M* so much, I said to the two of them, 'You know, you would get a lot of values here out of utilizing the double chase idea you had in *M*. You know—the police looking for him, as well as the beggars and thieves, out of self-protection, also looking for him.' I think it was at that time I invented the character of the Czech magnate—Gene Lockhart in the movie. The Gestapo now searches for Donlevy, and the underground is after Lockhart because he was exposing them.

"But getting to the credit thing, the agent Sam Jaffe called and asked in a shamefaced way if I would consider letting Bert come in on the screenplay. It had already been decided that it would be screenplay by me and let them share the story. At that time the writer regarded his credit as a woman regarded her wedding certificate. It would have been as silly and unjust for him to get that as for me to get the authorship of his next play."

Would it? Wexley made another such invidious comparison moments later: "After Sam Jaffe spoke to me I had lunch with Brecht, who was very shamefaced about the whole affair. I remember I said, 'I don't think you should do this.' And I explained why. I said I would like to do it, but I don't think I should go this far. But I said I would help him if I could. And then I talked to Lang, who said he was shocked that Brecht or Jaffe should made such a request. It would have been like me asking him for codirecting credit. Then I said to Brecht, 'Who put you up to this?' Then I had a shock when I found out he wanted arbitration on the matter. I asked him, 'Are you sure you want to go there? You have to come up with scripts and so on.' Brecht hadn't written anything that could be presented to the Guild. It was all oral. It was a three-man board. They examined the material, and of course Brecht had no written material. Fritz was up there, too, of course. He just squirmed."

But of course Fritz Lang claimed that he did a good deal more than squirm. He claimed to have testified in Brecht's behalf. Yet why should he have been there at all, since the original assignment of credits had to have come from him and Arnold Pressburger? And as for Lang's claim that the screenplay credit was awarded to Wexley on the basis of need—Wexley would remain, but Brecht would return to Germany—"the assumption here is that I needed the credit. Whereas the truth is that while every credit is important to a writer, nevertheless it is not the basis on which the Guild gives credit—that is, need. No, if that were so, it would have made a mess of arbitration long ago."[23]

In any case, John Wexley was awarded sole screenplay credit on *Hangmen Also Die*. According to him, he resumed seeing all the people involved in the matter socially for the seven months he remained in Hollywood before going into the army. After the war, Wexley says he saw Brecht in Europe: "It was in Zurich in the spring of 'forty-eight. We renewed our in-quotes friendship. The thing had worn off a bit with him, and he was a little shamefaced about it all. This was while he was waiting to get into the DDR [East Germany]."

There is no mention of any such visit to Brecht in Europe in the *Work Journal* for that period in Zurich.

We are left with a set of inconsistent interpretations and implications, and even a few facts that are quite simply in conflict. What are we to do with them? Shall we play *Rashomon* and keep digging and sifting through them with the intention of ultimately assigning blame in this affair? Perhaps so, but if we do, I think no special weight should be given to Brecht's version of the events. He was as inclined as the next man to see things his way and conveniently forget facts and details that did not suit his case. Yet today it seems that Brecht's dated account in his *Work Journal* has been accepted as the true one.

One thing to keep in mind in discussing the question of blame here is that there really need not be much given. To accept Brecht's version—or Wexley's—we must concur in the judgment that *Hangmen Also Die* was an artistic failure; actually, it was nothing of the kind. The film was, in many ways, the most "European" of any Fritz Lang had done to date in America: it re-creates Prague under German occupation perfectly—from the convincing and quite detailed sets to the feeling it conveys of a people subdued but unconquered. Its starless cast makes the most of roles that are of necessity rather schematic; they make people out of types. Walter Brennan, as the professor who shelters Heydrich's assassin and then is himself taken hostage, is particularly memorable—as is Gene Lockhart in the part of the Czech traitor. Best of all, however, is Alexander Granach as the Gestapo inspector in pursuit of the killers. Granach, an old friend of Brecht's from Berlin, creates a portrayal that is at once subtle and gross, as far removed from the usual iron-jawed movie Nazi as reality from fantasy. *Hangmen Also Die* stands with Fred Zinnemann's *The Seventh Cross* as easily the best of the wartime films offering a look at life under Nazi rule.

Another point to bear in mind in judging the success or failure of *Hangmen Also Die* is that while Brecht may have failed to get from it what he wanted, he certainly got what he needed. What did he want? What he always did: total control. In the theater his rehearsal tantrums are legendary; he nearly always managed to get what he wanted by pure unpleasantness. In working with Lang and later with Wexley, however, he found himself in a situation where that sort of behavior got him nothing, indeed was out of the question. But as Christopher Isherwood has said of him, "Brecht could be charming when it suited him," and certainly he did try charm—first with Lang (there was a good deal of friendly visiting between them in the beginning and even some discussion of bringing *Fear and Misery in the Third Reich* to the screen), and then with Wexley (all that colleague talk at Brecht's was surely to win him over to the ideal-script plan). None of it worked, of course: Wexley wrote the movie Lang wanted him to write, and Lang shot it the way he had intended. Would it have been a better film if it had been done Brecht's way? Possibly so, but probably not. The proof, after all, is in the movie that was actually made—and it is, in spite of Brecht's opinion of it, a good one.

What was it Brecht *needed* that his involvement with the production gave him? Money. Just how much it was is open to question. Evidently, the original agreement called for Brecht to be paid $5,000 for his work on the film. But John Wexley insists that he, Wexley, was "very helpful in getting him an additional three thousand dollars on the project. I put in a big campaign on it to Arnold Pressburger." The higher figure may indeed be the correct one, for Brecht is known to have bought a secondhand Ford auto at about this time, and there is this note in his *Work Journal* on June 24, 1943, the last entry in which the film is mentioned: "The Lang film (now known as *Hangmen Also Die*) has given me space for three plays. *(The Visions of Simone Machard, The Duchess of Malfi, Schweyk)*."

Brecht was, after all, first and foremost a playwright. His real ambition in America was to be produced on Broadway, and he eventually achieved it with *Galileo*. If he may have expected more from Hollywood at the outset, by the time he finished with *Hangmen Also Die* he saw movie work strictly as a means of making money. Later, there were a number of occasions when, collaborating with others, he would again try to turn out original stories for the movie market; but none of them sold. He did, however, share in the sale to M-G-M of *Simone*, a novel that was based on the play he wrote in collaboration with Lion Feuchtwanger. At the instigation of Charles Laughton he was brought in to do a few weeks work on the script of *Arch of Triumph*; he went uncredited on the film, though; that was in 1947, the year Brecht returned to Europe. When he did leave he took with him a whole suitcase full of play manuscripts—all of his best work and some of it still unproduced. Brecht had bought himself time to write most of them with money he made from working on movies.

5

SUNDAYS
IN MABERY ROAD

The house was at the foot of Santa Monica Canyon, only a few steps from the beach. To the west lay the Pacific, that vast ocean, which probably made this point seem to any European a kind of Ultima Thule, the absolute end of the line.

That, at any rate, must have been what it meant to Salka Viertel: she had gone about as far as she could go. Born in Galicia late in the last century, when that piece of Poland was still attached to the Hapsburg Empire, she had made her way to Vienna at her earliest opportunity to pursue a career on the stage. There, after an apprenticeship that had taken her as far afield as Berlin and Max Reinhardt's Deutsches Theater, she was established as a leading actress with the Neue Wiener Bühne when she met a young director, who was also a poet, named Berthold Viertel. World War I was in its third year. Viertel was on leave from the front, married, and with no apparent resources except his own overweening self-confidence. He swore when he first came to know Salka that they would soon be married. Before the war was ended, he kept that promise. Their alliance proved for a time to be one of the firmest professional partnerships in the German theater; and it was to the very end one of the most engaging. Immediately after the war the two settled in Berlin, where, it seems, they worked with or came to know nearly everyone involved in the Berlin theater world of the twenties—among them, playwrights Brecht, Bronnen, Kaiser, Zuckmayer, and players Kortner, Homolka, Granach, and Lorre. Somehow, between their involvement as founders of an avant-garde theater company, Die Truppe, and Berthold's additional work with F. W. Murnau in films, the busy couple even managed to bring three sons—Hans, Peter, and Thomas—into the world.

The association with Murnau was what brought them, together with their children, all the way across an ocean and a continent to come at last to a halt on that farthest shore. In 1928 Berthold Viertel was invited to Hollywood to write the screenplay for F. W. Murnau's second American film, *The Four Devils.* He had every intention of staying on to direct films of his own, and so the whole family came along. Once Salka set eyes upon the Pacific, she knew that she had reached her destination, attained a kind of goal. "Everything was so lovely and peaceful," she remembers in her autobiography, *The Kindness of Strangers,* "the people on the pier and the merry-go-round and the swaying boats. I begged Berthold to let us live in Santa Monica."[1] She had that passion for the beach and broad ocean that perhaps only a landlocked middle-European could generate. Her husband, for one, could not. Yet to satisfy her, he consented, and eventually Salka got her house by the ocean.

The address of the place she chose was 165 Mabery Road, and it was not at all grand by Hollywood standards. It became quite well known, however, among a certain select though ever growing contingent of residents, émigrés, and visitors. In the beginning, their guests were newcomers from Europe like themselves—people such as Fred Zinnemann, the young Viennese film editor and soon-to-be director, and William Dieterle, the director whom the Viertels had known as an actor in Max Reinhardt's company. Or, if not European, then they were those who, like Paul Muni, had something of Europe about them: he had come from New York's Yiddish theater to star in Berthold's second Hollywood film as a director, *The Seven Faces.*

What established Salka most firmly as a hostess, however, was her friendship with Greta Garbo. That began at a party given by Ernst Lubitsch. Upon meeting, the two women hit it off marvelously well, and Garbo, it turned out, lived quite near the Viertels. She began dropping by very early in the morning, and the two would take long walks together along the beach. On one of them Garbo asked Salka why she did not write. While Salka might have answered that the reason was, of course, that she was an actress, she knew that she had not worked in that capacity since coming to Hollywood from Germany. And here was Garbo—Garbo!—asking Salka to write something suitable for her. Who could decline such an opportunity? Teamed with another woman of like interest, one whose command of English was much surer than Salka's, she produced the screen story *Queen Christina*, which, on Garbo's say-so, was promptly bought by Metro-Goldwyn-Mayer. She was put on the payroll to work on the script.

Thus began Salka's career as a "Garbo specialist." It seemed quite a blessing, for at just about that time Berthold's luck gave out in Hollywood and he returned to Berlin to look for film work during the period when the country was teetering on the brink of Nazism. This new source of income enabled her to stay on in Santa Monica with their three sons until he could return. In the final reckoning, however, although it meant a decade of full-time employment for her, hitching her wagon to a star would prove somewhat risky.

As the crisis deepened in Germany, Salka became increasingly anxious for her husband's safety. He was under contract to a German film company and writing a screenplay when Hitler came to power. Boldly, perhaps even foolishly, Berthold Viertel, a Jew and an outspoken enemy of the Nazis, stayed on to finish the job. Only with the burning of the Reichstag did he and so many others—Thomas and Heinrich Mann, Bertolt Brecht, Ernst Toller, Kurt Weill, Alfred Döblin, and Anna Seghers among them—give in at last and depart. Salka was expecting him to return to his family in Santa Monica, but instead he went off to London on the promise of a directing assignment from Alexander Korda.

The name of the picture was *Little Friend*, and with it Berthold

Viertel took his place in English literature—not a very prominent place, to be sure, but, say, one that is high up in one corner of the gallery in a seat beside Gerald Hamilton, who was the original for Christopher Isherwood's Mr. Norris. Berthold himself became raw material for Isherwood, who was his screenwriter on the production; as Friedrich Bergmann in Isherwood's rather short novel, *Prater Violet*, Berthold made his own quite indelible impression on readers. Here is how he is described by Isherwood at their first meeting:

> Bergmann jerked to his feet with startling suddenness, like Punch in a show. "A tragic Punch," I said to myself. I couldn't help smiling as we shook hands, because our introduction seemed so superfluous. There are meetings which are more like recognitions—this was one of them. Of course we knew each other. The name, the voice, the features were inessential, I knew that face. It was the face of a political situation, an epoch. The face of Central Europe.[2]

No doubt that was the face, brooding and explosive, that Berthold Viertel presented to the world, for in the weeks of wide-ranging conversations that followed that first meeting the two talked at length of Berlin (which, of course, they had in common), of Hitler and his Nazis, and of the Reichstag trial that proceeded day by day even as they met and discussed the script of *Little Friend*. There was probably not a better companion for Berthold in all of England during those dark days than Isherwood.

He also talked about his family back in California—of Salka and his sons, and of their life there. As Isherwood recalled in his factual treatment of this episode in his third-person autobiography, *Christopher and His Kind*:

> Viertel described their white house with its green roof, standing amidst the subtropical vegetation of Santa Monica Canyon, three minutes from the Pacific Ocean. 165 Mabery Road— the British-sounding address became wildly exotic when Christopher tried to relate it to his idea of a canyon, a gigantic romantic ravine. He began to yearn to see this place; Viertel took it for granted that he would be visiting them there before long.[3]

Eventually he did. Five years later when Isherwood emigrated to America, he made for Los Angeles and settled—where else?—in the Santa Monica Canyon. (Once, when I had occasion to visit him in his home, he stood at a window looking down upon the canyon and remarked that he had lived in five different places in America and they were all within sight at that moment.)

Aldous Huxley preceded Isherwood to America by two years and the returning Berthold Viertel by one. In the beginning Huxley had come for no more than an extended tour, expecting to stay about a year. However, having seen something of the American West and having renewed his friendship with that knockabout mystic, Gerald Heard, he decided to stay on somewhat longer in Los Angeles. The news from Europe, after all, was getting worse by the day! To make it easier for the Huxleys to remain, Anita Loos (the brunette who wrote *Gentlemen Prefer Blondes*), whom they had met years before in New York, offered to see what she could do about getting him a film writing job at M-G-M. This was 1938. Salka Viertel was now a veteran screenwriter there and especially well thought of because of her proven ability to create roles for Greta Garbo (*Queen Christina* and *Conquest* had both originated with her). Salka's latest project for the actress was a story built around the role of Madame Curie, the Polish woman who, with her husband Pierre, discovered radium. She had read the biography of the scientist and suggested it to Garbo, who was most enthusiastic. Anita Loos knew all about this; and also knowing that Salka always worked with a second writer, she brought her together with Huxley one evening in her home. Perhaps a collaboration on the Madame Curie story?

That was just about how it was managed. George Cukor was to be the director. The writing team turned out a "treatment" that satisfied them both but seemed to the M-G-M producer involved excessively "scientific." Through the next two years the screenplay of *Madame Curie* went through successive—and, no doubt, excessive—rewrites (even F. Scott Fitzgerald had a shot at it) in the course of which Greta Garbo lost interest in the project. When the film was finally produced in 1941, it starred Greer Garson and Walter Pidgeon; and while it was not at all bad, it was certainly not the scientific epic that Huxley and Salka had envisioned. Their names, by the way, did not appear on the screen—nor, for that matter, did F. Scott Fitzgerald's; the last team to rewrite usually wins that prize. In fact, the picture would not be worth mentioning here, except that it brought Aldous Huxley and Salka Viertel together, and while their professional association lasted only eight weeks, they remained friends until Huxley's death. When he and his wife, Maria, at last admitted to themselves that they would be living in Los Angeles for quite some time, they bought a house in Pacific Palisades, just north of Salka's place. They were frequent guests at dinner and regular attendants when, during the war, she began her regular Sundays.

Both Huxley and Isherwood chose to remain in America because of the war. Both were committed pacifists by the time they arrived; Isherwood, in fact, put in time at a Quaker work camp when the United States did at last declare hostilities. It was because of Hitler and the war, too, that Hollywood's German colony began to grow so astonishingly—not just in quantity, but in variety as well. There had always been movie people. Beginning with Erich von Stroheim, German and Austrian directors and actors had begun to find their way over during the silent era, when the language barrier seemed not quite so formidable; and the Viertels, of course, were among them. But with Hitler's seizure of power in 1934, the trickle became a steady stream. Then, with the coming of the war, the stream became a river on which were borne not just movie people, but also playwrights, novelists, composers, and philosophers. The situation was such that by 1941 Aldous Huxley could remark casually of his new neighbors in a letter, "We were polite to the Feuchtwangers, and the Manns live exactly opposite so we meet on our walks."[4]

"The Manns," in this case, were the Thomas Manns. They had moved only recently to Pacific Palisades, having come there by stages from Zurich and Princeton. Mann, by far the brightest star in the émigré constellation, had come only with misgivings to California; although once settled, he liked it well enough and found no trouble whatever in writing there. But his wife Katia never came to terms with their new home (the Manns were among the first of the intellectual refugees to take out citizenship papers). Maria Huxley, again in a letter, described them at a dinner: "He was peaceful and pacifying; she was hating and violent and we would not discuss it; besides—to be rude about America while you have to remain in it."[5]

Heinrich Mann, Thomas's brother, was also there, a late arrival from France. Both he and Lion Feuchtwanger had been in Paris at the time of the fall of France. Mann effected an immediate escape over the Pyrenees to Spain and out by way of Portugal. Feuchtwanger made it to the south of France, where he was interned for a year by the Vichy government before he, too, managed an exit by the same route. Feuchtwanger, Franz Werfel, and Thomas Mann were about the only émigré novelists who were able to live on their book royalties once they had arrived in the United States. Others were in real financial difficulties during their entire stay, and had to depend upon secondary employment or the generosity of friends.

It wasn't long before Brecht was in close and frequent contact with Salka Viertel. They had known one another since the twenties in Berlin. Berthold and Salka both liked Brecht; and that in itself was significant, for he was not a likable man. They were willing to go that extra distance he seemed to require of everyone. Salka, in fact, made it possible for Brecht to solve the inevitable problem that arose with wife and mistress under the same roof. She offered to take in Ruth Berlau, and put her up in the apartment above her garage. When Brecht was able, he moved to a house in Santa Monica in order to be nearer to her. When he did, he became a constant visitor at Mabery Road.

Salka's son, the novelist and screenwriter Peter Viertel, remembers him well from that period. He told me in an interview: "I've known three or four men who have been recognized as geniuses. Hemingway was, Schönberg was, and Aldous Huxley was recognized by some, as he should have been. And Brecht, of course, has had the term applied to him, and he certainly was a genius. Like all the rest, he had that characteristic of being so God-damned sure of what he was doing and what he thought. He was *very* sure of his political convictions, for instance. He would get into *terrific* political arguments.

"What was he like personally? Well, there was the tremendous presence of the man. He would come into a room, and you knew it immediately. He had a manner that was shy and arrogant at the same time. I also remember that he had a rather strange way of walking and even standing in a room, a hesitance in his gait, as though he were on the point of moving, but then not moving. The majority of writers I've known speak quite a bit—but not Brecht. He was reticent, not voluble."[6]

Brecht grew quite close to Salka Viertel. One night she, Brecht, and Ruth Berlau sat up late having what Brecht would later term a "refugee conversation." Salka, who had not been able to get all her family out of Poland, confessed to them that she often felt guilty that she had been "spared." Brecht told her that he, too, had had these feelings. The next morning she found tucked under her door a poem that he had written:

> I know of course: it's simply luck
> That I've survived so many friends. But last night in a dream
> I heard those friends say of me: "Survival of the fittest"
> And I hated myself.[7]

She knew that he understood.

Among those whom Salka had been able to bring out of Europe was her mother, who arrived, even later than Brecht, by the same route, traveling all the way across wartime Russia and Siberia and then across the Pacific. Her mother was able to bring with her not much more than the clothes on her back and her recipe for chocolate cake; and it is with those chocolate cakes she baked on Mabery Road that Brecht is forever associated in the minds of some of those who knew him there at Salka's. The American movie comedy writer and director Mel Frank remembers that, as if by magic, Brecht would appear, with or without Berlau, whenever a cake was in the oven.

By the middle of the war, Salka Viertel's regular Sundays in Mabery Road had become perhaps the last great salon, one attended by Europe's exiled intellectual elite, as well as by some of Hollywood's most glamorous figures. But it should be evident that hers was a salon of a rather special sort— *heimisch, gemütlich, bequem*—one where chocolate cake was more likely to be eaten than canapés, one that perfectly suited the relaxed and generous style of the hostess. Yet she attracted Hollywood's serious people—the writers, the directors, the émigré novelists, the theater people just in from New York. Where did Christopher Isherwood at last meet Bertolt Brecht? At Salka's. Where was George Cukor a regular? At Salka's. Where was the first place Harold Clurman headed when he jumped off the Santa Fe Chief? To Salka's. "I remember it," Mel Frank told me in an interview, "as a complete striation, an incredible spectrum of Hollywood's most interesting people. You might meet Chaplin, Garbo, and Dietrich there—and only there!—as well as the in-people and the out-people, all the serious composers and writers in town, including, of course, that whole émigré community. She was very good about bringing people together. She was very helpful that way."[8]

How? She got jobs for a few, and arranged informal charity from rich movie patrons for the rest. She served as intermediary between Brecht and Berthold Viertel in the early stages of negotiations for a New York production of *The Private Life of the Master Race.* She had her own agent, Frederick Kohner, handle some of the more employable émigrés.

Of course, things did not always work out as she hoped. One of the first people she had tried to help was the composer, Arnold Schön-berg, with whom her brother Edward had studied in Berlin years before. When Schönberg arrived in Hollywood in the thirties, she suspected that he was in rather difficult circumstances. After making a few discreet inquiries, she went to him and offered to arrange a meeting between him and her boss at M-G-M, Irving Thalberg, about the possibility of scoring the film *The Good Earth,* which was about to begin shooting. She told Schönberg not to consider doing it unless he was willing to compromise. He agreed that he was ready to do that; and so she did as she had offered, and brought the two together. She was present at the meeting in Thalberg's office, and she listened dumbstruck as Schönberg explained that of course he could not agree to work unless he was given complete control over the film. What did that entail? He would write the score *first,* of course; and then coach the actors and actresses in delivering their lines in the proper key and right rhythm. Clearly, what he had in mind was turning *The Good Earth* into a work for *Sprechstimme* on the order of his earlier *Pierrot Lunaire.* Thalberg, although truly impressed by Schönberg, declined the opportunity the composer had given him to turn the movie into a "serious" work of art.

In spite of the fact that her reputation as a Hollywood hostess was made during the war years, they were very hard years for Salka personally. There were general worries about the war; and there was the despair she felt for the many she had known in Vienna and Berlin and Poland who had not been able to get out. Her own life was emp-tier than ever before. The years of separation endured by Salka and Berthold had at last taken their final toll: the two were divorced in 1944.

The year before she had lost her screenwriting job at Metro-Gold-wyn-Mayer. Of course the difficulty was Salka's role as the "Garbo specialist." She had worked on other things, but in the minds of the studio executives she was still the writer they had hired to turn out stories and scripts for Garbo; and, as the Swedish actress turned down project after project and became more and more reclusive, Salka herself began to seem to them somewhat superfluous. The last thing she worked on for Garbo was *Song of Russia*. Like *Madame Curie*, it was turned down by the star and passed on to another actress: Jean Peters played it opposite Robert Taylor. The studio took its revenge on Garbo by firing Salka.

Thrown onto her own, she had no immediate choice but to try another Garbo project, this time for an independent producer in collaboration with a French screenwriter of Russian parentage, Vladimir Pozner. Garbo seemed behind them on this one. She dropped by Mabery Road frequently to read what the two had done and to offer encouragement. In the end, however, she was no more willing to go with this script than with any of the others that had been offered her at M-G-M. That ended Salka Viertel's professional association with Greta Garbo.

Another of Salka's sons, Hans Viertel, became Brecht's collaborator on a number of screen stories. He was politically attuned to Marxism and provided the playwright with a worthy opponent in argument. "My parents were never Party members," he said in an interview, "but they were always of the Left."[9] A mere reading of *The Communist Manifesto* in high school inspired him to declare himself a Marxist, but then the Moscow Trials and the contradictions of the Popular Front period estranged him from the Soviet brand of communism. A term or two at the University of California made a Trotskyist of him.

"I first met Brecht in 1941," he remembers, "just after he arrived in America. My father took me to meet him. I'm not sure when it was clear to me that he was one of the greatest dramatists of our time. Not that he told me so—though he did say it in so many words. He didn't believe in false modesty.

"At the time we started collaborating I was working in a shipyard in San Pedro, then later as a mechanic at Pan American. We tried to write original stories from films and sell them. As I knew English and at that time he really didn't, he asked me to collaborate with him. I would put our work into English as we went along. What kind of things did we do? Well, I remember there was one story about a museum director who steals a statue of Venus to keep it from falling into the hands of the Germans. We never sold it, but there was a film in French that followed a story line that was strangely close to ours. I remember it had Erich von Stroheim in it.

"This was the routine. Brecht got up at seven and did his serious writing until 1 P.M. Then I would come, and after lunch we would work on film projects . . . eventually. Actually, he would lie down for a while with a detective story, and I would talk to Helli, his wife, and Stef, his son, in the kitchen. But we would finally get to work and go at it the rest of the afternoon. He had the ability to sit back in a chair and simply develop scenes. He could map them out and pare them down with such ease! The fertility and facility of his imagination was unbelievable. But it was a real collaboration. He invited that. He wanted it. In the fall of 1944 I had an emotional involvement with a woman, and I was leaving town to be with her. I was short of money, and he knew that and knew how much I wanted to go, and so he wrote me out a check for a hundred dollars—which was a lot of money to him—and said, 'I owe you this for the work we did together.' I took it and left town, but shortly after that I was drafted, anyway. After that? Well, my mother worked with him after I left."[10]

Brecht approached Salka, proposing that they collaborate on a screen story. "Why shouldn't we be able to do as well as any Hollywood hack?" he wanted to know. Yet, as they met daily at Salka's to shape the story, she soon found that although Brecht had always promoted team authorship, he certainly demanded to be captain of the team. At last, in desperation, she asked that they bring another writer in on the project, one who might serve as referee to their battles. Brecht was willing, and so Vladimir Pozner was welcomed aboard. The fights continued, however; by Pozner's own account, Brecht seems to have been just as autocratic as before. The playwright would lay down the law on a scene; Salka would demand an explanation, motivation, a justification. "Why?" she would ask. "I want to know why!" "Because I said so," Brecht would shout. "That's enough!" Finally, as things calmed down, he would say something conciliatory. Once: "Above all, let us not for one moment forget that we are writing this scenario to sell it."[11]

But they never did sell the story, which was called *Silent Witness* and was set in France just after liberation. By that late date, 1945, producers may have felt that the war was going out of style. In their own crude fashion, they were right, of course. The war was over in Europe, and would soon come to a sudden, startling end in the Pacific as well. With peace came the inevitable breakup of the émigré community in Hollywood. Even many of those who had taken out citizenship papers had no real intention of staying on; they were refugees now ready to return.

Eventually, Salka Viertel returned as well. Things grew increasingly difficult for her financially. She managed to stay more or less active as a screenwriter, and had two more of her scripts produced. But assignments were few and far between; and free-lance projects of the kind she engaged in with Brecht and Pozner were always risky. Finally, after decades in the house on Mabery Road, she said goodbye to it and to the ocean she loved, and left Los Angeles for good. After some passport difficulties—her associations with Brecht and others had left her with that curious label, "premature anti-Fascist"—she departed in 1953 for Klosters in Switzerland, where she lived near her son, Peter Viertel. Years before, when she was not much more than a girl, a gypsy had told her that she would know her greatest happiness near water, and that had been so. Writing her autobiography, it seemed to her that the best part of her life had been spent there in Santa Monica—the Sundays and the dinner parties, the walks along the beach. There was no body of water of any considerable size near her there in Klosters; only mountains. She died there in 1978.

6

BRECHT AND
THE BROTHERS MANN

It was as inevitable that Bertolt Brecht should have come to despise Thomas Mann as that he should have revered Heinrich Mann. To young Germans of the World War I generation like Brecht the two novelists represented almost totally opposite views of the national catastrophe they had been lucky enough to survive. Heinrich, the Francophile, had fought the narrowness and authoritarianism of the old Kaiser regime for two decades; he opposed the war he saw coming and, even as it proceeded, bravely declared himself a socialist and cried out against it. Thomas, then profoundly convinced of the superiority of *deutsche Kultur*, not only made speeches and wrote essays supporting the war but also expounded his antidemocratic views at length in *The Reflections of a Nonpolitical Man*.

Although more conservative by nature, Thomas was the younger of the two. Heinrich, the eldest child of an established Lübeck trader, was born in 1871. Soon after Thomas came along four years later, the two brothers were in almost constant conflict. Angry memories of their extraordinary sibling rivalry in childhood were carried by the younger Mann well into adulthood. "Heinrich could be *so* hurtful," Thomas told his daughter Erika many years later.[1] And we have it on the authority of his wife, Katia Mann, that during one whole year while growing up the two brothers did not speak to each other (as they again did not during World War I).

But if Heinrich fought bitterly with Thomas as a child, he got along no better with their parents. He refused to follow his father into the family business, and when he insisted he wanted to be a writer, he was simply shipped off as an apprentice to a bookseller. By the time Thomas was ready to begin to make his own way as a writer, their father had died and their mother offered him no resistance— partly no doubt because Heinrich had already managed to achieve some success. Thus, in spite of his hostility to Heinrich, Thomas was not only inspired in his vocation by Heinrich but had the way cleared for him by his brother as well. His debt to Heinrich was considerable.

Heinrich Mann's early novels and essays, most of them written from expatriate havens in France and Italy, did a good deal to inspire the poets and playwrights of the Expressionist movement. One of these, Kurt Pinthus, wrote that he "inspired all of us, speaking with a quiet voice and aristocratic poise. . . ."[2] Yet it was not the style or even the substance of his books that influenced them so much as their attitude: he was steadfastly antiauthoritarian, cosmopolitan, and liberal in an age when most German writers felt an overwhelming obligation to the fatherland. In novels such as *Professor Unrat*, which Josef von Sternberg adapted years later as *The Blue Angel*, and *Der Untertan*, finished just before World War I but judged too incendiary to be published until the war was lost, and in essays such as *Voltaire-Goethe* and *Mind and Deed*, Heinrich Mann established himself as the voice—at the time it may have seemed the *only* voice—of German liberalism. However, with the end of the war and the final revelation of the moral bankruptcy of the old regime, he suddenly found himself the literary hero of an entire generation. Bertolt Brecht, for example, would write of Mann's novel *Der Untertan* that it was "to my knowledge the first great satirical political novel of German literature" and an inspiration to him in his own politically pointed writing.[3]

For Thomas Mann it was much different. From the time of the publication of *Buddenbrooks* in 1901, he was one of the most widely read writers in Germany and would remain so until he was declared persona non grata by the Nazis. Even the position he had taken during World War I was not held against him by his large reading public, for after all it was the stand *they* had taken, too. Thomas reconciled with Heinrich after the war; he quite sincerely admitted that his faith in the Kaiser had been misplaced, and somewhat stiffly embraced democracy. With *The Magic Mountain*, published in 1924, in which he continued to analyze his own "nonpolitical" attitudes to the forces of culture and history, Thomas Mann achieved international fame as a novelist. It was at a reading from that novel-in-progress at Augsburg in 1920 that Brecht made his first public comment on Thomas Mann and his work. Actually, he did no more than report it as an event to the local newspaper, but in doing so he parodied Mann's overblown and slightly pompous style, giving his own sly criticism of the writer who was even then considered by some to be Germany's greatest novelist.

Even during the twenties there seemed an almost personal animosity between Brecht and Thomas Mann. Although both lived for a few years in the same city (Munich), they were not to meet for nearly two decades (in California). Nevertheless they sniped back and forth relentlessly in print and conversation. Mann, in writing of the premiere of Brecht's *The Life of Edward the Second of England* for the American magazine *The Dial*, described the playwright as "a strong but somewhat careless talent who has been pampered by the public in Germany." The performance of the play itself he called "one of the most unpleasant sights I have ever witnessed."[4] For his part, Brecht declared in 1927 that Thomas Mann was a "bourgeois producer of artificial, empty and useless books." He went on to say, "I frankly admit I would actually make financial sacrifices to prevent the publication of certain books"[5] (meaning Thomas Mann's, Franz Werfel's, and others of their generation).

But it was more than a generation gap that separated the two. To Thomas Mann, Bertolt Brecht grew to be a kind of *bête noire*, the incarnation of all that was pernicious and morally corrupt in Weimar culture. In *Unwritten Memories*, Katia Mann recalls that the actress Therese Giehse, who was a friend of both Brecht's and Erika Mann's, brought a play by Brecht to Thomas Mann and urged him to read it. He did, and later returned it, saying, "Just imagine, the monster has talent." Giehse went to Brecht with this, and he replied, "As a matter of fact, I always found his short stories quite good."[6] Which is surely what Pope meant by damning with faint praise.

If Thomas Mann saw Brecht as "the monster," Brecht regarded him during the last Weimar years as one whose aloof devotion to his art fed a kind of aesthetic quietism among the Germans that would pave the way for a Nazi takeover. In his long poem "Ballad on Approving the World," in which he ironically applauded the villains of the German tragedy, Brecht included an angry quatrain aimed squarely at Mann:

The author has us read his Magic Mountain
What he wrote there (for money) was well thought up.
What he suppressed (for free): that was the real thing.
I say that he's blind; he's not been bought up.[7]

In this, as was often the case, Brecht was being a good deal less than fair. For by the time it was written, the writer who had once said, "I hate democracy," had come so far around to his brother Heinrich's position that he had campaigned publicly for the Social Democratic Party. At a large political rally held in Berlin in 1930, Thomas Mann gave a long, heavy, and characteristically philosophical address that was later reprinted as "An Appeal to Reason." Replete as it is with reference to Fichte and Goethe, the speech reads like anything but campaign rhetoric; nevertheless, it struck out directly at the Nazis, whom Mann perhaps did not take quite seriously enough as a threat to Germany's frail democracy:

Is there any deep stratum of the German soul where all that fanaticism, that bacchantic frenzy, that orgiastic denial of reason and human dignity is really at home? Do the heralds of radical nationalism plume themselves all too much upon their success at the polls? Is National-Socialism, regarded as a party, just possibly a colossus with feet of clay, whose prospects of endurance cannot compare with those of the Social-Democratic organization of the masses?[8]

If as a political analyst and prognosticator Thomas Mann, like so many other German intellectuals of the day, proved less than astute, these remarks so enraged the band of Nazis who were in the audience that they tried to shout him down. They were led, incidentally, by Arnolt Bronnen, an old friend and colleague of Brecht's from the early twenties who had gone over to Hitler.

During the last few years before the Nazi takeover, Heinrich Mann devoted himself to political writing somewhat to the neglect of his creative work. He managed somehow to continue turning out novels and stories and a play or two—he was always a rapid, prolific writer, as his brother was not—but none of it was very distinguished stuff. Most of his attention was given to essays, articles, and speeches, all of them concentrated on issues and crises of the moment. His literary standing may have fallen slightly during this period but nobody noticed: Heinrich himself had become such a prominent figure that in his own time and place he had managed to exceed his old idol, Emile Zola. He was even seriously put forward as a presidential candidate by a socialist literary group who argued that he was the only man who could unite the German Left. He was not interested.

Heinrich Mann was actually more involved in literary work at this time than his production would have indicated. As early as 1927, he had become interested in Henri IV of France (Henry of Navarre) as a possible subject for a novel, and all during those years of deepening crisis he had been reading and taking notes, planning the long, two-part historical novel that would become his masterpiece. On February 22, 1933, less than a month after Hitler's appointment as chancellor and only five days before the burning of the Reichstag, Heinrich slipped across the border by train into France with his wife Nelly. So as not to call attention to their departure, they carried only a bare minimum of hand luggage, but packed away securely in a briefcase that never left his side were the voluminous notes and opening chapters of *Young Henry of Navarre*, at which he would work steadily in exile.

That he was able to complete it and its sequel, *Henry, King of France*, which together comprise a work of about the size of *War and Peace*, is a tribute to the industry and discipline of this great man of letters of the old school; he was then in his sixties. He not only worked at great speed on this vast project, but also threw himself completely into the political war against Hitler that was mounted outside Germany. In exile he proved even more effective politically than he had earlier, for, after all, this was essentially a war of words that was fought from France, Holland, Austria, and Czechoslovakia—and who was better equipped than he to fight it? Not even his brother, Thomas, could have done as well, for Heinrich Mann had the confidence and respect of exiles from every position on the political compass. He rallied them, mobilized the writers among them, and put them to work. With regard to his ability to hold together those of widely differing political views who would have found it impossible to work together in Germany, the novelist and historian of the Left David Caute called him, in *The Fellow-Travellers*, "the Hindenburg of the Left."⁹

Caute also called him, with some justice, "the greatest of German fellow-travellers." For it is true that writing from Paris during these years of the Popular Front era his orientation began shifting discernibly toward Moscow. In his essays in the émigré publications *Die Sammlung*, which was edited by his nephew Klaus, and *Das Wort*, issued out of Moscow, it gradually became his theme that it was not enough simply to oppose Hitler; one must also oppose international capitalism. As Hindenburg became a prisoner of the Far Right, Heinrich Mann became a prisoner of the Far Left.

Bertolt Brecht, who had by this time met Heinrich Mann in Paris and had shared a few platforms with him, was unreserved in his admiration of the older writer—partly because their political views were now so compatible, but also no doubt partly because it pleased him to place one of the Mann brothers so high above the other. Heinrich was the stick he used to beat Thomas. Reviewing a collection of political essays, *Mut* (Courage), published by Heinrich in exile, Brecht wrote:

It is not the German working class to whom Heinrich calls, *courage!* It is the middle stratum. They need courage. For they need an insight that requires courage in order to be free. They must draw the same conclusion from their oppression and proletarianization that the workers have drawn from theirs: and that is, to struggle against a social and economic system that for the purposes of profit by men requires the oppression of men by other men—indeed increasing oppression! So they must become people who have actually only one conception whenever "the people" is referred to.[10]

By the time that Brecht wrote this in 1939, it was probably an accurate summary of Heinrich Mann's position with regard to the "necessity" of a socialist revolution in Germany.

· ● ·

Thomas Mann's protracted passage into exile was more comfortable than his brother's and considerably less dramatic. He and his wife Katia were out of the country at the time of the Reichstag fire and decided to remain away until after the March 5 election, which the Nazis felt would give them the mandate they hoped would legitimize and complete their takeover. As it turned out, having jailed most of the democratic opposition, the Nazis got exactly what they expected. A week later, Katia Mann called home and talked to two of their children, Klaus and Erika, in Munich. "I don't know," she asked them, "but don't you think that this would be time for a spring cleaning?" (She was asking them whether she and her husband should return home.) Erika Mann replied from Munich, "No, no, and besides the weather is terrible. Just stay there for a little while; you're not missing a thing."[11] They did as she advised. That "little while" stretched into a very long while, and Thomas Mann did not return to Germany until after the war, and then only as a visitor.

The Nazis' feelings toward Thomas Mann were somewhat ambivalent. While they were well aware of his political opposition to them, they were not anxious to denounce him and burn his books, as they had done with his brother, with Brecht, and the many other writers who had openly fought them. He was by then, after all, a Nobel Prize winner and was regarded in international literary circles as the very soul of Germany. In the early years of the Hitler regime, they were quite sensitive to world opinion and were especially concerned that they retain some degree of intellectual respectability in foreign eyes. It was decided that as long as Mann made no direct attack upon them, he would simply be considered a German resident abroad and not a refugee. He could retain his citizenship, and his books would continue to be published in Germany.

For his part, Thomas kept the unspoken pact with the Hitler government—though he did so with great misgivings. A good deal was involved in this decision. He had by then completed *The Tales of Jacob*, the first novel in his *Joseph* tetralogy, and wanted to see it published in Germany. He was also given to understand by his publisher that whether or not this Jewish-owned firm was allowed to continue operation would depend in part on whether or not it continued to publish Thomas Mann—whether or not, that is, Mann remained "publishable" in the view of the government. In any case, the Nazis kept him quiet in this way for three years. As Nigel Hamilton says in his dual biography, *The Brothers Mann*, "The poet had been allowed to speak; but the contemporary moralist, political and cultural, had *de facto* been silenced."[12] This, of course, did nothing to endear him to the more militant exiles such as Brecht and the Communist Party poet Johannes R. Becher. His brother Heinrich, however, supported him strongly in the decision, and on a couple of occasions when Thomas was tempted to break silence, argued against it. As a result of Thomas Mann's decision, S. Fischer was allowed to publish both *The Tales of Jacob* and *Young Joseph* in Berlin.

Although publicly mute, he criticized the Nazis bitterly in private, both in conversation and in letters. In fact, it was the publication of a letter that evidenced his first statement against the Nazi government. Heinrich had been quietly urging the award of the Nobel Peace Prize to Carl von Ossietzky, the former editor of *Die Weltbühne*, who was then in a concentration camp. He appealed to Thomas—after all, a letter from a Nobel laureate!—who came through with a strong recommendation to the Nobel Committee that they consider von Ossietzky for the Peace Prize as a gesture of criticism of the regime that had imprisoned him. After the award had been made to von Ossietzky early in 1936—in absentia, of course—the Nobel Committee released the letter to the press.

By this time, S. Fischer, Thomas Mann's publisher, had been sold at the insistence of the government, and the Jewish proprietors had been allowed to leave for Switzerland, so there was no longer any need for him to keep quiet on their behalf. However, when they tried to set up business in Zurich the Swiss refused to grant permission for fear of offending the German government. When Mann heard of the situation, he sent a letter to the editor of the *Neue Züricher Zeitung* that was blisteringly critical of the Nazis for forcing the Fischer people out and of the Swiss for their cowardice. It did no good, however. The firm of Bermann-Fischer, as it then became known, moved on to Vienna, where it published *Joseph in Egypt* in 1936, and then to Stockholm where it brought out the last book in the tetralogy, *Joseph the Provider.*

Cut off from most of his German reading public, Thomas Mann was increasingly dependent, as were all the exiled writers, on royalties from translations. Of them all he was in the most favorable position in this regard because of his reputation and because of his American publisher, Alfred Knopf. Translations of *The Magic Mountain* and the first books of the *Joseph* tetralogy by Helen Lowe-Porter had sold magnificently in America. Knopf invited him over for the publication of *The Tales of Jacob* in 1934, and the author was given such a welcome—it included a motorcycle escort through the streets of Manhattan—that he began eventually to think about settling in America. This did not come about, however, until 1939; he and his wife left Europe only days after the beginning of World War II. A visiting professorship had been arranged for him at Princeton, where he stayed for two years, then in 1940 he and Katia moved on to Pacific Palisades, California, which was his home for the next twelve years.

•   •   •

As usual, things were much harder for Heinrich. He hung on in France to the end—and beyond—leaving Paris at the collapse for the unoccupied zone in the south that was controlled by the Fascist French from Vichy. This would provide no sanctuary for him, and he knew it. Heinrich appealed for help to Thomas, who arranged an entry visa into America for him. Still, the problem was getting there to use it. As the Vichy government began rounding up refugee Germans, Heinrich and his wife Nelly slipped away to the Pyrenees in the company of Lion Feuchtwanger and his wife Marthe, Franz and Alma Werfel, and Thomas Mann's younger son, Golo. There, shown the way by a Basque guide, the party of German intellectuals by night crossed the border illegally into Spain. From there they made their way into Portugal and took a Greek tramp steamer to America.

By the time Heinrich and Nelly arrived in New York, Thomas and Katia had moved to California. Because he was there and was who he was, Thomas managed to arrange a job for his brother as a screenwriter at Warner Brothers. This was remarkable enough in itself, for Heinrich had no real experience with films (he had given some advice to von Sternberg regarding the screenplay of *The Blue Angel*, most of it ignored), but he *was* a needy refugee author, and some of the motion picture studios, to their everlasting credit, gave a number in this situation a year's employment to make emigration easier for them. At sixty-nine, Heinrich had not much English and was reluctant to speak the little he knew. He was not likely to continue in films, and he knew it. In fact, during the nine years of life left to him after the Warner Brothers contract gave out, he was unable to earn a living for himself and was financially dependent on the European Film Fund and ultimately upon the generosity of his brother Thomas and Lion Feuchtwanger. The only literary success he had enjoyed in America was with the publication of the translation of *Young Henry of Navarre* in 1937. When *Henry, King of France* was published by Knopf during the war and failed to sell, Heinrich gave up any hope of duplicating Thomas's success here and resigned himself during his last years to writing his memoirs for the drawer (they were published posthumously but have never been translated into English).

Considering all this, a number of the German refugee writers in Los Angeles thought it would be proper to honor Heinrich on his seventieth birthday. Salka Viertel offered her house, and all the arrangements were made. But it was soon found that it would be impossible to have the planned dinner on the date in question, for Heinrich's brother could not be there. Thomas was to be at the University of California at Berkeley to receive an honorary degree (one of about a dozen he received during his stay in America); he was then scheduled to give a series of lectures that would hold him at the university many weeks more. So, some three months after Heinrich Mann's actual birthday, a number of German writers in exile, including both brothers, Bruno Frank, Alfred Döblin, Franz Werfel, Lion Feuchtwanger, and Ludwig Marcuse, gathered with their wives to celebrate a ceremonial anniversary in his honor. Novelist Alfred Döblin, a good friend of Heinrich's, described the scene in a letter to another refugee novelist, Hermann Kesten:

> When we recently celebrated Heinrich Mann's seventieth birthday at Salka Viertel's, it was as it once had been: Thomas Mann drew out a manuscript and congratulated him from it. Then the brother pulled out his paper and read the thanks written on it as we sat at dessert—about twenty husbands and wives listened to German literature discussed. Feuchtwanger, Walter Mehring, the Reinhardts were there, as well as some from films. The war seemed a long way off.[13]

Afterward, as Salka Viertel tells it in her autobiography, *The Kindness of Strangers*, she remarked to novelist Bruno Frank how moved she had been by the mutual tributes read by the two brothers (even though Thomas Mann's had been so long it caused the roast to be served overdone). "Yes," said Bruno Frank. "They write and read such ceremonial evaluations of each other every ten years."[14]

. • .

One German writer absent from that birthday gathering was Bertolt Brecht. He was by then such a good friend of Heinrich's, or at least such a good comrade, that he would surely have been invited, even over Thomas's objections. But at the time that august assemblage sat around the table in Santa Monica listening to the mutual praise of the brothers Mann, Brecht was just preparing for his arrival from Russia at San Pedro, the port of Los Angeles.

Once settled in California (first in Hollywood, but soon in Santa Monica), Brecht began seeing Heinrich with fair frequency. This was about the time that Heinrich lost his screenwriting job at Warner Brothers, and Brecht was sympathetic to the point that he seems to have felt that the studio actually had an obligation to keep the novelist on. In any case, the contrast between Heinrich's financial situation and Thomas's was very much on Brecht's mind after an evening spent with the elder Mann and some others at Lion Feuchtwanger's. Afterward he thought it important enough to mention the evening in his *Work Journal*, noting that the conversation had mostly to do with the progress of the war (this was only days before America's entry) and that Heinrich was especially pleased at some good news from Russia. Then he went on to say of Mann: "He is on relief, every week picks up $18.50 unemployment benefits, since his contract with the film firm . . . has run out. He is over 70. His brother Thomas is building a grand villa."[15] The implication is obvious.

If anything, Brecht's hostility toward Thomas increased considerably once he had arrived in America. According to James K. Lyon in *Bertolt Brecht in America*, he was given reason to bear a grudge even before he got here: "While trying to flee Finland in 1941, Brecht had written friends in America asking for affidavits of support for his family. Someone must have mentioned his plight to Mann, who had been living in America since 1938. This was reported back to Brecht; his daughter Barbara remembers hearing in her family that Mann had refused to provide affidavits for them. Even among the worst of refugee enemies, this would have been tantamount to treason."[16]

Still, in spite of his personal dislike, his feeling of betrayal, and his sense of outrage at the "neglect" of Heinrich, Brecht was forced by the circumstances of exile life in California to be at least civil to Thomas, for Thomas was easily the most eminent German in America during World War II. Rumor had it that this noble incarnation of "the other Germany" had the ear of President Roosevelt himself; he was, in any case, in close communication with a member of the State Department. He had to be treated with a certain amount of deference—especially since his name and support were needed for any sort of political initiative undertaken by the German refugees.

Such support Thomas Mann gave only very reluctantly, as his brother, Brecht, and a number of other exile intellectuals found out in August 1943. On the first day of that month a party of them comprised of the two Mann brothers, Lion Feuchtwanger, Bruno Frank, Bertolt Brecht, Berthold Viertel, Hans Reichenbach, and Ludwig Marcuse met at Salka Viertel's in Santa Monica. At hand was a three-part statement to be signed by these writers and intellectuals, the most important point of which was the second, which was to stand as a refutation of the so-called Vansittart thesis. This was a proposition widely bandied about during World War II that was more or less attributed to Robert Gilbert Lord Vansittart, the English *revanchiste* who contended that the German national character was such that the Nazis and the German people could be considered as one and the same—so that rather than a master race, it was a blighted, evil one. Thomas Mann had already taken exception to this in a radio broadcast, and so it was quite naturally assumed that he would go along with the second point, which said simply: "We also hold it necessary to make a sharp distinction between the Hitler regime and its allied strata on the one hand, and the German people on the other." There was some debate over the phrase "allied strata" and at one point Thomas suggested that this be changed to "those who share their guilt," but in the end he did not insist, and the phrase finally stood as originally written. All this, as described to me by Marthe Feuchtwanger,[17] took place in one of the second-floor rooms of the Viertel house. After the discussion, the men brought the document downstairs and signed it before the waiting wives, thus lending a certain sense of pomp to the occasion.

The next morning, however, Mann called Lion Feuchtwanger and asked that his name be taken off the document. Why? "Since it might cause a big mess," according to Brecht. But according to Marthe Feuchtwanger: "Mann didn't want to be involved in something he considered pro-Communistic." Was it simply because Brecht was involved that Mann thought it such? Perhaps. Who could have warned him that if he signed the document it might cause "a big mess"? Well, it was hoped that such a declaration of eminent writers and intellectuals might lead to the formation of a permanent "Free Germany" committee that would work to transplant democracy in postwar Germany—and in fact such a committee was formed and, in spite of his earlier reticence, Thomas Mann was offered the chairmanship of it. After a meeting with Under Secretary of State Adolf A. Berle, Thomas not only refused to be chairman but also refused even to serve on the Council for a Democratic Germany, as it came to be known. The implication made by an Office of Strategic Services document in which reference is made to this meeting is that Thomas acted on Berle's advice. (Who, after all, was Adolf A. Berle? He was the man in the State Department to whom Whittaker Chambers went in 1939 when he first accused Alger Hiss of being a Communist.) It seems likely that Thomas consulted with Berle earlier when he reversed himself overnight on the anti-Vansittart statement and asked that his signature be removed.

Brecht was furious at Thomas. Yet he held himself in check and said nothing until the latter had refused to have anything to do with the Council for a Democratic Germany . Even then the letter that he wrote, though it put a considerable onus upon Thomas, was essentially a plea that he reconsider his position with regard to the Council—and the Vansittart thesis. The letter from Brecht to Thomas concluded:

> I also declare a real fear to our friends—that you, most respected Herr Mann, who more than any other of us has America's ear, propagate doubt of the existence of meaningful democratic strength in Germany; for after all, the future of not only Germany, but also of Europe, depends on these powers being aided by the [Allied] victory. I write this letter because I am honestly convinced it may be very important that you put our friends at ease by speaking out on these most important questions.[18]

The letter had considerable impact upon Thomas Mann. In fact, he noted its reception in *The Story of a Novel*, his *Doctor Faustus* diary: "One letter from Bert Brecht, taking me to task for my lack of faith in German democracy. In what way had I shown it, this lack of faith? And was the charge justified?" The letter did not have the desired effect: Mann steadfastly refused to change his mind. Yet he felt called upon to defend himself to Brecht in a letter to him:

> Where will we be, if we have prematurely vouched for the victory of the better and higher impulses within Germany? Let her military defeat take place, let the hour ripen when the Germans themselves settle accounts with the villains with a thoroughness, such as the world scarcely dares to hope for from our unrevolutionary people. That will be the moment for us on the outside to testify that Germany is free, that Germany has truly cleansed herself, that Germany must live.[19]

Brecht was neither convinced nor mollified by Mann's rhetoric. "It would be no exaggeration to say that Brecht hated him," Marthe Feuchtwanger had told me.

· ● ·

That substantially ended things between Brecht and the brothers Mann. Brecht continued to grumble in his *Work Journal* about

Thomas's fiction (*Joseph*—"the encyclopedia of philistine education"). There were a few more meetings between him and Heinrich, mainly at the Feuchtwanger home. Eventually, when Heinrich's wife Nelly committed suicide, the elder brother moved to a small apartment that Katia Mann found him in Santa Monica. (He was by that time totally dependent on Thomas.) That was where Heinrich was when he died in 1950 at the age of seventy-nine. He had then, however already made preparations to leave for East Germany, where he had waiting for him an official welcome, a home, and a sinecure as president of the Academy of Letters in East Berlin. A year after his death, Heinrich's body was moved to East Berlin, where it was reinterred with all the ceremony thought due to a laureate of socialism.

Brecht had settled there, in East Berlin, in October 1948, a year after his appearance before the House Committee on Un-American Activities and his hasty departure from America. Although Thomas Mann had no love, or even much respect, for Brecht, the latter's persecution by the right-wing elements that came to be known as McCarthyites both disturbed and frightened Mann. He saw in it convincing proof of America's movement toward fascism. In the next few years, as McCarthy emerged and the Cold War hysteria increased, he saw his worst fears about life in America realized, and finally left the country in 1952. Mann, by then an American citizen, called this his "second exile." He died in Switzerland in 1955 at the age of eighty.

In their attitudes toward each other, these three, who were arguably the greatest German authors of the twentieth century, were clearly influenced far more by political considerations than by literary ones. After all, writers are no more pure than others in their appreciations—perhaps a little less so. But in a better world, one not riven by the hostile politics of this century, could they perhaps have played Goethe and Schiller to one another? Had they anything to teach each other? Certainly. Better to ask: Could they have learned? Sadly, probably, no.

7

BRECHT AND KURT WEILL

Whatever god or fate it was that stuck Brecht in the United States for the better part of the war must surely have had a sense of humor. America—and particularly Chicago— loom large in Brecht's early work, yet it was never a real place he wrote about, but rather some violent land of heart's desire in which his larger-than-life characters might freely act out their crude passions without restraint of law or custom. In the beginning, as he described the struggles of Shlink and Garga in *The Jungle of the Cities*, and the manipulations of Pierpont Mauler in *St. Joan of the Stockyards*, you sense that Brecht was both attracted and repelled by this America of his own imagining. Later, as the more or less orthodox Marxist who wrote *Mahagonny* and *Arturo Ui*, he seems to be merely repelled. Of course it was Brecht the Marxist who landed in Hollywood in the summer of 1941, and like the good Communist he wanted to be, managed to remain virtually indifferent to the real America—in spite of seeing a good deal of it during the six years he was here.

Most of it was along the route from Los Angeles to New York. The first time he crossed the country, he remarked only on the American soldiers with whom he shared the train, "assuredly 'nice boys' with very good manners, playing cards, drinking lemonade and beer, hearing music on the radio," and on the Western landscape: "Arizona and Texas reminded me very much of Siberia from the train."[1] On that same trip he changed trains in Chicago, as one always had to do then on transcontinental journeys. He was curious enough to take that opportunity to go out and visit the Chicago stockyards, which he had used as a setting on a couple of occasions, yet not impressed enough by what he saw to record in his *Work Journal* what he thought of it.

On that first trip and on the four that followed, he was traveling to New York in hopes of cracking Broadway. It is easy to understand why. Since fleeing Germany in 1933, he had had only two fully professional productions of his works—a 1935 staging of *The Mother* by the Theatre Union in New York, and the premiere of *Mother Courage* at the Zurich Schauspielhaus in 1941 (which, of course, he was unable to attend). Nevertheless, he had kept writing steadily during those years of exile, and by 1943 he had a suitcase full of unproduced plays that included *Galileo*, *The Good Woman of Setzuan*, and *Puntila and Matti*. Never one to write purely for the printed page, Brecht required a theater to function truly as a playwright.

A couple of his German contemporaries had already attempted what he was about to try, with no success whatever. Ernst Toller, who had made such a brilliant beginning in Munich in the twenties, was so discouraged by his poor prospects in the New York theater and so depressed by his life as an exile that he committed suicide in a Manhattan hotel in 1939. Carl Zuckmayer, whose play *The Captain from Köpenick* had been an international hit, failed in his attempts to get it produced on Broadway and finally retired to a chicken farm in Vermont where he sat out the war.

Why did Brecht, living in California and making some money working on films, bother at all with New York? Because, first of all, he was a playwright and not a screenwriter. His experience with Fritz

Lang on *Hangmen Also Die* had left a bad taste in his mouth; Brecht was simply not by nature disposed to work in a medium as truly collaborative as film—certainly not one in which the final authority rested with the *director*. Secondly, Brecht had received assurance from Hollywood intellectuals such as Ben Hecht, Arch Oboler, and Clifford Odets that the American theater was badly in need of his talents (even though Broadway might then be unaware of him). There is an amusing note in Brecht's *Work Journal* concerning an evening spent at the home of Herman Mankiewicz shortly after Brecht's arrival in Hollywood. Broadway was the subject of discussion.

> Ben Hecht, who has just come from New York, gives Man-
> kiewicz a delicious account of all the New York flops—a gift
> to the host, so to speak. "Nobody writes serious plays any-
> more," he says. The effect produced by the crisis of '29 and
> of the New Deal seems to have been too weak to put the drama
> on its two feet. Broadway won the victory and demonstrated
> its Mithridates-like tolerance for small doses of poison. The
> clouds kicked up [by the Depression] have now changed to gold
> dust.[2]

With the right English adaptation for his work, Brecht might manage to collect a bit of that gold himself.

He never wanted for collaborators. In fact, the first to translate and adapt his work into English during the war sought him out even before his arrival in America. Hoffman R. Hays, a young New York poet and playwright, was much taken with the work that Brecht and Kurt Weill had done, separately and as a team. The Theatre Union's 1935 production of *The Mother* had fascinated Hays so much that in 1937, when he had the opportunity to emulate Brecht in collaboration with Kurt Weill on a play with music, *The Ballad of Davy Crockett*, he jumped at the chance. (Hays's finished script was never brought to production.) In *Bertolt Brecht in America*, James K. Lyon tells how H. R. Hays (as he signed himself), when hearing from Hanns Eisler of Brecht's plight as a refugee in Europe, immediately offered to do whatever he could to help. He eventually wrote an affidavit that helped make it possible for the playwright and his family to emigrate to America.[3] Not only that: when Brecht was in Finland waiting for his visa, he received a package of manuscript containing a number of poems by Brecht that Hays had rendered into English (one of which he had even managed to get published in *New Masses*) and a translation of Brecht's play *The Trial of Lucullus*. Brecht had his pigeon. He courted Hays by mail from Finland and California and eventually got him to do a translation of *Mother Courage*, which was published in New Directions' 1941 annual, and a translation of *The Resistible Rise of Arturo Ui*, which Hays did without a contract, simply as a favor to Brecht. In addition, Hays continued translating Brecht's poems and eventually got a collection of them published in 1947.

When Brecht journeyed to New York for the first time in February 1943, he had arranged beforehand to undertake an adaptation of John Webster's *The Duchess of Malfi* in collaboration with Hays. This had been discussed in Hollywood with the producer Paul Czinner as a project for his wife, stage actress Elisabeth Bergner. Not long after Brecht's arrival in New York, he and Hays signed a contract with Czinner, and they began "rewriting" the play; Hays, of course, did most of the work, since Brecht's English was at that time quite rudimentary. However, after working intermittently with him for the better part of a year, Brecht decided that a Jacobean play might require an English collaborator, if possible with a bigger name than H. R. Hays's, and so he contacted W. H. Auden and invited him into the project. Hays was thus neatly squeezed out of the picture. About this time, too, Hays found out that after persuading him to undertake a translation of *Fear and Misery in the Third Reich*, on speculation, Brecht had invited Eric Bentley to have a shot at it as well. The Bentley version was published by New Directions in 1944. Despite the fact that he must have felt exploited, Hays kept working on Brecht's behalf, translating poems and promoting the playwright's reputation whenever he had the chance. He seems to have felt it a privilege, as did most of the other translators and collaborators whom Brecht exploited.

Another reason for that first visit by Brecht to New York and for all those that followed was Ruth Berlau. She was the mistress who had landed with him and his family in America. It had not gone well for her with them in Los Angeles, and she had left in 1942 for the East, settling in New York, where she had landed a job with the Danish section of the Office of War Information (a job "Red Ruth" eventually lost because of her outspoken Communist sympathies).

She was living in a walkup apartment on Fifty-seventh Street, and Brecht made it his base of operations during that stay there and on all subsequent visits. (It was there that his collaboration with H. R. Hays on *The Duchess of Malfi* took place.) Although Brecht and Berlau had exchanged house keys by mail, and he had extracted a promise of fidelity from her, he discovered to his consternation that she had been keeping company with a Danish sailor there in New York. However, once on the scene, he exercised his *droit du seigneur* and at least figuratively sent his rival packing. Since she is cited as his collaborator on *The Caucasian Chalk Circle* (the only one of his plays on which her name appears), it would be reasonable to assume that their preliminary discussions on the play took place during that first visit or the one that followed it in November 1943.

Still another reason for that trip to New York in February 1943 was the occasion that had been planned in his honor at the New School for Social Research. "A Brecht Evening" took place there about a month after his arrival, and Brecht himself took an active part in the preparation of the program, even directing the actors personally. The cast for the evening included a couple of stars, Elisabeth Bergner and Peter Lorre, who read poems. Paul Dessau, the composer who had provided the playwright with music on a number of his plays, sang songs on which the two had collaborated, including "The Ballad of the Straw Hats," from *St. Joan of the Stockyards*. The evening went over so well that the entire evening was repeated a month and a half later.

This was essentially an occasion for the German exile community in New York City. At that time it was of considerable size. As a matter of fact, the New School was founded and staffed largely by refugee scholars, many of them Jews and most of them German, who had fled to this country and been unable to find suitable faculty positions at established colleges and universities. "A Brecht Evening," an all-German-language program, brought together this large group and served as a reminder to all that one of the finest playwrights and best-known poets of the Weimar years had survived and was still quite active. To underline this, Brecht himself appeared onstage when the program was repeated and read a selection of his newer, unpublished works.

This stay in New York gave him an opportunity to renew old acquaintances with these people, some of whom had contacts in the

American theater that he wished to use. The poet and director Berthold Viertel was one of these; he was quite devoted to Brecht and a year before had even staged an abridged version of *Fear and Misery in the Third Reich* (in German) at the New School, which the playwright had been unable to attend. Brecht joined with Viertel and a number of other refugee writers in encouraging Wieland Herzfelde, whose Malik-Verlag had published Brecht in exile, to start a new German-language operation in New York (these discussions eventually resulted in the founding of the Aurora-Verlag, which began issuing books in 1945). In his *Work Journal*, he records meetings with his old Marxist tutor Karl Korsch, with his former collaborator and mistress Elisabeth Hauptmann, with the painter and fierce political cartoonist George Grosz, and with the theater director Erwin Piscator. Piscator invited Brecht to lecture on the Epic Theater at the New School, where he taught. The two, who had been among the most influential figures in the German avant-garde theater during the twenties and early thirties, had collaborated on a previous project, a free-wheeling adaptation of Jaroslav Hasek's funny antiwar novel *The Good Soldier Schweik*. They wanted to work together again. Why not update Schweik and send him off to war again?

Actually, Brecht had considered this idea as early as the middle of 1942, when he had thought of interspersing scenes of Schweik in World War II with others from Karl Kraus's *The Last Days of Mankind*. He had, however, pushed no further with the idea until he went to New York. There he came to give it considerable attention. As was his practice, once a project had begun to form in his mind, he enlisted as many people as possible in it as collaborators. Piscator was the first in. But Brecht felt he needed others—somebody, at least, who was better established in the New York theater. Who? From his *Work Journal:* "Weill has had considerable success on Broadway, but is no more very sure of his future here. Aufricht brings us together."[4]

"Aufricht" was Ernst-Josef Aufricht, who, as proprietor of the Theater am Schiffbauerdamm, had produced the 1928 work that made both Brecht and Kurt Weill internationally famous—*The Threepenny Opera*. Having had little success himself as an actor, Aufricht had turned to producing with considerable backing from his wealthy father. However, with a lease on a theater and no immediate prospects in sight for production, he had gone to Brecht and asked if he had a play that might be suitable—even an idea, perhaps. Well, it so happened that Brecht did have an idea (he always had ideas): his secretary and collaborator, Elisabeth Hauptmann, had brought to his attention the enormous success enjoyed by the London revival of John Gay's *The Beggar's Opera*, which had run there from 1920 to 1924; she had even made a rough, working translation of the play for him. He suggested an adaptation of this in collaboration with Kurt Weill, with whom he had already had some critical success with the *Mahagonny Songspiel* (an earlier version of their opera *The Rise and Fall of the City of Mahagonny*). Thus with not much more than an idea to work on—and a borrowed idea at that—Brecht and Weill got to work and in no more than several weeks during the summer of 1929, *The Threepenny Opera* was born.

The Brecht-Weill collaboration was one of the most fruitful the German theater has ever known. Besides *Threepenny* and *Mahagonny* it resulted in two other full-length works, *Happy End* and *The Seven Deadly Sins* (both of which Brecht, for whatever reason, eventually disowned), and a number of shorter pieces—the *Mahagonny Songspiel*, *Berlin Requiem*, *Lindbergh's Flight*, and *The Yea-Sayer and the Nay-Sayer*. The two had a synergistic effect on each other. Together their separate talents had exploded into something grander and stronger than they had ever been before. This being the case, why then was it necessary now for a third party to bring together these two who had earlier worked so closely and so well? To answer that fully, we must go back and trace the conflicts between them that ended their working collaboration, conflicts that ended in hostility that erased the last vestiges of a friendship they once shared. Brecht liked his collaborators to be far more docile than Weill proved to be; he was used to working with second-rate people he could dominate. By the time Brecht teamed up with him, Weill had served an apprenticeship as an opera conductor, had himself written and had performed a number of operas and orchestral pieces, and was in general firmly established as one of Germany's musical avant-garde of the twenties. What's more, he knew something about writing; he had distinguished himself as music critic for *Der deutsche Rundfunk*, the national weekly of broadcasting. To some it seemed that his collaboration with the shrill, rowdy playwright was a step down for Weill.

But their success—even though it was more often than not *succès de scandale*—stilled most such critics. After the triumph they enjoyed with *The Threepenny Opera* in 1928, all of Europe wondered what they would do next. Ernst-Josef Aufricht signed them for another production. This one was to be a freewheeling satire of the Salvation Army set in Chicago and complete with gangsters. Again, Elisabeth Hauptmann had come up with the model—George Bernard Shaw's *Major Barbara*. After writing two acts and a number of the song lyrics for the new play, Brecht suddenly lost interest in the project; he was undergoing his conversion to Marxism. When he was forced to return to work because of the production deadline, he managed to slap together some sort of final act, and took over the production himself when the director walked out in exasperation. It was a doomed effort, and he knew it. And so, ignominiously enough, Brecht took his name off the play—*Happy End* opened in 1929 as the work of Elisabeth Hauptmann—although he did take credit for the lyrics to the songs he had written with Weill. They were among their best, and included "The Sailor's Tango" and "Surabaya Johnny."

Brecht's new political commitment proved troublesome to Weill in a number of ways. Although he was certainly well to the Left of center in his own politics, Weill was no Communist. As a Jew and a producer of officially designated "degenerate art," he was at least as strongly opposed to the Nazis as Brecht; however, he was far more democratic in his outlook. Their first artistic disagreements came when Brecht tried to politicize their opera *The Rise and Fall of the City of Mahagonny*, as he had also attempted to do with *Happy End*. As Weill's biographer Ronald Sanders says in *The Days Grow Short*: "In general, if Brecht saw the play as a parable of capitalism, Weill became less and less inclined to take this view of it and preferred looking upon it as a parable of human greed. By this time, Weill was clearly moving away from the bitterness of the original conception."[5]

Similarly, and perhaps even more significantly in the light of what later developed, Weill objected to Brecht's treatment of America in *Mahagonny*. He was not won over by Brecht's view of this country as a kind of never-never land of greed and violence. He was interested in the *reality* of America, especially in its music—jazz and Tin Pan Alley. Again, quoting Sanders: "Another factor conditioning his attitude toward America may have been his Jewish origins. In the postwar era, the United States had clearly emerged as the country of the world that offered the fewest obstacles for Jews in the realization of social equality and freedom from opprobrium. Weill, who had even met such a uniquely *American* Jewish phenomenon as George Gershwin, must have been fully appreciative of this fact, even long before he knew that the United States was going to be his own home one day."[6] By the time he voiced his objections to Brecht, there was not much that could be done to alter the setting or the tone of the play. However, according to Sanders, he did attempt to influence him to tone down some of *Mahagonny*'s more blatant anti-Americanism and to generalize its setting somewhat.

As they pushed and pulled at one another, the two found it harder and harder to collaborate. Aufricht produced *Mahagonny* in Berlin as well. As he tells it, their first "final" falling out came during rehearsals, when they came into the inevitable conflict between playwright and composer over who would hold sway. Weill was insistent: this was to be an *opera*, after all. Yet Brecht attempted to dominate in this instance as he had in all the others. It ended in shouting and screaming (at which Brecht had no equal), and in lawyers' communications, and, finally, with Brecht's threat to throw Weill down the stairs.

When the two parted company after *Mahagonny*, Brecht used Hanns Eisler and Paul Dessau to provide songs for his increasingly strident Marxist dramatic works. Weill teamed up with Brecht's long-time collaborator and boyhood friend, the designer Casper Neher, to do an opera, *Die Bürgschaft*, and later with Georg Kaiser on a play with music, *Die Silbersee*. Weeks after the latter work was produced, Hitler came to power; months after that the Reichstag burned, and Hitler demanded dictatorial powers. Brecht got out of Germany so fast that he even left his daughter behind. Weill, though a Jew, stayed on for some weeks to work on the musical score to a film, *Little Man, What Now?* Finally, when he received direct word that he was about to be arrested, he fled to France.

Once settled there, he found that he was best known as the musical half of *The Threepenny Opera* team. A Paris production had had a successful run, and G. W. Pabst's film adaptation had been shot in French as well as the German version and had also done quite well. George Balanchine let it be known that he would be willing to mount a new Brecht-Weill production for his company *Les Ballets*. And so Weill resigned himself and brought Brecht to Paris. Their collaboration on *The Seven Deadly Sins* was in at least one way a rerun of

Mahagonny, although evidently without the earlier emotional fireworks. Out of necessity both men were committed to cooperation.
Ronald Sanders suggests that Weill was just as keenly troubled by
the anti-Americanism of Brecht's new text as he had been before with
Mahagonny. If, however, it became an issue between them, then
Brecht prevailed. For it is a rather Freudian tale of two sisters who
share the same name, Anna I and Anna II (suggesting a kind of ego
and superego division in a single personality), who leave their home
in Louisiana and go wandering through America, where their misad-
ventures slyly suggest that nowhere is economic sin and social
depravity more rampant than in the forty-eight states. One reason
that Weill may have chosen to keep quiet about this is that the production promised a part for his wife, Lotte Lenya. She sang the role
of Anna I (the superego sister), while the Austrian dancer Tillie Losch
danced as Anna II when the work had its premiere in Paris. The
production set no records, however, and achieved only modest critical
success. Each of the two went his own way once more—not to meet
again until a decade later in New York.

By the time they did, Weill had achieved some success in the
American musical theater. Working with Paul Green, he had a crit-
ical success with the rather Brechtian antiwar play with music,
Johnny Johnson. He collaborated with Franz Werfel and the great
Austrian Max Reinhardt on an ambitious pageant of Jewish history,
The Eternal Road. With his friend Maxwell Anderson, he had done
Knickerbocker Holiday and had made his first appearance on the
"Hit Parade" with "September Song." In a distinguished company
of Broadway veterans that included Moss Hart and Ira Gershwin, he
had had his first real hit on Broadway, *Lady in the Dark*.

Brecht watched Weill's success from Europe and later from Hollywood with growing envy and contempt. On April 15, 1942, for
instance, there is this entry in his *Work Journal*:

> Since Weill made difficulties for the project of a Negro pro-
> duction of *The Threepenny Opera*, I had Weisengrund-
> Adorno write him. Weill answered him with an angry letter full
> of attacks on me and with a love song to Broadway which [he
> says] accepts everything as long as it is good and has pushed
> the European experiments further along. The last piece for
> which Weill did the music has run 14 months. It is called *Lady*

in the Dark. (It should be an amusing thriller.) Since he wrote this letter in English, it begins, "It's easier for me and I like it better."[7]

Across from this entry he has pasted a photograph, evidently cut from *Life* magazine, showing Weill and Maxwell Anderson serving as civilian aircraft spotters from a perch atop High Tor, a mountain near their homes in New City, New York. Although it is there without comment, one can sense the sneer on his face when he cut it out of the magazine.

The letter to Theodor Adorno, with its alleged attacks on Brecht, simply does not sound much like Weill. He was a far gentler, more forgiving sort than his erstwhile collaborator. Remember that it was Weill who extended the invitation to Brecht to come to Paris to work together with him on *The Seven Deadly Sins.* For that matter, he may simply have cited his grievances against the playwright, which were many and real. Brecht was used to riding roughshod over all those around him; he was inclined to view even legitimate complaints regarding his behavior as unfair personal attacks. As for Weill's alleged efforts to block the black production of *The Threepenny Opera,* they may well have had something to do with his feelings for George Gershwin's *Porgy and Bess.* He had great respect for Gershwin, whom he counted as a friend until the latter's untimely death in 1938. And he regarded *Porgy and Bess* as Gershwin's finest work, one that achieved stunningly many of the things that he had been trying to do in Europe. If it had failed on Broadway—as indeed the original production did—then what chance had a bastard version of a European musical (a parody of the German operetta form) acted and sung by blacks? He may even have thought that such a show may have been disrespectful of George Gershwin's memory. Ira Gershwin told of sitting next to Kurt Weill during rehearsals of *Porgy and Bess.* Weill listened in wonder and whispered to him, "It's a great country where music like that can be written—and played."[8]

He wasn't kidding. If Weill had been respectful of America from Europe, he became positively maniacal about this country once he was here. He wanted more than anything to be accepted as an *American* composer. That is why he willingly sought work on Broadway and wrote for the movies. He wanted to *be* an American. When he applied for citizenship, he did so with the utmost seriousness and not simply (as many refugee artists did) as a means of further legitimizing his residence in the United States (even Brecht took out first papers). Weill took his studies for the examination quite seriously and became fascinated by American history. When at last he received his final papers, he referred to the event as one of the most important of his lifetime. He not only wrote letters in English; he is said even to have become angry occasionally when he was addressed in German.

Given all this, it is easy to understand why it took an intermediary, such as Aufricht, to bring Weill and Brecht together in New York. Weill seems to have regarded his former partner as an unwelcome visitor from his past, at least at first. Brecht's stay in Hollywood had not lessened his anti-American feelings; if anything, they were more intense. It must have been deeply annoying for Weill to listen to him rasping on and on about the greed of Hollywood and how he had been forced into "gold-digging" with all the rest, and sneering at Los Angeles as "Tahiti in big-city form." And Weill was quite frankly frightened by Brecht's politics, which were as hard-edged and Stalinist in their orientation as ever. Imagine how Weill felt, practically on the eve of his citizenship, hearing Brecht complain about how the American Communist Party had sold out by forswearing political activity for the duration of the war (a favorite topic of Brecht's about that time).

Nevertheless, the two got together and seriously discussed collaborating on future projects. As Brecht notes all too briefly in his *Work Journal*, "Weill wants to produce the *Setzuan* play and we are planning a *Schweyk*."[9] Weill's intention was to do a musical version of *The Good Woman of Setzuan*, which had been completed in 1941. It was one of the few new plays by Brecht that were actually produced during the war. The Zürich Schauspielhaus had done a production a few months before his arrival in New York. Weill seems to have intended to do it as an opera, for it was not really the stuff from which Broadway musical comedies are made. They discussed it at length, though. Weill had Brecht out to his home in New City, New York, where for a week they "worked on a *Setzuan* adaptation for here."

As for the update of *Schweyk*, Brecht's shrewd strategy was to interest Weill in the project by pointing out to him that there would be in it an excellent part for Mrs. Weill, Lotte Lenya. She would play Anna Kopecka, the palm-reading owner of The Flagon, the Prague bar where much of the play's action takes place. On that basis—and perhaps on that basis only—Weill was interested. Although Lenya had been a star in Germany, she had at that time never even appeared on the American stage. She herself clearly wanted the role, and as an earnest of her interest recorded a number of Brecht's songs for propaganda broadcasts to Germany for the Office of War Information. With no more than a handshake from Weill, Brecht returned from New York after a three-month stay promising to show him a script as soon as one was available.

Once back in California, Brecht set to work on *Schweyk in the Second World War*. In writing it, he seems to have drawn heavily upon the research done by him and Fritz Lang on conditions in wartime Prague for *Hangmen Also Die*. Prague is the setting, and the passive resistance of the Czech people provides most of the action. Also Brettschneider, the Gestapo agent in *Schweyk*, has a good deal in common with the one in the film played so brilliantly by Alexander Granach; he may even have had Granach in mind for the part. He certainly set about casting the play as it was being written; he got Peter Lorre seriously interested in the title role, and he also had some wild notion of getting W. C. Fields into the play, probably in the role of Baloun, the fat photographer. Lorre, as close to a friend as Brecht had in the movies, eventually paid the American writer Alfred Kreymborg to write an acting translation of the play. From Kreymborg, Erwin Piscator first heard that Brecht had gone ahead with the *Schweyk* idea. It was to have been a collaboration; Piscator felt cheated.

When Brecht had been at work on the project about a month, Weill showed up in Hollywood. Brecht notes their meeting in his *Work Journal* on June 28, 1943: "Weill here to plan a revue. He has good dramaturgical judgment. For example, he finds lacking the element of Schweyk's survival that I had in the short story outline. I outline the dog-catching business for this purpose."[10] After that, there is no mention of Weill's reaction to *Schweyk*. This is odd, for it proved to be strongly negative. Weill especially objected to the play's conclusion, in which Schweyk and Hitler meet out on the frozen plains of Russia; he thought it contrived and silly. The play, Weill quite rightly saw, was altogether unsuitable for Broadway. He suggested changes, but Brecht refused on political grounds. Although from the published text of the play it is hard to see why there should have been any discussion of politics with regard to it, Lotte Lenya herself has declared that it was there that the final break between the two of them came. Not long before her death, she told a magazine interviewer, "Do you know why he stopped working with Brecht? Because he told Brecht, 'I don't want to compose *Das Kapital.*'"[11]

In any case, the old Brecht-Weill combination did break up once and for all over *Schweyk in the Second World War.* With that eventually went Weill's interest in *The Good Woman of Setzuan* as well. After all, he now had *One Touch of Venus* to work on. Brecht, who had always been so difficult as a collaborator, was now regarded by Weill as an undesirable political contact. Why should Weill jeopardize his new standing as a naturalized American just to help out one who had always treated him so shabbily? Perhaps it was not a brave attitude but it was certainly a practical one. From Weill's point of view, and emphatically from Brecht's, their dubious friendship was now ended; they would go their separate ways.

· ● ·

Brecht's way took him back to New York again and again in search of success on Broadway. He came close a number of times. On another long stay from mid-November 1943 to March 1944, he started back to work with H. R. Hays on the *Duchess of Malfi* adaptation. Finally, Hays was forced out in December 1943, and Auden, who had been originally introduced into the project as an adviser, started to work with him on the text. They seem to have felt no great urgency. Once back in Los Angeles, Brecht turned to other matters. The enterprise did not come to a boil until early in 1946, when producer Paul Czinner declared himself ready to mount a production, as planned all along, with his wife, Elisabeth Bergner, in the title role. Evidently it was she who was responsible for putting the adaptation through so many rewrites and versions. Bergner called for the introduction of material from two of John Webster's other plays and one of John Ford's into the text. Brecht complied willingly, Auden unwillingly. In the meantime, a very successful production of an unrevised version of *The Duchess of Malfi* had been mounted in London. Paul Czinner decided to bring over its director, George Rylands, to bring their new and improved *Duchess* to Broadway. Rylands came, ignorant of the changes that had been made in the text. When he learned of them he demanded that they be thrown out and that nothing more or less than the original text be performed. This battle was fought through tryout runs in Providence and Boston, but the director won out, and in the end only one of the additions was retained. Brecht, sure that the production would fail, had his name taken off the program, not wishing to be associated with a Broadway flop. Only Auden's name remained as adapter. In the end, Brecht's judgment proved correct. The production opened in mid-October 1946, received bad reviews, and closed after thirty-one days.

In the summary report in his *Work Journal* of that second trip to New York, Brecht notes: "Contract with Broadway for a *Chalk Circle*, negotiated through Luise Rainer. Piece begun."[12] That entry, of course, marked the beginning of *The Caucasian Chalk Circle*. It had its origin in a short story he had written years before, "The Augsburg Chalk Circle." His reason for switching the setting from his native city during the Thirty Years' War to Soviet Socialist Republic of Georgia at the end of World War II (with the body of the play a flashback to Georgia's dim past) was probably propagandistic. He seems to have wanted to present Stalin's home province in the comfortable, appealing light of a folktale. In any case, he evidently did not consider using this material or writing the play until he made the contact with Rainer, the Viennese actress who had won two Academy Awards for her performances in *The Great Ziegfeld* in 1937 and again in *The Good Earth* in 1938. Although the two had discussed the idea in general terms in Los Angeles, Brecht did no writing on it until he returned from New York with a Dramatists Guild contract from Jules J. Leventhal, who wanted to produce a play on Broadway starring Rainer. In the *Journal* entries that follow he merely complains of the difficulty he is having with the play—in particular with the character of Azdak, the comically unscrupulous judge who doles out justice without regard for the law. Finally, on June 6, 1944 (the date of the Allied invasion of France): "Yesterday afternoon finished *The Caucasian Chalk Circle* and sent the piece to Rainer."[13] She didn't like it, although she did not reveal, in an interview with James K. Lyon, just what her objections to it were. Nevertheless, after seeing a rough translation of the play, Leventhal was still willing to produce it on Broadway. At one point, Elsa Lanchester, Charles Laughton's wife, was considered for the leading role of Grusha. W.

H. Auden did a more finished adaptation (though one that failed to satisfy Brecht), and *The Caucasian Chalk Circle* was alive as a project when Brecht left for Europe in 1947. Perhaps it finally fell through *because* he left for Europe.

When his play *Fear and Misery in the Third Reich* was published by New Directions in 1944 under the title Brecht had chosen for it, *The Private Life of the Master Race*, its translator, Eric Bentley, gave permission for an Off Broadway production of the play at City College. Erwin Piscator was to direct it and was to assemble a cast from émigré German actors in New York and from his own workshop group at the New School. As the production was being mounted in 1945, Brecht came east from Los Angeles to make sure things were done his way. He soon fell into such furious disagreements with Piscator that the director withdrew from the production altogether. Brecht took over rehearsals himself and began his usual routine of screaming abuse and yelling orders as he attempted to put them through a short course in the Epic Theater. Berthold Viertel was brought in to serve as the nominal director of the production but actually did no more than act as a buffer between Brecht and the actors. It was the opinion of at least one who attended the rehearsals (Brecht's publisher, James Laughlin) that the playwright systematically undermined the production. It must have been Brecht who ruined it, for *Fear and Misery in the Third Reich* (under whatever name) is *not* a bad play. But the critics, some of whom were inclined to be friendly to him, were virtually unanimous in attacking the production and dismissing the work itself. Brecht was angry at them, but most of all he was angry at New York, for it had failed to live up to his high standards of playwriting and production.

It has continued to do so. Brecht has never been successful on Broadway. He might have come close with the Charles Laughton *Galileo*, the only one of his plays to reach that goal he had set for himself in his lifetime. But *Galileo* is another story entirely and its failure resulted from reasons more complicated than mere aesthetics. What success the playwright's work has enjoyed in New York has been in Off Broadway productions, notably the long-running production of *The Threepenny Opera* in Marc Blitzstein's adaptation during the fifties, which starred Lotte Lenya, and Joseph Papp's production of the same play at Lincoln Center in 1976. By and large, his considerable reputation in America has been earned on college stages and in regional theaters. Will he ever be successful in the commercial theater? Can he be? Probably not—certainly not on his own terms—for Brecht, who pretended to himself to be most accommodating to audiences, was quite unwilling to make a compromise with popular taste. Like so many other artists who have been animated by Marxist ideals, he was heart and soul an elitist.

8

BRECHT AND
HIS WOMEN

Think of Brecht as a Jonah—or perhaps more accurately as a sort of Typhoid Mary of misfortune, carrying it with him wherever he went and spreading it like a disease. He himself, however, remained relatively unafflicted. Scrambling across Europe with so many other political refugees during the years leading up to and during World War II, he always managed to dance away from danger just in time, while many of those close to him proved to be not nearly so nimble. Walter Benjamin committed suicide at the French-Spanish border; Lion Feuchtwanger was turned back at the border and tossed into a Vichy concentration camp; Sergei Tretyakov, Brecht's friend and theatrical advocate in the Soviet Union, died in a Siberian prison camp; Frank, Brecht's illegitimate first son by his Augsburg girl friend Paula Banholzer, also died in Russia—

with the German Army near Porchov. But Brecht not only survived; once in America, he prospered.

At its most virulent, Brecht's bad-luck malady seemed to operate like some form of venereal infection. For if, in general, he was bad news to those close to him, then he was a walking disaster to the women in his life. Death, attempted suicide, mental disorder, alcoholism—these were Brecht's benefactions to his mistresses. And yet he always had so many women about. When John Houseman worked with Brecht in Hollywood on the production of *Galileo* that starred Charles Laughton, he was impressed by the playwright's "harem." Houseman writes in his book *Front and Center*: "It was one of Brecht's well-known peculiarities that, regardless of his circumstances, he was constantly surrounded by a retinue of handsome, dedicated ladies, some of whom had accompanied him for years on his wanderings around the world."[1]

What was the source of his appeal? After all, at just about the same time, screenwriter Albert Maltz, one of the Hollywood Ten, met him in the course of the meetings held by the subpoenaed "unfriendly" witnesses to organize their defense before the House Committee on Un-American Activities. Maltz, a rather fastidious man, remembered Brecht in an interview as "one of the most repulsive men I ever met. He stank!"[2]

Physically Brecht was a most unprepossessing man. One has only to consider the photographs to realize how little he had to offer in the way of conventional good looks. The younger Bertolt Brecht was skinny, with a face so narrow that it seemed to exist only in profile; the big, rudderlike nose and the prominent Adam's apple were all that could be seen. The older Brecht's face widened, took on flesh; the nose spread to Karl Malden size, the Adam's apple obscured by a modest double chin. The remarkable thing, however, is that between such "before" and "after" pictures, there is no "during." Brecht seemed physically to leap from adolescence into middle age. But none of that mattered to the women who surrounded him. Whatever face he presented to them, women—young or old, ferret or old fox—offered themselves to him eagerly, pursued him ardently, and earnestly sought from him what he was apparently least able to give—his love.

It would be a mistake to read a contradiction in this. His very real appeal to women had little to do with his physical attractiveness or lack of it, and still less to do with how often he bathed. They found in him a far more powerful aphrodisiac than any dispensed in soap or deodorant. They were attracted to him by what they perceived as his genius, hoping—what?—perhaps only to serve it, or to benefit from it indirectly by association; or some of them may even have hoped that a bit of it might rub off on them. The rawest, most direct expression of this attitude came from Ruth Berlau, the mistress who traveled with him and his family from Europe to America. She is quoted in James K. Lyon's *Bertolt Brecht in America* as having boasted to co-workers at the Office of War Information that she was the "whore of a classical writer."[3]

That was the way it had always been. Back in Augsburg, where he was born, he grew up sure of his own genius, probably convinced of it by his mother, who it is said gave him all the encouragement he needed to plan for a life as a poet. With no more than a handful of youthful ballads to croon as he twanged his guitar, he managed to communicate to his contemporaries a sense of his own greatness, or greatness-to-be. He was accepted by them very early on, on the strength of his own assessment, as nothing less than a genius.

Among his contemporaries, crowding in the first rank, were the women, then no more than girls. There was Rose Marie Aman, who claimed Brecht was the first ever to kiss her, an occasion he memorialized in "Remembering Marie A":

It was a day in that blue month September
Silent beneath a plum tree's slender shade
I held her there, my love so pale and silent
As if she were a dream that must not fade.[4]

And there was Hedda Kuhn, the medical student he met in Munich. When she left for Berlin, he remembered her less sentimentally in the poem "Of He":

Listen, friends, I'll sing you the song
of He, the dark-skinned girl, my sweet-
heart for the sixteen months before she
fell apart.[5]

There are others, too, who pop up unnamed in those early poems of his. In fact, a surprising amount—surprising for Brecht—of the early poetry is written to or about women.

By far the two most important to him in those early years were Paula Banholzer and Marianne Zoff. Banholzer, to whom Brecht referred always by her nickname, "Bi," was the daughter of an Augsburg physician. The two met in 1915, when Brecht was just seventeen; in 1919, their son Frank was born. Both parents were then still living with their respective families; the baby was put out immediately to board with a peasant family. Bi and Brecht then got on with their lives. Oddly enough, however, although he had shown no inclination to marry her before the baby was born, Brecht continued to see her afterward on a fairly regular basis and even toyed with the idea of marrying her well into 1922.

That was about the time he was becoming most exasperated with Marianne Zoff. An opera singer of some talent from Vienna, she had come to Augsburg on a contract with the Augsburg municipal theater. They met, were attracted, and became lovers. When she became pregnant in 1922, Brecht declared his willingness to marry her though she was more or less already promised to another man. The two rivals tugged away at her for weeks and weeks as Brecht considered giving up the competition altogether and going back to Paula Banholzer. Finally, on a trip to Berlin (financed, incidentally, by Hedda Kuhn), he fell ill and Marianne rushed there to nurse him back to health. Once together, they married. Their daughter, Hanne (who became the actress Hanne Hiob), was born in 1923.

Brecht's diaries from this period have been published, and they are especially interesting for what they tell us about his pride and ambition and about his arrogant attitude toward women. The two were, surely, very closely related. Only a young man who was as completely wrapped up in himself and his nascent career as he was could, at the age of twenty-two, have written about women in this way:

> What I want is to bottle them and preserve them and caress them and make do with those solid clouds, with whatever's crooked, tangled, misplaced; want to be able to beat them up, knock sense into them, love them down and joke with my

thighs. Better to stuff some old virgin with a skin like a dog
than poke around in everybody's pet little hole.[6]

Perhaps the most revealing, and indeed almost prophetic, passage in
these early diaries, however, is a simple notation by Brecht of a passage he had come across in his reading: "Meier-Graefe says of Dela-
croix that here was a warm heart beating in a cold person. And when
you come down to it that's a possible recipe for greatness." This was
important to him; even months later he referred to it. In his introduction to the diaries John Willett says quite accurately of this rather
obscure quotation that so gripped Brecht that "it sums up much that
was remarkable about him." Very much indeed—for it foreshadows
Brecht's thinking in theater theory and stagecraft, suggests why his
politics took the turn they did, and also tells us why he often behaved
as badly as he did with others, male and female.

Was that how he would have characterized himself? As a cold
person with a warm heart? I believe he must have set this as a sort
of operating ideal for himself even years before he happened to have
come across the quotation, and that is why he responded to it so
profoundly. Doesn't that phrase fairly sum up Baal, the poet-hero of
Brecht's first play? We are told that Baal, whose very name recalls
the pagan god of the big belly and the gaping maw, feeds his feverish
appetites in the most cold-blooded manner:

> Once a woman, Baal says, gives her all
> Leave her; that's as far as she can go.[7]

Or again, from Baal himself:

> But love is also like a coconut that's good as long as it's fresh;
> but you have to spit it out once its juice is squeezed dry, and
> all that remains is the meat which is bitter.[8]

And leave them Baal does. He squeezes his women dry—Emilie,
Johanna, Sophie—and spits them out. The gross, greedy child-man
has no regrets and offers no justification. He needs none; he is a poet.

Baal was Brecht's first play; its earliest version goes back to
1918, when he was just twenty. Was it in some sense autobiograph-

ical? Only in that Baal behaved consistently in a way that Brecht managed to do only intermittently. His was the standard of absolute ruthlessness to which Brecht aspired—if not the one he always managed to live up to.

It should probably be added that when Baal at last goes soft and declares his love, it is to a man—Eckart, the composer. Would it be likely that in the same way this directly reflected Brecht's sexual preference? Well, it is certainly possible and quite consistent with his attitude toward women at the time. You get the feeling here, though, and perhaps a little later on from his behavior with the boxer Paul Samson-Körner in Berlin, that Brecht must have tried homosexuality and decided he had no vocation for it.

• • •

Once married to Marianne Zoff, Brecht settled for a while with her and their child in Munich. There he had produced his second play, *Drums in the Night.* Its success brought him eventually to Berlin, alone of course. The two parted amicably enough; Marianne, given no choice, obliged him with a divorce, and went on with her own career. Even so, Brecht had two children, and less than a year after arriving in Berlin would have a third, Stefan. For by then he had begun a liaison with the actress Helene Weigel that would eventually lead to his second marriage.

Success, when it came to him in Munich and as it continued in Berlin, meant more women. He had extracted from Marianne Zoff a promise that she would allow him complete independence in extramarital relationships. What did he expect in return? Absolute fidelity. He was a very jealous man. In Munich, there were—among others— Blandine Ebinger, Gerda Muller, and Carola Neher (who would reenter his life later on in Berlin), all actresses. In Berlin, he had so many mistresses that according to one of them, Marieluise Fleisser, he began to insist that they adopt a kind of uniform so that they could be identified as "his" women. The uniform consisted of a tight, black ankle-length wool coat. Klaus Völker quotes Fleisser in *Brecht: A Biography*: "And the coat, which was never buttoned, had to be held close to the body with one's elbow over one's stomach—this was the height of fashion in Berlin."[9]

Of them all, the most important to Brecht professionally was Elisabeth Hauptmann. An exception to the rest—and in every way an exceptional woman—she was not an actress, but rather an intellectual and a writer of real, if unproven, talent. He engaged her as his secretary and used her as his mistress. Hauptmann could read English and introduced him to the works from which he borrowed and adapted so freely—works such as John Gay's *The Beggar's Opera* (which of course provided the basis for *The Threepenny Opera*), and George Bernard Shaw's *Major Barbara* (*Happy End* and *St. Joan of the Stockyards*). She was Brecht's first important collaborator. She freely contributed her own ideas; in return she received little credit (a line on the back of the title page), and on the single occasion when there was blame to be assigned she was made to take it (see Prologue, page 6, and chapter 7, page 131).

Brecht and Carola Neher resumed in Berlin the relationship they had begun in Munich. She was an actress and quite the most beautiful woman who had ever taken up with him. Gina Kaus, the Austrian novelist and screenwriter, who was introduced to Brecht by Neher, told me in an interview that her friend "was always with him and that they were in love, though at the time she was married to Klabund, the poet, who was sick with tuberculosis."[10] Brecht, in fact, wrote the part of Polly Peachum in *The Threepenny Opera* for her, and she was pleased to take it. She went into rehearsals with the play, though not without some misgivings. Klabund (the Munich Expressionist, whose real name was Alfred Henschke) was then so seriously ill that he had been taken to a tuberculosis sanitarium in Davos, Switzerland. When he suddenly took a turn for the worse, she felt she had to leave the play just fourteen days before it was scheduled to open and go to him; and in fact only days after it did open without her, Klabund died. In Brecht's mind, however, Carola Neher was still his Polly Peachum, and when *The Threepenny Opera* came to be shot as a film, he prevailed upon G. W. Pabst, the director, and she was cast in the role he had written for her.

All through these years in Berlin he had maintained his relationship with Helene Weigel, sometimes sharing quarters with her and sometimes not. In any case, he continued his involvement with other women unimpeded by his ties to Weigel. Yet she brought increasing pressure on him to marry, and at last he gave in. They were married on April 10, 1929. He indicated his attitude toward his union with Weigel when he informed Carola Neher of it and assured her that it meant nothing. Neher evidently took him at his word, and she continued with him as before. Elisabeth Hauptmann, however, took a far more serious view of this development; she attempted suicide. Upon her recovery, however, she continued as his secretary, collaborator, and mistress.

· ● ·

Helene Weigel had been introduced to Bertolt Brecht by Arnolt Bronnen, the avant-garde playwright who later became sympathetic to the Nazi cause. She had appeared in a production of Bronnen's play, *Vatermord* ("Patricide"), and he believed, quite rightly, that the two would be attracted to one another. She was Viennese, half-Jewish, and was recognized from the start as an actress of considerable promise. Although she was a small woman of almost gnomish aspect, she had trained as a dancer and was quite graceful. She was strong-featured rather than beautiful, and gradually matured into the character roles *(Señora Carrar's Rifles, The Mother,* and *Mother Courage)* that eventually established her as the leading female interpreter of Brecht. From the start, she believed passionately in his genius, and that is why she put up with him as long and patiently as she did. Their first child, Stefan, was born in 1924, almost five years before their marriage, but Brecht certainly acknowledged him and even contributed to his support. Eventually they arranged that his son by Paula Banholzer (Frank) be sent to live with relatives of Weigel's in Austria. Then, as later, a very strong-willed woman, she prevailed at last on the question of marriage, and their second child, Barbara, was born in 1930, one year after they married.

Although he never took seriously the marital vow of fidelity, Brecht did, in his fashion, honor his obligations as a family man. When he left Germany in 1933 at the time of the Nazi takeover, Brecht was seeking first to ensure the safety of Weigel and their children. Carola Neher and Elisabeth Hauptmann were left to fend for themselves. Hauptmann, in fact, did well on her own; she made it early and safely to St. Louis (of all places) but was in New York to welcome Brecht on his first visit to the city in 1935. Neher, however, was not nearly so lucky. In the company of a German Communist refugee, she sought sanctuary in the Soviet Union. There they remained in comparative safety for a few years. But at the time of the Nazi invasion in June 1941, she was picked up by the Russian police and interned as a part of the general roundup of German refugees. What happened then? Nobody is quite sure. Her friend Gina Kaus says simply, "She died in Russia during the war. It was never really clear whether she died in internment, or whether she was killed."[11]

After a few months wandering around Europe, Brecht settled with his family in Denmark on the island of Funen near the town of Svendborg. Not long after his arrival, he was visited by a Danish actress named Ruth Berlau. Something of a radical chic celebrity in Copenhagen, she was known there as "Red Ruth." Berlau had returned from a trip to the Soviet Union proclaiming herself a Communist and promoting the cause of revolutionary theater—this under the protective wing of her husband, an eminent Danish physician considerably older than she. She came to see Brecht to beg from him a copy of his play *The Mother*, which she hoped to translate into Danish for production in Copenhagen. Reportedly a beautiful woman (though, frankly, most photos of her fail to show it), she attracted Brecht's attentions immediately, and he boldly propositioned her. The two began a relationship that lasted, for better or for worse, throughout the rest of his life.

Berlau, however, was not Brecht's only long-standing mistress during his years of exile. His deepest involvement at this time—always, of course, apart from his marriage to Helene Weigel—was with a young, working-class Communist girl from Berlin named Margarete Steffin. She had had a minor part in a play of his (again, *The Mother*, in the 1932 production that starred Weigel), and he had taken up with her then. At the time of the Nazi takeover, she had fled to Paris, where she found work with the refugee publisher and Communist propagandist Willi Muenzenberg. Brecht found many occasions to take him there from Svendborg, some of them managed by Steffin herself in the course of editing a collection of his poetry for Muenzenberg's Editions du Carrefour. Yet he certainly did not hesitate to bring her up to Denmark. In spite of the distance that separated them, he had pressed her into Elisabeth Hauptmann's multiple role of secretary, editor, and collaborator.

It is interesting to reflect what it was about Steffin that attracted him to her. She was a plain woman with none of the glamour and good looks of Marianne Zoff or Carola Neher. Possessed of a rather austere personality, she lacked altogether the warm good spirits of his old Augsburg girl friend, Bi Banholzer. Perhaps it was her ill health—she was a chronic consumptive—that brought him around to her. Not that he was much given to pity; no, her tuberculosis may have been to him rather an emblem of her working-class origins. To Brecht, the son of a prosperous managing director of a paper mill who was still helping to support him with money sent out of Germany, Margarete Steffin was an *authentic* Communist, and not one of those of the middle class with whom he had generally associated in Berlin. She was his "good comrade," or that, at least, was how he described her in this poem addressed from Denmark to the German Communists:

> I came to you all as a teacher, and as a teacher
> I could have left you. As I was learning however
> I stayed. For even after that
> Fleeing for shelter beneath the Danish thatch
> I did not leave you.
> And you gave me one of you
> To go with me.
>
> So that she could examine
> All I said; so that she could improve
> Every line from then on.
> Schooled in the school of fighters
> Against oppression.[12]

Did he really depend on her so completely? Well, she is named as collaborator on every play written in his European exile except *Mother Courage*—and these include some of his best and worst works. (*Never* expect consistency from Brecht in anything!) Not really a writer and not even a trained actress, she may have contributed little directly to the writing of the plays, yet she seems to have served him as a kind of Marxist voice of conscience:

> Since then she has been my support—
> In poor health but
> High spirits, not to be suborned
> Even by me. Many a time
> I cross out a line myself, laughing as I imagine
> What she would say about it.[13]

Yet none of this held him back in his pursuit of Ruth Berlau. The Danish actress proceeded with her plans to bring *The Mother* to the stage in Copenhagen, and in fact it did take place at last in 1935 with both Brecht and Helene Weigel on hand to tell them how to do it right. The Revolutionary Theatre was actually an amateur group of Danish working-class players who came, even according to Berlau, about as much for the free coffee and sandwiches as for any abiding interest in the theater.

As the era of the Popular Front dawned in the East, there were petitions to sign and writers' congresses to attend. Brecht went off to one in Paris in the company of Ruth Berlau. This was in 1937, however, and civil war was raging in Spain. A few of the delegates, André Malraux among them, had taken leave from the fighting especially to attend the congress. When Malraux moved that the meeting adjourn to Madrid as a gesture of solidarity by the writers with their Spanish comrades, his proposal was met with thunderous approval from all those present—except one. Brecht tended toward physical cowardice, and he had no intention of going off to the war zone and exposing himself to Fascist bombs and artillery fire. Berlau was greatly disappointed in him—so much so, in fact, that she flew off to Spain with the others to teach him a lesson (see chapter 1, page 27). He, in turn, was disappointed in her when, meeting the ship on which she was to return from Spain, he learned that she had taken up with a Swede on the voyage and had gone on to take him home with her instead. Brecht felt betrayed; whose mistress was she, anyway?

Yet they reconciled. What is more remarkable still, Red Ruth continued to live with her husband, who permitted her every liberty. At her urging, he even treated Margarete Steffin for her tuberculosis on one of the good comrade's frequent visits to Denmark. She, however, wanted out. When war seemed imminent, and Sweden looked to Brecht a safer sanctuary, Berlau arranged for the necessary visas to permit Brecht and his family to travel there, and then she left her husband and followed Brecht there but kept her distance. The war began with them all in Stockholm. Brecht, fearing for Margarete Steffin's safety in France, brought her up to Sweden as well. The party of refugee Germans applied for visas to America, hoping to sail soon from Finland.

Invited there to wait by the Finnish novelist Hella Wuolijoki, the Brechts and Margarete Steffin went to live at their hostess's country home outside Helsinki. Again, Berlau followed them there. At that Helene Weigel put her foot down: one mistress was too many, but *two*! But Berlau was not to be put off. When she was not allowed into the house, she pitched a tent on the lawn. She prevailed upon Brecht. After all, the Germans had by then occupied Denmark. How could she, Red Ruth, return there now? Brecht listened and agreed. There was only one solution, of course: Berlau would accompany them to America. He was firm, and Weigel backed down—as, in the end, she nearly always did with him.

Hella Wuolijoki was forced for financial reasons to sell her house in the fall of 1940, and so the entire party—Brecht, Weigel, their two children, Margarete Steffin, and Ruth Berlau—moved into an apartment in Helsinki. (What a prison that must have been for them all!) Not Berlau's but Steffin's visa was what delayed their departure, and Brecht had determined that they would all leave together, or not at all. By the spring of 1941, when Steffin's entry visa at last came through, she was gravely ill; in her consumptive condition, the Finnish winter had simply been too much for her. With the Baltic the private pond of the German fleet, and the North Atlantic infested with Nazi submarines, sea passage seemed closed to them, even in a Finnish or Swedish vessel. So Brecht made plans for them all to cross Russia on the Trans-Siberian Railway and booked passage on a Swedish ship sailing from Vladivostok to San Pedro.

They departed Helsinki on May 13, 1941, passed through Leningrad, and arrived in Moscow a few days later, where they put up at the Hotel Metropol. There Margarete Steffin collapsed. In her already weakened condition, she fell victim to an infection that quickly advanced to pneumonia. When she entered the hospital in Moscow, a lobe of one of her lungs had filled completely with fluid. With a sailing date to make, it now appeared that it would be necessary to leave her behind. Brecht was assured by no less a personage than Alexander Fedayev, a Soviet novelist who was a great power in the Writers' Union, that she would be sent on as soon as she was well and that, under any circumstances, her passage from Vladivostok was assured.

And so Brecht made plans to leave her there. On their last day in Moscow, May 30, 1941, he went to visit Steffin in the hospital. They said a painful farewell. Brecht, his family, and Ruth Berlau then left for Vladivostok. Along the way he sent telegrams to Steffin and received them in reply. After two days, her answers ceased. Finally, on June 4, 1941, just beyond Lake Baikal in Siberia, he received a telegram from Fedayev informing him that Margarete Steffin had died that day in the hospital. The next day in Vladivostok he received a longer telegram from Maria Grasshohner, a friend who had attended her in the hospital:

> Grete did not want to die and thought only of living. She asked for books, thought of you and wanted to be well soon so that she might follow you. After her last night she ate breakfast easily, read your telegram carefully and asked for champagne. Soon she felt ill and shivered but thought she would be better. At that moment the doctor came. The next moment she repeated three times the word "doctor." She died peacefully. In the post-mortem examination the doctor found both lungs in the last stages. Great cavities, heart and liver considerably enlarged. A death-mask of her face was made for you.[14]

· ● ·

A small house had been rented for Brecht and his party in Hollywood. During his first days there he did nothing but complain about his situation. He groused about nearly everything *except* the immediate cause of his unease, and that was the daily conflict between his wife and Ruth Berlau. Once more Weigel had drawn the line: she would no longer have the woman in the same house; Berlau would have to go. This time she made it stick. Regretfully, Brecht arranged a place for Berlau with Salka Viertel in Santa Monica.

It is worth noting that within a month of Berlau's leaving, Brecht moved his family from the house in Hollywood to one in Santa Monica so that he could be nearer to her. Did he continue to see her? Yes, and often. Gina Kaus remembers hearing tales of Brecht's coming late at night and climbing into the little garage apartment by a window left open for him.

With Margarete Steffin gone, Berlau became the collaborator and secretary that Brecht seemed to require. Although she is actually named on only one play, *The Caucasian Chalk Circle*, Berlau is remembered by no less than Marthe Feuchtwanger as the source of the original idea that led to *The Visions of Simone Machard*, the play the late novelist Lion Feuchtwanger wrote with Brecht shortly after the latter's arrival in America. As for Berlau's contribution to *The Caucasian Chalk Circle*, it was evidently considerable. It may even be true, as she later claimed, that she, and not Brecht, wrote the two love scenes in the play.

By the time the two of them worked together on *The Caucasian Chalk Circle*, Ruth Berlau had moved to New York. Things were evidently not so smooth between them. Brecht continued to mourn quite openly the loss of Margarete Steffin. If Berlau had found her a formidable rival while alive, Steffin must have seemed virtually unbeatable dead. The truth was, Berlau was not very stable. In *Bertolt Brecht in America*, James K. Lyon presents a very graphic picture of their relationship. Berlau alternated near-worship of Brecht with attempts to make him jealous that were often quite successful (he was, after all, very possessive). She sought—demanded—from him constant assurances and demonstrations of his love for her. Her love for him was quite literally driving her mad. In her high-strung state, she must have been moved by a desire to show him that she could live a life of her own when, on a trip to Washington to speak to a group of Danish refugees, she impulsively accepted the offer of a job with the Office of War Information to do propaganda broadcasts on shortwave from New York.

Away from Brecht, Berlau became even more demanding in her letters. When she had barely settled in New York, she asked him to join her there, pointing out that he had as yet failed to achieve any sort of foothold in the movie industry, so he might as well come to New York where he might have better luck in the theater. But by this time he was beginning discussions with Fritz Lang on the project that would become *Hangmen Also Die*, and so he refused. For months they wrote back and forth, she in an increasingly hysterical tone, and he pledging his love for her and sending poems. When she lost her job with the OWI in early 1943 because of her Communist past, he made her his New York agent, and she set out energetically to promote his fortunes there. He made the first of five trips to New York in February 1943, for a "Brecht Evening" at the New School. During his time there, he stayed with Ruth Berlau at her apartment on Fifty-seventh Street (as he would do during all successive trips to the city, one of which kept him there for a period of eight months).

Yet Brecht's visits came nowhere near satisfying her. She began drinking heavily. This may have been a factor in her frequent job changes in New York. Because, of course, there was little or no money for her in the work she did for Brecht, she had to make a living for herself, and she worked variously as a factory worker, a scrubwoman, and (unwisely) as a barmaid. During one of Brecht's stays, she became pregnant by him. With money given to her by Peter Lorre, who was a friend of Brecht's, she returned to the West Coast, supposedly to have the baby there. Yet it was discovered that she had a tumor on an ovary and had to be operated on immediately. As a result of the operation, the child, a boy, was born prematurely and lived only a few days. She returned to New York shortly afterward.

During the year that followed, her drinking continued. She began acting oddly, erratically. In 1945 she had an affair with a Danish sailor in New York and boasted to Brecht about it in a letter. Finally, on one occasion near the end of the year, she became violent, and a doctor was summoned. The next day she was in Bellevue, and a few days after that she was in a Long Island mental institution receiving shock treatments. Brecht returned then to New York expressly to see her.

Ruth Berlau made only one more trip back to California after that, during the rehearsals for the production of Brecht's *Galileo*. It had been translated and rewritten with the help of Charles Laughton in order to provide Laughton with a vehicle to use to return to the stage and ride off to Broadway. The pressure was on Laughton, whose career could then scarcely be said to be in the ascendant, and who had not appeared on the stage in years. Never a confident actor, he had a case of the jitters even during the dress rehearsal at which Berlau was present, busily occupied shooting photographs for publicity purposes. As John Houseman recalls the occasion in *Front and Center*: "From the orchestra floor I was dimly aware of a figure moving around upstairs and of the repeated, unpredictable click and slither. . . ." And then quite suddenly:

Laughton broke off in the middle of a scene and came slowly down to the edge of the stage. He glared up at the balcony, his face twisted into a strange grimace that made him look as though he were about to burst into tears. Then he started to howl at her. He accused her of violating him as an artist, of trying to ruin his performance and to destroy him as a man.

The more he raged, the wilder he became: he threatened to smash her cameras; he said he would kill her if he ever saw her again in the theater. He was still yelling long after she had fled into La Cienega Boulevard.[15]

Then, most significantly, Houseman recalls: "Brecht was in the theater and said not a word. He knew, as we all did, that Berlau and her cameras were the scapegoats for Charles's long pent-up and finally erupting emotion." As Houseman, the producer, interpreted his star's outburst, it was actually directed against Brecht, "a man he loved and revered but whom he held responsible for luring him, with his accursed play, out of the secure and lucrative backwater of his movie career. . . ."[16]

• • •

What of Helene Weigel? She had been an actress of considerable reputation in the German theater, although she had subordinated her career before and after marriage completely to Brecht's: during their European exile she had had only a couple of opportunities (in refugee productions of *Fear and Misery in the Third Reich* and *Señora Carrar's Rifles*) to return to the stage and prove even to herself that she was still an actress. Otherwise, she was simply Brecht's wife, the mother of his children, the woman of the house who was made to put up with his mistresses.

She had reason to hope that things would be different in Hollywood. After all, by the time they arrived there in 1941, there was a whole company of German character actors in American films, many of whom (Peter Lorre and Oscar Homolka, for example) had done quite well there. With America's entry into the war, and the consequent proliferation of anti-Nazi films, there would be even more parts for German actors. True, her English was not good—worse than Brecht's when they arrived, though eventually she surpassed him— but others had made do with as little. Besides, she knew many directors and producers there—among them Dieterle, Siodmak, Lang. She had even worked for Lang in Germany; she had been an extra in a number of the great director's early films and had had a small featured role in *Metropolis*. That, however, was not enough to win her the speaking part she sought in *Hangmen Also Die*, even though Brecht himself had written the film in collaboration with Lang and

John Wexley. In the end she worked in only one American film, quite a good one as it turned out—Fred Zinnemann's 1944 production of *The Seventh Cross*, which starred Spencer Tracy, an actor whom both she and Brecht greatly admired. And so she passed her time in Santa Monica as she had in Svendborg—as wife, mother, and chief concubine. In an interview, Hans Viertel, Salka's son, remembered her well from his many visits to their home: "I got to be very fond of Helli, although as far as I could tell then she was mainly a housewife. I had no idea she was one of the greatest actresses of our time."[17]

Brecht continued to surround himself with women in California. The fact that Ruth Berlau had removed herself to New York really altered nothing in that regard. He continued to see her on his long visits to the East, and at home there were others to take her place. John Houseman specifically recalls one of them, "a tall, Walkyrian blonde who, besides her Nordic beauty, was reputed to have money."[18] Elsa Lanchester, Charles Laughton's wife, remembers Brecht surrounded by "a coterie of mistresses." She guessed at their effect on Weigel:

> She was very loyal to him; they understood each other. . . . I think Helene Weigel obviously is a great actress. But at that time I had no opportunity to see that she was, because Brecht himself, and I think she went along with it, did not want her— he would not allow her—to appear in Hollywood films in small character parts. . . . I myself, if I were her, would have been much happier working at something. But obviously she had [worked]—her greatness had to be preserved. And so she was rather an unhappy woman. I don't blame her, but I think that it might have changed her life and even the children's lives if she'd worked. She must have been absolutely boiling inside.[19]

Did she sometimes boil over? Often? We know that on a number of occasions she demanded that Ruth Berlau be sent away—and on nearly as many she was overruled by Brecht. When he told her he was bringing Berlau to Hollywood for the *Galileo* opening, Weigel reluctantly consented, but she insisted the woman be kept out of her sight (she wasn't, of course). But did she ever confide her feelings to anyone? If so, only one of her friends from that period has ever gone on record—Marthe Feuchtwanger, who remembered Weigel's breaking down in tears once when the two of them were together: "She said to me, 'I don't know if I can go on taking these women of his.' I think she told me about it because my husband also had this weakness."[20]

Suffering then, even long-suffering, yet not mute. In this, as in so much else, Helene Weigel herself seems to have behaved as a typical Brecht heroine. Was it by mere coincidence? A case of life imitating art? Neither, I think. For far from conforming to some external model of behavior sketched out for her by her husband, Weigel seems much more likely to have provided *him* with whatever living model he needed from which to draw those powerful female characters who give such life and inherent dignity to his major plays. Not many would dispute that Brecht's reputation rests mainly on five plays that were written between 1937 and 1945—*Galileo*, *Mother Courage*, *The Good Woman of Setzuan*, *Puntila and Matti*, and *The Caucasian Chalk Circle*. Remarkably enough, three of the five have women in their leading roles—women who are, in fact (rather in spite of him), real heroines. Why should this be remarkable? Because with one notable exception, in his early work Brecht seemed little interested in creating strong roles for women. That exception was *The Mother*, his dramatic adaptation of the Maxim Gorky novel. Significantly, the play was written about the time he and Helene Weigel at last were married, and the leading role in it, that of Pelegea Vlassova, may have been the only one he ever wrote for Weigel. In any case, she played the mother of the World War I Russian soldier who is gradually won away from patriotic support of the war to Communist activism against it. Weigel played the role with such subtlety and style that she gave life, strength, and humor to this play, which (putting it mildly) his didactic propaganda works of that period lacked.

The five major plays of Brecht's exile were certainly not propaganda pieces. They were not even—no matter how furiously he rewrote to make them so—especially political. They dealt with human nature in an impressive variety of manifestations. It is interesting that when he set out to give flesh to certain human qualities (one is almost tempted to say virtues—but after all, it is Brecht we are dealing with here), he felt obliged to give them female form.

Goodness, for example. Shen Teh, *The Good Woman of Setzuan*, is truly good. Yet the entire action of the play is directed toward showing the impossibility of accomplishing good in a corrupt and unjust world. Whether he intended it to or not, the play serves as a dramatic illustration of Brecht's dictum: *Erst kommt das Fressen, und dann kommt die Moral* ("First feed yourself, and then worry about morality"). It does so by showing the disastrous consequences that result when the order is reversed.

Shen Teh certainly *tries* to do good. She is left a thousand silver dollars by gods visiting the city incognito because she was the only one in the city kind enough to take them in. With the money, she opens a tobacco shop and soon finds herself beset by beggars and squatters. She gives them rice and allows them to stay, and although she earns herself the title the Angel of the Slums, they make it impossible for her even to conduct business. In desperation, she invents a male cousin, Shui Ta—herself in male clothing and mask—who ruthlessly casts out the squatters and coldly refuses the beggars, then sums up the fundamental problem: "The trouble is there's so much poverty in this city that no one person can hope to relieve it."[21] With things set right once again, Shen Teh reappears as herself and promptly falls in love with an unemployed pilot, Yang Sun. In need of money for a bribe to restore him to his place on the air-mail roster, she again calls in Shui Ta, who raises the money by questionable means. And yet again, pregnant by her young pilot, Shen Teh is about to lose everything—and once again Shui Ta comes to the rescue. This time he not only saves Shen Teh's little tobacco shop; he even expands it into a tobacco factory and stays on to run it, with the help of the pilot Sun, in his characteristically ruthless fashion. When he is haled into court for supposedly doing away with Shen Teh, other accusations are hurled at him: "He ruined us!—He blackmailed me!—He made me do wicked things!—Exploited the helpless!—Lied!—Swindled!"[22] etc. His judges are the three gods whose gift set in motion this course of events. To them alone Shui Ta reveals he is Shen Teh in disguise. She pleads her case: "To be good and yet to live tore me like lightning into two halves."[23] The gods find themselves in a dilemma: rather than admit that the world they have given to men is such an impossible one to live in, they admonish her weakly: "Just be good and everything will turn out all right!"[24] And Shui Ta? She is to resort to him only once a month. And so the ending remains unresolved. In an epilogue the problem is posed to the audience in a series of questions:

> But what's *your* answer to the situation?
> For love nor money we could find no out:
> Refashion man? Or change the world about?
> Or turn to different gods? Or don't we need
> Any? Our bewilderment is great indeed.[25]

The Caucasian Chalk Circle is fundamentally a play about sacrifice. That, after all, is what that troublesome first scene is all about. It was omitted from the initial performances of the play in West Germany because it seemed to smack too much of Soviet propaganda— peasants arguing out their future, voting, determining their joint destiny—and was a little too far removed from Soviet reality. The scene is Georgia toward the end of World War II. Peasants have been asked to join their valley with a neighboring one in a water project that would completely change their old way of life. In the end, of course, they subordinate their wishes to the greater good and join the water project: they sacrifice.

In the remaining five scenes that make up the body of the play (it is supposedly offered as an entertainment for the assembled peasants and government representatives), this theme of sacrifice is restated more satisfyingly in the story of Grusha Vachnadze, probably the most attractive of all Brecht's characters. During some civil war of the vague past, she rescues the infant male heir of the governor when the governor's wife flees for her life, leaving her child behind. At great risk to herself, pursued by soldiers of the rebellion who want the child dead, she takes him off to the mountains and raises him as her own. She bravely bears the stigma of the baby's presumed illegitimacy, but finally consents to a marriage of convenience with a man who is supposedly dying but proves to be only malingering to avoid military service, thus complicating things considerably when Simon, the soldier to whom she promised herself, returns for her from the war. With order restored, she is apprehended at last with "her" child and taken back to stand trial before the judge Azdak. At this point, it is usually said that Azdak "takes over" the play, but the long flashback that makes up scene 5 and deals solely with the rise of the scalawag judge during the period of disorder seems nothing more or less than an intrusion on the main action and a sign of the slapdash construction of which Brecht was sometimes guilty. (Why couldn't the story of Azdak have been told concurrently with Grusha's?) At any rate, Grusha is brought before the judge by the governor's wife, who now expects to reclaim the boy and through him the property of his murdered father. But after hearing both sides, the unpredictable Azdak has a chalk circle drawn and the child placed in the middle. He then instructs the two mothers each to grab an arm and pull; the one who succeeds in pulling the boy out of the circle will get to keep him. The governor's widow wins easily. Grusha has refused even to take hold: "I raised him!" she cries. "Do you want me to tear him to pieces?"[26] And so Azdak, impressed by Grusha's willingness to sacrifice even her own motherhood rather than hurt the boy, reverses himself and awards him to her as the "true" mother. In the bargain, Azdak impulsively divorces Grusha from her malingering husband, leaving her free to marry her soldier, Simon. The peasants dance. Azdak departs. Everyone lives happily ever after.

If the strong matter of *The Good Woman of Setzuan* and *The Caucasian Chalk Circle* is relieved somewhat by their qualities of fairy tale and legend, there is little in *Mother Courage and Her Children* to lighten its heavy load. It is, quite in spite of Brecht, a tragedy. Courage is even provided by him with a tragic flaw: rapaciousness. Yet where he clearly wished her to seem *merely* greedy—a crude, penny-ante capitalist, a caricature of a war profiteer—she grew out of his control in the writing and took on strength and tragic dimension that he never intended her to have. Mother Courage, for all her faults, is the very embodiment of those qualities of fortitude and endurance that saw so many through those brutal, soul-testing years of World War II.

Mother Courage follows the bloody and devastating Thirty Years' War with her three children—selling, bartering, doing anything she can to get by. In the beginning, her two sons pull the canteen wagon (oxen and horses have long since been eaten), and her daughter Kattrin, dumb since she was raped by a soldier, rides beside her on the wagon box. In the course of the play, her children are taken from her one by one. The boys, inspired by soldiers' tales of glory, want to join the fighting; one of them, Eilif, runs off with a recruiting sergeant, and the other, Swisscheese, is forcibly enlisted. Eilif simply disappears, never to be heard from. Swisscheese returns, now working as a paymaster, but is set upon by soldiers who think he has hidden away his cash box (actually he has thrown it away to keep it from them). They hold him hostage and Courage is forced to bargain with them for her son's life. In the end, she offers them all she has — but too late, for they have murdered her son. "I think I've haggled too long," she says bleakly. But she presses on, only to lose her daughter when, in her absence, Kattrin hears of a surprise attack against the city of Halle and climbs up on a rooftop and beats a drum to wake the sleeping city. The girl is shot down, but her alarm saves the city. In the play's last short scene, Mother Courage is left alone, her only wish to find Eilif, if he still lives. With no other choice she picks up the traces of the wagon. "Let's hope I can pull the wagon alone. I'll make it — there's not much inside." And she hauls away singing an angry song, determined to keep on selling to any who may survive the war's destruction.

Helene Weigel scored her greatest personal success in this role in the Berliner Ensemble production of *Mother Courage and Her Children*, which was directed by Brecht himself. Did he originally intend it for her? Evidently not. He wrote the play in Denmark in hopes of Swedish translation and production and is said to have inserted the role of the dumb daughter Kattrin so that Weigel might appear in it despite her ignorance of the language. In fact, none of the three leading roles — and they are among the finest for actresses in the modern theater — was written expressly for her. This is remarkable only because Brecht made it a practice to tailor roles for specific actors: *The Good Woman of Setzuan* was, he said, written with Elisabeth Bergner in mind, and *The Caucasian Chalk Circle* was written for Luise Rainer.

On none of the three — on none of his plays at all — does Weigel's name appear as collaborator. Yet her influence can, in a sense, be felt in all of them. She was with him when he wrote them, always there to be read to, always there to comment and criticize and certainly willing to do so. More than that, living with her through so much, he must have drawn a good deal from her; that strength of personality that all three of these Brechtian heroines share must surely have been hers. The fortitude that characterized Courage was displayed by Weigel in all the moves from country to country — moves that required enduring not just physical hardships but also the indignity of sharing her roof with her husband's mistresses. Like Grusha, she was willing to sacrifice—not her claim to her children but her claim to her career, and it was all done to further Brecht's. Was Shen Teh's sort of goodness hers? Probably so, because it was goodness tempered with shrewdness. Shen Teh knew her limitations, and she knew, too, that to act forcefully and effectively in her world she had to play the part of a man. In a way, Weigel did that, too, when, upon their return to Germany, she took on the artistic directorship of the Berliner Ensemble, organizing things and running them (some hint that it was with the ruthlessness of Shui Ta), so that Brecht might be free to work.

In most other ways, their relationship stayed the same in East Berlin. Although Brecht and Weigel continued to live together until his death in 1956, he was also continually involved with other women—most of them young actresses in the Berliner Ensemble. Among them were Käthe Reichel, who reminded Brecht of Margarete Steffin and whose first role in the Ensemble was the role his "good comrade" had played in the original production of *The Mother*. Another was Käthe Rülicke, an assistant director who took over as Brecht's secretary and was trained in her job by Elisabeth Hauptmann. A third was Isot Kilian, whom Brecht enjoyed the last two years of his life. Klaus Völker tells of an occasion on which Weigel noticed a visiting Polish director flirting openly with Kilian: "Helene Weigel asked him to go to her office, where she discreetly explained the situation. It distracted the playwright when other men behaved intimately with the women he loved."[27]

For a time, Ruth Berlau was there in East Berlin, too. She had followed Brecht there from New York as soon as he was established. Failing as thoroughly as before to win his complete attention, she began (or rather continued) to drink heavily. She was picked up a number of times by the police for drunkenness and on each occasion was sent off to a hospital to dry out. At last she became an embarrassment to Brecht, and in 1955 he asked her to return to Copenhagen. She died in 1974 at the age of sixty-eight.

Yet in spite of all these disruptions and the gossip they caused, the company prospered and became one of, or perhaps *the* leading theater troupe in Europe. Hans Viertel, collaborator of Brecht and friend of Weigel back in Santa Monica, remembered a meeting at the moment of their greatest triumph: "While I was in London in 1954, I heard that the Berliner Ensemble was in Paris doing *Mother Cour-*

age. Well, I hitchhiked there and got to the theater just a half hour before curtain and found Weigel. She was a square woman, a commissar type, and she really knew how to give orders. 'Get him a seat where he can hear,' she said, and, believe me, I got one. Well, I saw the play, and I saw her performance, and all I can say is there's been nothing like it in the theater. Naturally I went backstage afterward to congratulate her and, when I did, she laughed and said, 'You didn't know I could do anything but cook, did you?' Brecht wasn't around, but I remember when I left the theater with Helli, there was still a crowd in the foyer. She nudged me and pointed. 'There's Ruth [Berlau],' she said. 'You must say hello to her.' And so of course I did."[28]

· ● ·

Bertolt Brecht and his women. To say that he used them would be true, of course, but it would not be the complete truth, for each in her own way, and to some degree, used him as well. Invoking the bohemian prerogative, he dismissed notions of fidelity as merely "bourgeois," but only as they impinged upon *his* freedom. He expected—and usually got—complete, sometimes abject, devotion from his mistresses and wives. In all this, his justification and theirs was talent, his genius. Was it sufficient? That was for them to answer, each according to whatever spoken or unspoken bargain may have been struck. In any objective sense, however, it should be evident that as individuals he exploited them shamefully.

And yet he did give something in return. Of course he helped them along: actresses were given parts; Hauptmann, Steffin, and Berlau were given the chance to "share" in his creation as collaborators; Weigel was "given" a theater with which she established an international reputation for herself. Moreover, he gave to the theater and to womankind three female roles of heroic dimensions. But with his history and his apparent attitude, how did he manage to do it? Perhaps in the way that the true artist always seems to excel the man. The artist knows more, feels more truly, and gives more generously. The best of the man—sometimes the only good in him—is always in his art.

9

GALILEO IN HOLLYWOOD

Many years after the brief wartime era of Hollywood's intellectual and artistic glory had passed, Vera Stravinsky wrote to a cousin in Moscow contrasting Hollywood then (1962)—"a cemetery with lights, as the Americans say"—with what it had been during the war:

> The ferment of composers, writers, scientists, artists, actors, philosophers and genuine phoneys did exist, and we often attended the lectures, exhibitions, concerts, and other performances of these people. To compare *that* Hollywood with the Hollywood of today, consider the fact that the premiere of one version of Brecht's *Galileo*, with the collaboration of Eisler and Charles Laughton took place here, and think of the inconceiv-

ably remote prospects of such an event now. Igor was so
deeply impressed by the *Galileo*, incidentally, that the play
was directly responsible for one of his rare public political acts.
He protested Eisler's deportation because, as he said, he could
see no possibility of harm from the man, and he thought the
exile of the artist, or of any artist, a loss. But, then, at the time
of the political fears of the immediate postwar years, culture
decamped like Cambyses' army—culture, as we knew it, that
is, for Hollywood continues to boom unmindful of the phase I
have tried to distinguish.[1]

The Brecht-Laughton production of *Galileo* impressed even the Stra-
vinskys. It was not just a social event, nor even a cultural event of
the routine sort. There was nothing routine about it.

To the émigré intellectuals who attended, and even more to those
who took part, the Hollywood *Galileo* gave dignity and purpose to
their anomalous and perhaps superfluous presence there in the movie
capital. Imperfect though it may have been, racked by dissension
though it certainly was, the production nevertheless appears in retrospect to be the most important single event of the exile years. Why?
Not so much for what it was, but as an indication of what the era
could have produced. There was so much émigré talent, so much
artistry there through the war—a little before and after—and yet
except for a handful of motion pictures by Fritz Lang and some others
(count *Hangmen Also Die*, *The Seventh Cross*, *Ninotchka*, and *Letter from an Unknown Woman* among them), there was little real
evidence of the European sensibility at work in Hollywood. Billy Wilder Americanized completely; Fritz Lang survived as long as he did
by making films that were essentially *American*.

It was suitable, if a little surprising, that Brecht and Laughton
achieved what they did on the stage. In spite of the talent on hand,
there was little theater activity there in Los Angeles—far less than
today. But perhaps it had to be theater. Brecht had tried movies, and
though he had made enough money to sustain himself and his family,
he had decided that that sort of work wasn't for him. When Charles
Laughton undertook the *Galileo* project, he felt (quite wrongly as it
turned out) that his film career was coming to an end.

Bertolt Brecht is unjustly famed for his "generous" practice of
working with collaborators. Except in a couple of instances when his

co-workers were too tough or big to be bullied, as was the case with Kurt Weill and Lion Feuchtwanger, he generally "collaborated" with those bright enough to offer ideas but too weak to give him resistance—usually his mistresses. In a way, however, his work with Laughton on the adaptation and production of *Galileo* was a truer sort of joint effort. There was, of course, already a German text at hand. The original version of the play was written in Denmark in 1938 and had, in fact, been produced in Zurich in 1943. Not long after that, however, Brecht met Laughton at one of Salka Viertel's Sunday afternoon salons. He knew Laughton's work from films and thought well enough of him as an actor; more important, he knew the actor had sufficient star power in America to carry a play of Brecht's on Broadway. Which one? There could be no doubt. *Galileo* might well have been written with Laughton in mind—although of course it wasn't. Long before he met Laughton, Brecht described the character in this way: "My Galileo is a powerful physicist with a belly on him, a face like Socrates, a vociferous, full-blooded man with a sense of humor, the new type of physicist, earthy, a great talker."

Brecht set about to cultivate the actor's friendship. They visited back and forth. Laughton was fond of reading aloud from Shakespeare and the Bible, and he did this on a couple of occasions at Brecht's home. From the *Work Journal*, July 30, 1944: "Laughton reads . . . the first three acts of *Lear*. He brings out excellently the Lear of the first act, grown inhuman through kingship, obtaining 10 pounds of filial love for 1,000 square meters of land." And so on. The playwright passed on to the actor the English adaptation of *Schweyk in the Second World War* that he had prepared for Peter Lorre with Broadway in mind; Laughton read it aloud, too, and was most flattering. Brecht curried his favor. After visiting the actor's home and watching him at work in the garden he loved, Brecht (who had repeatedly declared in his *Journal* that he loathed the natural beauty of southern California) wrote a long poem in praise of it, "Garden in Progress." When a rockslide took part of the garden away, Brecht was forced to tack on a rather weak ending:

> Alas, the lovely garden, placed high above the coast
> Is built on crumbling rock. Landslides
> Drag parts of it into the depths without warning. Seemingly
> There is not much time left in which to complete it.[2]

But at last Brecht found the right bait to land his big fish. According to James K. Lyon, "[Laughton's] widow recalls that this great interpreter of English literature never became what he most wanted to be—a writer."[3] The playwright produced a terribly literal and Germanic translation of the original text of *Galileo* (probably by Elisabeth Hauptmann) and invited the actor to work with him in an adaptation of it for the American stage. Laughton read it and must have said something like, "This will never do, old chap—not even for a start." For he immediately employed two young M-G-M screenwriters, who had virtually no German between them, to turn the crude translation into an acting adaptation. Only with their work in hand did Brecht and Laughton begin on the text.

Brecht described their collaboration in uncharacteristically idyllic terms:

> We used to work in L's small library in the mornings. But often L would come and meet me in the garden, running barefoot in shirt and trousers over the damp grass, and would show me some changes in his flowerbeds, for his garden always occupied him, providing many problems and subtleties. The gaiety and the beautiful proportions of this world of flowers overlapped in a most pleasant way into our work.[4]

According to Brecht—and, for that matter, according to Laughton as well—all that passed between them was sweetness and light during this period when they worked together on the adaptation. What Brecht has to say is contained in a foreword, "Building Up a Part: Laughton's Galileo," to the 1956 German version of the play. In it, Brecht is purposely misleading on a couple of points. First of all, he neglects to make any mention of either of the two English translations that existed before he and Laughton started their work. The implication is that the two worked directly from the 1938 German version:

> The awkward circumstance that one translator knew no German and the other scarcely any English compelled us, as can be seen, from the outset to use acting as our means of translation. We were forced to do what better equipped translators should do too: to translate gests. For language is theatrical in so far as it primarily expresses the mutual attitude of the

speakers. . . . In a most striking and occasionally brutal way L showed his lack of interest in the "book," to an extent that the author could not always share. What we were making was just a text; the performance was all that counted.[5]

Here, too, Brecht is being a little less than forthright, for his English was not nearly as sketchy as he lets on. No doubt they did act out a good many lines between them, but Brecht could also have talked them through, and no doubt did.

Whatever the true nature of their collaboration, it began in December 1944 (the first mention of it in the *Work Journal* is dated December 10) and continued for just about a year. They did not work steadily on the project of course. Laughton broke things off to do two films—*Captain Kidd* and *Because of Him*—and Brecht, as always, had other irons in the fire. They had a "final" text by December 1945, which Brecht, typically, kept right on revising with the help of others. Laughton, however, took their version to Orson Welles, who was quite enthusiastic about it and agreed to direct the play. Mike Todd was then brought in as producer, and it looked for a while in 1946 as though they were headed directly for Broadway. By mid-year, however, Brecht and Laughton had become annoyed at both Welles and Todd when no move was made toward production. It was the old story in show business—prior commitments, other projects, hurry-up-and-wait. Well, they chose not to wait. They took back their handshakes—nothing had gone down on paper—and began looking elsewhere for a backer and a director. Because Laughton felt responsible for tying them up with Welles and because he had accepted another motion picture role (in Alfred Hitchcock's *The Paradine Case*) and had thus delayed things further, Laughton generously offered to pay Brecht $5,000 in compensation. Brecht generously accepted.

At last they found their producer in T. Edward Hambleton, described by John Houseman (who later became involved in the Hollywood production of *Galileo*) as "a stubborn Maecenas from Baltimore with an astonishing record of creating and supporting some of the American theater's most daring and valuable projects over the past forty years."[6] Hambleton was to be best known as founder and backer of New York's Phoenix Theatre, but all that was ahead of him. When he agreed to coproduce *Galileo*—and right from the start a Broadway production was planned—he was a comparative beginner. The choice of director this time was Brecht's, and Joseph Losey was his man. Losey had been involved in the left-wing theater in New York during the thirties. He had directed an experimental and quite successful production of *The Living Newspaper* for the W.P.A. Theatre Project and *Conjur' Man Dies* for the Negro Theatre, and he had gotten to know Brecht in 1935 when the latter came to New York for the Theatre Union production of *The Mother*. Deeply impressed by the playwright and fascinated by his Epic Theater theories, Losey was a natural choice for director; Brecht felt sure he could dominate him. He had hoped from the beginning to direct the production himself. Because Losey was then at work in Hollywood on *The Boy with Green Hair* at RKO, the first feature in his long and distinguished career as a motion picture director, and because Laughton had still another part in still another film (*The Big Clock*), it began to seem most practical to mount a production in Hollywood that might then be taken to Broadway.

The opportunity to do just that came early in 1947 when John Houseman and the actor-director Norman Lloyd joined forces to form Pelican Productions. They rented the Coronet Theatre on La Cienega Boulevard in West Hollywood and began looking around for plays, old and new, to produce. Norman Lloyd brought in *Galileo Galilei*, as they were calling it then, and Houseman was eager to do it. They worked out a coproduction deal. "T. Edward Hambleton would put up the money if we would contribute the theater," Houseman recalled in an interview. "There was more to it than that, there always is. We also contributed certain other things—our technical facilities, including the costume shop, which were under Kate Drain Lawson."[7]

Rehearsals began June 24, 1947. The huge cast—fifty in all—included the established movie character actor Hugo Haas as Cardinal Barberini, who later becomes Pope Urban VIII; Frances Heflin as the physicist's daughter, Virginia; and Mickey Knox as the Little Monk. Most of the roles were filled by young movie hopefuls, students of Laughton's and members of the Actors' Lab, with which Norman Lloyd was associated. From the beginning the rehearsal sessions were stormy. Brecht was determined to see the play done according to his Epic Theater theories, which most of the cast, schooled in the Stanislavsky method, had not even heard of. And Joseph Losey proved to be not quite as pliable as Brecht had expected. In fact, at one point

Losey walked out on the production and was persuaded to return only by an impassioned personal appeal from Laughton.

The trouble was Brecht, of course. As far back as 1935 John Houseman had heard rumors of Brecht's screaming, abusive fits of rage during rehearsals of *The Mother*—and as an old theater hand he was used to displays of temperament. But what he saw and heard from the playwright then and there far exceeded anything he had previously experienced. "Brecht was impossible and behaved vilely throughout," said Houseman. "But I have to admit that he was dead right most of the time."[8]

The effect this had on the cast? Houseman: "They resented it, of course, as all actors do. They were getting orders from two different people—from Brecht, of course, and from Losey, the titular director, who was caught in the middle. Even Laughton was throwing out advice and instructions."[9] (The star escaped the playwright/director's acid criticism, except for one minor disagreement when he was told not to "pout and act like a baby.")

Is *that* what it was like to work with Brecht? Was he really such a monster? Some say no. And, in spite of all declarations to the contrary, they say it so emphatically that some of this testimony should also go on the record.

Frances Heflin is one of his defenders. The actress who is now known and loved by the daytime millions as Mona Kane, the brave matriarch in the fabulously successful soap opera *All My Children*, first met the playwright when she was cast as Galileo's daughter in the Hollywood production. She had been one of a group that met informally over a period of months with Laughton and was in that sense one of his students. She had also appeared in Pelican's first production of that 1947 season, *The Skin of Our Teeth*, and had been sent a copy of the *Galileo* script. To Norman Lloyd and John Houseman she expressed her interest in the play, and so was passed on to Brecht. "We had lunch," she recalled in an interview. "He never asked me to read. I just talked to him and got the part. It was only afterward that I met Losey."

Frances Heflin is, of course, the sister of the late actor Van Heflin. (I say "of course" because if you have ever seen her on television you must have noticed the unmistakable resemblance.) We talked in her apartment on the upper West Side of Manhattan. Through most of our conversation her husband, the musician and composer Sol

Kaplan, was present and contributed a few remarks of his own. But it was she who had worked with Brecht and knew him best, and it was she who responded to my blunt question: What was Brecht like? "I found him the most interesting man I ever met," she declared. "He was thoroughly charming but not intentionally so. He had an old-world politeness together with an impatience with formality—and bright, outspoken! He had an energy that came out of every pore. His eyes darted. You could see his mind racing a mile a minute."

But in rehearsals? How was he with the cast? She admitted that he could and did carry on a bit: "He was terribly impatient with any act he felt was put on for effect. When an actor would come on too grand, well, it just drove him crazy. But he would often take time and give his reasons for demanding what he did. I remember there was an actor who was playing the part of a merchant in too grand a manner. Brecht felt he was not getting to what was in the play, and so he gave him a history lecture on the merchant's place in society at that point. He said that merchants were among the most important people in society at that time but were still not recognized by the aristocracy. Yet they played an important role, helping artists and scientists. All *this* just to set an actor straight. I thought it was an unusual way to get what he wanted.

"Look, it was hard for him. He wanted it all to be *right*—all the details, that it should look a certain way, that it should *sound* a certain way. He was *very* interested in the music. But it was also very hard for Joe Losey, too, because he was even then a very good director. I *don't* think Brecht wanted to direct the play, really. I think he wanted it done by an American director. Brecht was around as the author. He just wanted to be consulted as the author. But he wanted it *right*."

Did he try to educate the actors in his Epic Theater style?

"No, he just said he didn't want a lot of emotion spilled on the stage. He said, 'In the theater I work in I don't believe in interfering with the emotions of the actor on or off the stage. But I am determined that the audience should hear the words and understand the ideas. How the actor gets to the emotion is up to him.' It wasn't that he denied the actor the right to get to the emotion, but he believed it was up to an American actor to get to it in whatever way was best for him. How? Well, he believed that the emotional life of the actors should develop as the emotional life of the play.

"One thing I should say is that he was totally a man of the theater and could be very helpful in all kinds of ways—for instance, with hair and makeup, where you might think he wouldn't be interested. Most playwrights aren't. In that play, as I guess you know, the scenes switch rapidly, and it jumps back and forth. It calls for a lot of quick costume changes. He told us what to do, how to handle it. Brecht had an instinct for what was right in costuming. He liked rough fabrics. Kate Lawson did the costumes with a lot of help from Helene Weigel, but they did them the way he wanted them—not in bright colors. I wore white. There were a lot of blacks and whites and grays. He loved suede and rough wools.

"What else? Let me see. Oh, yes, he gave us tips on makeup. I remember he showed us what to do in order to age—the play covers a lot of years. He showed us that if we put on cold cream—patted on the cold cream—and then put powder over it and wiped it slightly, we would get the delineation we wanted."

Frances Heflin enjoyed a closer relationship with Brecht than did most members of the cast. The two obviously liked each other. "There were cherry sodas after rehearsals. We had these long discussions on soda stools. I was pregnant at the time, only he didn't know that. It only came out later when he found out why I couldn't do the New York production. I had to faint in the play—hit the floor and everything—and I remember he asked me, 'Do you know how to do that without hurting yourself?' And I told him, 'Sure. It's okay,' and so on, and it was, too, because I did it every night onstage. But afterward, when he found out I had been pregnant all through the run, he told me, 'There was no reason for you to faint. I'm a writer. I could have rewritten so you didn't have to faint.'"[10]

. ● .

Yes, during the rehearsals of *Galileo*, Brecht stood ready to rewrite, even (perhaps especially) when he was not asked to do so. Yes, he did fiddle with the text to the dismay of some; and he did fire at least one member of the company—the American choreographer Anna Sokolow. She had been recommended by Joseph Losey, with whom she had worked, and by Norman Lloyd and John Houseman. Houseman recalled: "From the first day, because she was not wholly pliable and subordinate to his ideas, Brecht insulted and vilified her. Declaring that he had no use for a 'lot of Broadway commercial shit,' he insisted on her dismissal."[11] He hired an émigré pantomimist Lotte Goslar, who apparently was quite overcome at the honor of working with him and gave him just what he wanted.

At last, in spite of Brecht's fits of rage, in spite of Joseph Losey's temporary walkout, in spite of the dismissal of the choreographer and her hasty replacement, and in spite of a one-week postponement caused by these problems and others, *Galileo* opened at last on July 30, 1947, in the middle of a long heat spell during which temperatures hit the mid-nineties every day. Brecht says in his essay, "Building Up a Part: Laughton's *Galileo*," that "L's chief worry was the prevailing heat. He asked that trucks full of ice should be parked against the theater walls, and fans be set in motion 'so that the audience can think.'"[12] Perhaps, but that justification sounds terribly Brechtian; one wonders if it was truly Laughton who did the asking (or insisting); or if, on the other hand, the star of the show was by then so truly imbued with the principles of the Epic Theater that he played back precisely what the playwright wanted to hear.

In any case, the heat did nothing to hold down attendance. At its opening the small (260-seat) theater was sold out for the length of its four-week run. Opening night was a celebrity-hound's dream; in attendance were some of Hollywood's stars of the first and second magnitude, among them Ingrid Bergman, Charles Boyer, Charlie Chaplin, John Garfield, and Anthony Quinn. There were exiles and émigrés aplenty: Billy Wilder, Lion Feuchtwanger, and Igor and Vera Stravinsky.

During preview performances before the opening, Laughton, who was so nervous that he had no idea what he was doing, showed an unconscious propensity for a game that is known to adolescent boys as "pocket pool." The costume trousers he wore had large pockets into which he would thrust his hands as he walked ceaselessly about the stage. Inside, they agitated ceaselessly about his private parts. The audience noticed, all right. There were snickers and even a few laughs at quite inappropriate moments. What to do? Frances Heflin: "Helli [Weigel] got his pants away on the pretext of pressing them. She wanted his hands out of his pockets, so she sewed them up."[13] Laughton reportedly was beside himself when he found out what had been done and why. He roared mightily until the stitches were removed. But the lesson was not lost on him: from then on he kept his hands where they belonged.

Had he not done so, that fact would almost certainly have found its way into at least one of the reviews following opening night. Patterson Greene of the Hearst chain's *Los Angeles Examiner* vilified the play as "a harrangue—and a fussy, juvenile harrangue at that."[14] He said the play was anticlerical (it is not; in fact, it presents Pope Urban VIII quite sympathetically) and Red propaganda (it is one of the least tendentious of Brecht's plays). Laughton he called "a porcine boor."

But by and large the reviews were not at all bad. In fact the most important of them, Edwin Schallert's in the *Los Angeles Times*, was quite favorable. He hailed it as "an arresting footlight event" and predicted that it would "unquestionably arouse marked controversial interest."[15] In the *Los Angeles Daily News*, now long since merged into the *Times*, Virginia Wright called it "good theater, exciting theater, provocative theater,"[16] and she showed that she understood perfectly what the play is about.

• • •

What is *Galileo* about? What does it say? There is, after all, reason to doubt that it actually says what Bertolt Brecht intended. In the basic sense, of course, it is about Galileo Galilei, the Italian astronomer and physicist who lived from 1564 to 1642 and challenged the prevailing notions of astronomy by suggesting that the earth was not the still center of the universe, and that the sun did not revolve around the earth but rather vice versa. In doing this, he came up against the authority of the Catholic Church, which supported the old Ptolemaic conception of the universe. Under threat of torture by the Inquisition, he recanted his position completely; but then, upon his release, he beat the ground with his foot and was heard to say, *"Eppur si muove!"* ("And yet it [the earth] moves!") In his old age, under virtual house arrest, he wrote his *Discorsi*, in which he restated and defended his views. He had them smuggled out of Italy, and they were published after his death.

Now, while Brecht altered certain historical details, he certainly remained true to the story in broad outline in the versions of the play that he wrote—although in the original (1938) text he was evidently *truer* to the facts. I say "evidently" because since this version has never been published and I was not on hand in Zurich on the only occasion when it was performed, I am relying on Eric Bentley, who has read it, probably at the Brecht Archive in East Berlin. In his excellent essay, "The Science Fiction of Bertolt Brecht," Bentley contrasts the original version with the one performed by Charles Laughton in Hollywood and New York. In the earlier one he sees an "analogy between the seventeenth-century scientist's underground activities and those of twentieth-century left-wingers in Germany." He calls it "propaganda for thinking," referring directly to a line in the play, "Propaganda that stimulates thinking, in no matter what field, is useful to the cause of the oppressed." Brecht, Bentley says, so stresses the physicist's "slyness and cunning" in writing his *Discorsi* and smuggling them out for publication that he virtually excuses him for his weakness in giving in to the Church.[17]

On the other hand, there is some evidence that even at the time that Brecht first wrote the play, he could not find it in his heart to forgive Galileo his cowardice. In researching his subject Brecht not only consulted books but also had talks with a Danish physicist, Professor C. Møller, who was a co-worker of the great Niels Bohr himself. To a German critic, Ernst Schumacher, Møller recalled his conversations with Brecht. Møller said that between them "there arose a certain difference of opinion" on a crucial point:

> Since the *Discourses* would never have been composed if Galileo had not many years before submitted to the Catholic Church, I regarded this step as justified. Only in this way could he have finally won a victory over the Inquisition. Brecht, however, was of the opinion that Galileo's recantation of his theory of the motion of the earth in 1633 represented a defeat, which was in years to come to lead to a serious schism between science and human society. I could never understand this point of view, and even today I do not understand it after reading Brecht's *Life of Galileo*, which does not prevent this play from affecting and impressing me deeply.[18]

Since the *Galileo* that Møller read was probably the Laughton version—though it may possibly have been a third version prepared by Brecht for the Berliner Ensemble production of the play in 1953—the point is that *both* these later versions strongly stress Galileo's defeat by the Church over the later victory he won with his *Discorsi*.

In fact, as Brecht himself later declared in "Building Up a Part," this is what the revised work is all about:

> The atomic age made its debut at Hiroshima in the middle of our work. Overnight the biography of the new system of physics read differently. . . .
> Galileo's crime can be regarded as the "original sin" of modern natural sciences. From the new astronomy, which deeply interested a new class—the bourgeoisie—since it gave an impetus to the revolutionary social current of the time, he made a special science which—admittedly through its very "purity," i.e., its indifference to modes of production—was able to develop comparatively undisturbed. The atom bomb is, both as a technical and social phenomenon, the classical end product of his contribution to science and his failure to society.[19]

By whatever tortuous logic, Brecht came to the conclusion that if Galileo had not given in to the Pope and the Inquisition, the modern world would have been spared the horror of the atomic bomb. It could as easily be said that if Galileo had been more sincere in his recantation and had *not* written the *Discorsi*, Ptolemaic astronomy would have prevailed and World War II would have been fought with seventeenth-century weaponry. But that, of course, would be nonsense too.

At any rate, with the advent of the nuclear age Brecht set about with Laughton's assistance not only to translate and adapt the original text but to revise it substantially to sharpen his indictment of the physicist for his cowardice and betrayal. Most of these revisions were made in the latter part of the play. For instance, Galileo's defiant and historically verified line, *"Eppur si muove!,"* had previously seemed so important to Brecht that he used it for the title of the play's first draft—*And Yet It Moves!* It has been deleted from the second version altogether. In its place is this brilliant, if ambiguous, exchange between Galileo, who enters "changed, almost unrecognizable," from his ordeal with the Inquisition, and Andrea, his student and disciple, who looks at him in dismay, knowing he has recanted:

ANDREA *(in the door)*: Unhappy is the land that breeds no hero.
GALILEO: No, Andrea: Unhappy is the land that needs a hero.[20]

We have Professor Møller's word that Galileo's recantation deeply troubled Brecht right from the start, and so the alterations Brecht made in the text may have been something in the nature of settling an old account. Still, it must be admitted that it is a *mea culpa* that he puts in Galileo's mouth in scene 13. In good dialectical style, Brecht brings up Møller's argument that the writing of the *Discorsi* completely justified the recantation—simply so that the argument could be demolished. After many years, his former disciple, Andrea, looks in on the physicist and is asked by him to take the manuscript to Holland. Andrea is overcome. "Everything is changed!" he cries. Galileo asks why; and then:

ANDREA: We lost our heads. With the crowd at the street corners we said: "He will die, he will never surrender!" You came back: "I surrendered but I am alive." We cried: "Your hands are stained!" You say: "Better stained than empty."[21]

Andrea, in other words, sees his mentor's surrender to authority simply as a sly tactic by which he may gain the time he needs to continue and complete his important work. But Galileo disabuses him of this:

GALILEO: I recanted because I was afraid of physical pain.
ANDREA: No!
GALILEO: They showed me the instruments.
ANDREA: It was not a plan?
GALILEO: It was not.[22]

In the long speech that follows, a tirade of self-loathing, Galileo sets forth Brecht's thesis that his sin was the "original sin" of science, declaring that if he had held his ground his scientific knowledge could have freed the people from their tormentors. In fact, he concludes:

As a scientist I had an almost unique opportunity. In my day astronomy emerged into the marketplace. At that particular time, had one man put up a fight, it could have had wide repercussions. I have come to believe that I was never in real danger; for some years I was as strong as the authorities, and I surrendered my knowledge to the powers-that-be, to use it, no, not *use* it, *abuse* it, as it suits their ends. I have betrayed my profession. Any man who does what I have done must not be tolerated in the ranks of science.[23]

There is no rejoinder from Andrea. This is the last word on the matter and clearly what Brecht would have us also believe.

Yet this is seldom what *is* believed. For example, critics at the Coronet Theatre on opening night were full of praise for Laughton's extremely human portrayal of the scientist who, as one of them put it, is "altogether heroic while professing to be a coward." In spite of the fact that he had collaborated in the adaptation, Laughton could not help but wring sympathy from the audience for the character. The actor got deeper into his role than the playwright had intended.

But in doing this, Laughton worked no unique magic. Other actors less skilled than he have managed to do the same. Audiences and readers alike respond with sympathy to Galileo; they even see him as "heroic." Why? First of all, because Brecht could not alter the fundamental facts: even though Galileo recanted to the Inquisition, he *did* write the *Discorsi* and had them smuggled out of the country. This is certainly a case where actions speak louder than words.

But what about Brecht's words? Do they really convince? No— and the reason they don't is that by the time we hear them from Galileo we have come to know him so well and believe in him so profoundly that we cannot bring ourselves to accept the verdict against him that he himself hands down. Brecht's Galileo is one of the most fully developed characters in modern drama. No mere great man, he has such appealing, vulgar, human qualities—gluttony, greed—that his cowardice before the Inquisition (if it is that and not cunning) may be disappointing, but it is not surprising. Frankly, it would be difficult to imagine this corpulent, sensuous man stretched out on the rack, emitting agonized howls interspersed with screams of defiance to his torturers right up until that awful, final moment when his bones snap. That's not *our* Galileo. No, our Galileo might, as Andrea supposed, have given in because he knew that it was more important for him to continue his work than to die in defense of it. Or, at the very least (for the bare facts support this), he might have recanted out of fear, knowing all the while that he was right *("Eppur si muove!")*, then, after a period of years, have decided that, even though there was real risk involved, he had to set down the principles of his new physics on paper and get them published. But would he, in either case, hate himself so for not having challenged authority? He might, for in their final years men do look back upon their lives and count the missed opportunities. But the long speech of self-denunciation that Brecht puts in Galileo's mouth does *not* convince us; it does not alter appreciably the estimate of the man formed from the many scenes that preceded it. It has, rather, the effect of deepening the character, giving a hint of the tragic to a man who now yearns to be the kind of hero he never could have been.

Brecht himself must have seen that this was so, for in that third version of the play, which he prepared for production in East Berlin, he made further changes in the text, and all of them were directed toward demeaning Galileo and making the self-contempt he voices at the end more truly justified. Yet, ultimately, not even this version (available in German and English editions) manages to convince us. The historical Galileo and the character created by Brecht join forces to resist every effort by the playwright to denigrate them. We have all heard of plays that are actor-proof and director-proof; *Galileo* seems to be one that is playwright-proof.

Yet it is not the only one. Brecht's own *Mother Courage* went through the same sort of revisions for the same reasons. Audiences and readers alike insist on sympathizing with this woman whom Brecht meant to be seen as a grasping, haggling war profiteer, a caricature in miniature of those capitalists who consider war in terms of the bottom line. Yet Courage, too, has survived all her creator's efforts to make her over into something she is not. There must be a moral here, somewhere, for *Mother Courage* and *Galileo* are certainly his two greatest plays.

• • •

Encouraged by their Hollywood run at the Coronet, Laughton, Brecht, and their backer, T. Edward Hambleton, were determined to take *Galileo* to Broadway. The opportunity to do so was extended to them by the American National Theater and Academy (ANTA), but it was to be only for a limited run. Nevertheless, they accepted. If reviews were good, another theater could probably be found.

Well, reviews were not good. The most important of them all, Brooks Atkinson's in *The New York Times*, not only attacked the play for its loose, episodic structure but also blasted Charles Laughton's performance as "ponderous and condescending." Notices were not universally bad, however. John Mason Brown praised both play and performances in the *New York Post*. On the strength of that and Charles Laughton's drawing power, the production played to good audiences—SRO on some nights—and extended its scheduled two-week run by another week. In the end, however, the Maxine Elliott Theatre had to be vacated for another show, and the production had nowhere to go.

What happened to *Galileo* on Broadway? According to John Houseman, "The play was far in advance of its day. To the majority of critics the play was just very talky, and so on." Houseman did have an interesting theory on the all-important Brooks Atkinson review: "It was an aberration. He seemed very sore at the whole production. I happen to know that he had been to Russia and had made friends there who were later executed. He chose to see this as a direct piece of Marxist propaganda."[24] Which it was not.

Sol Kaplan, husband of Frances Heflin, said that he was not at all surprised at the failure of *Galileo* in New York. In the shift to the East Coast too many changes had been made. "That was *not* a Broadway production—not even Off Broadway. It was just 'experimental theater.' Not many of the actors from the Hollywood production went to New York. Just Laughton and a few others."[25] Frances Heflin, newly a mother by the time the play opened on Broadway, was one of those who did not make the trip. Her place was taken by an actress-dancer who added a lot of dramatic movement to the part—just the sort of thing that would have driven Brecht into a fit of rage.

But he was not around to see it. By the time *Galileo* opened at the Maxine Elliott on December 7, 1947, he was in Zurich promoting his European comeback. That was not quite as he had planned it. He had certainly hoped to return to Europe with a Broadway success under his belt. However, a summons from the House Committee on Un-American Activities intervened. He was called to Washington as one of the "unfriendly nineteen," and there he himself played a role not unlike that of Galileo before the Inquisition. It is worth noting that as a witness he acquitted himself no better and no worse than Galileo had done. All the Committee had to do was show him the instruments of torture. That was enough.

10

THE HOLLYWOOD ELEVENTH

No matter what was soon to come, Bertolt Brecht had reason to be optimistic as autumn rolled around in 1947. *Galileo* closed its limited run at the Coronet Theatre in Hollywood after garnering some excellent reviews and playing to full houses for four weeks. A New York run seemed certain. There also seemed to be the possibility of a sale of the film rights to the play. For the first time it seemed that he might be offered a choice. He could either return to Europe, as he had more or less planned to do all along, or if *Galileo* was a success on Broadway and there was consequent interest in his other plays by American producers, he might stay on indefinitely in America.

In fact, as late as September he was telling people he meant to remain in California. That, at any rate, was what he said to Frances Heflin and her husband, composer Sol Kaplan. As Kaplan recalled,

"It looked as though a number of his other plays might be produced. He wanted to be known in America, to have his plays produced here."[1]

At the same time, as he often did when faced with a choice, Brecht made preparations so that he might also follow the opposite course of action if necessary. He applied for a permit to travel to Switzerland. He made inquiries about bookings, even asked about the possibility of taking a car to Europe. He also put his house up for sale.

Then on September 19, 1947, came a visitor to Brecht's house who immediately decided the question for him. It was a U.S. marshal with a summons for Brecht to appear before the House Committee on Un-American Activities in Washington on October 23, 1947. It seemed to Brecht then that whether or not *Galileo* succeeded or failed in New York, there was only one course open to him, and that one would lead him straight to Europe. But between him and that escape lay that appointment in Washington—one that had, in any case, to be kept. His fear was that wrong answers or a bad performance before the Committee might impede his exit from America.

Brecht was, of course, not the only one to receive a visit from the marshal during that week in September. In all, there were nineteen who were issued subpoenas. Invitations to testify had also gone out to members of the right-wing vigilante group of the movie industry known as the Motion Picture Alliance for the Preservation of American Ideals. And because those who merely received *invitations* to testify were designated by the Committee itself as "friendly" witnesses, those who were subpoenaed came to be known as the "unfriendly nineteen."* Most of them were writers, although there were also a few directors and producers, and a single actor (Larry Parks) among them.

Of the nineteen, Brecht was the only one who was not an American citizen. Except to John Howard Lawson and Albert Maltz, he was known to the rest only as a name. It was a puzzle to the rest why the German playwright had been pulled in with them. Although not

---

* They were, besides Bertolt Brecht, Alvah Bessie, Herbert Biberman, Lester Cole, Richard Collins, Edward Dmytryk, Gordon Kahn, Howard Koch, Ring Lardner, Jr., John Howard Lawson, Albert Maltz, Lewis Milestone, Samuel Ornitz, Larry Parks, Irving Pichel, Robert Rossen, Waldo Salt, Adrian Scott, and Dalton Trumbo.

all of them were then or had been members of the Communist Party of the United States of America (CPUSA), all were at least quite active politically on the Left in Hollywood. While it was true that any reading of certain of his works (those in question being, however, mostly untranslated) would reveal him to be a thoroughgoing Marxist very sympathetic to the Communist cause, Brecht himself had kept a low profile during the six years he had been in America. If the purpose of the upcoming hearings were truly, as had been announced, to examine the "Communist Infiltration of the Motion Picture Industry," then how much infiltrating could Brecht have accomplished? After all, he had only one movie credit to his name in America (shared-story with Fritz Lang on *Hangmen Also Die*) and had done odd-job work on only one or two other films. The thrust of the Committee hearings was to "prove" that Communist propaganda had been smuggled into a great many motion pictures viewed by an unsuspecting American public. But *Hangmen Also Die* was merely anti-Nazi—as indeed what American war movie during the forties was not? No, Brecht's inclusion with the rest of the "unfriendly nineteen," though not a mystery, had little or nothing to do with his movie work and not even much to do with his presence in Hollywood. His was clearly a special case.

•   •   •

The Federal Bureau of Investigation had been gathering information on Brecht since his arrival in America on July 21, 1941. In the beginning, the interest seems to have been only of the routine sort given to any alien coming to the United States during wartime. Information on Brecht's arrival at San Pedro was collected from the Bureau of Immigration and a file on him was started. When the United States officially entered the war against Germany, Brecht and his family automatically fell into the category of "enemy aliens," in spite of the fact that they had come to America as refugees from the Nazis. They were put under the same restrictions on travel as all Germans who were not U.S. citizens. And, like all the rest, they were subjected to a 10 P.M. curfew and to spot checks by FBI agents to make sure that they observed it. It is worth noting that, as though anticipating all this and hoping to ease things for himself, Brecht went downtown to the Immigration office in Los Angeles the day after

Pearl Harbor and declared his intention to become a citizen of the United States. There is some reason to suppose that at the time that may indeed have been his intention.

From that part of Brecht's FBI file that has been made available to the public under the Freedom of Information Act, it is immediately obvious that it was not Brecht's enemy-alien status that interested the Bureau but rather his supposed Communist past. From a report on him sent from the Los Angeles field office to Washington, D.C.: "Subject alleged to have been a Communist in Europe, where he engaged in Underground activity." And then, more specifically:

On February 26, 1943, [name deleted] advised that she knew Mr. and Mrs. BRECHT in Germany, where they were Communists. [name deleted] stated that there was no doubt about their political attitude at that time, as it was evidenced in their activities, associations and in the writings of BRECHT, who is a poet and author.

Was either Brecht or Helene Weigel a member of the Communist Party in Germany? Brecht denied that he was before the House Committee on Un-American Activities and, perhaps more important, went on to affirm that denial in his *Work Journal*. But it is certainly true that he was as openly sympathetic as he could be to the Communist cause from about 1929 until he fled Germany, with good reason, in 1933. And he remained in solid support of international communism all during his years of exile (and, for that matter, during the years that followed until his death in 1956), doing whatever he needed to do to adjust to the serpentine twists of Russian foreign policy.

But where did the FBI get the idea that Brecht had engaged in underground activity?

On March 5, 1943, [name deleted] advised that he knew BRECHT by reputation in Germany, where he was considered a radical and an associate of persons with Communistic inclinations. [name deleted] stated that he became acquainted with BRECHT personally in the United States and found him still a radical and an enemy of Capitalism. According to [name deleted], BRECHT recently finished work on the moving picture, "HANGMEN ALSO DIE," in the production of which he acted as storywriter and Technical Adviser on Underground activity in Europe. The authenticity of "HANGMEN ALSO DIE" is largely due, [name deleted] stated, to the work of Subject, whose knowledge of the Underground was attained through personal experience. [name deleted] stated that Subject was imprisoned by the Nazis at one time and is believed to have been severely treated by them.

Except for a few pamphlets and poems written at a safe distance in Denmark for clandestine distribution in Nazi Germany, Brecht seems to have engaged in no underground activity; certainly there is nothing on record. And of course there is nothing to the tale that he was "imprisoned by the Nazis" and "severely treated by them." Where could this have come from? From Fritz Lang perhaps, who coauthored the screen story and directed the film, or from Arnold Pressburger, who produced it. They may have wished to give a sort of inside-story glamour to the production. (Background information on the workings of the Czech underground was actually supplied by U.S. government sources.) In any case, it is not likely to have come from Brecht himself because, for all his faults, he was not one to fabricate and brag about his degree of involvement as a political activist.

This inaccuracy or untruth goes a long way toward explaining the interest of the FBI, and later the HCUA, in *Hangmen Also Die*, and also in Brecht as a supposed undercover operative for international communism. They seem to have assumed that he was engaged in similar activity here in America. About the only support for this is a series of contacts by Brecht with one Gregori Kheifets reported by one of the FBI's many helpful sources. Kheifets, according to the field-office report of these meetings (October 2, 1944), "is known to this office as the Soviet Consul of San Francisco, who has been alleged to have been engaged in a military and political investigation on the West Coast as a close assistant of the high NKVD officer heading the Soviet Secret Police in the United States. It has been ascertained that KHEIFETS was engaged in espionage in Los Angeles."

The story of Brecht's imprisonment and the implication that he was tortured by the Nazis is far from the only inaccuracy in his FBI file.* Hearsay, supposition, and false speculation abound. To cite a few examples, Brecht is reported to have journeyed to America aboard the "SS Annie Jackson from Helsingfors, Finland." He actually came here on the SS Annie *Johnson* from *Vladivostok*, *USSR*. (When the mistake was discovered, a great deal was made of the fact that he had embarked from the Soviet Union.) According to one source, Brecht "was in Los Angeles in the early part of 1936." He wasn't; although he came to the United States for the Theatre Union's production of *The Mother* in the fall of 1935, there was no record of any such visit to Los Angeles, as the FBI later found out, and he evidently remained in New York until his departure for Europe on December 29, 1935. It is stated in one report from Los Angeles that *The Threepenny Opera* had at that time (1952) never been produced on the stage in the United States; the truth was it had been done in New York as early as 1933. As if these were not bad enough, it is more than a little disturbing to find the FBI reports filled out with excerpts from *Twentieth Century Authors*; Eric Bentley's introduction to the New Directions edition of *The Private Life of the Master Race; The New York Times* morgue (which then evidently allowed the Bureau access); a number of reviews reproduced in toto from *The New York Times Book Review, The Daily Worker, The New Leader,* and a magazine of uncertain parentage known as *Top Secret;* and, most dismaying of all, an item from a Walter Winchell column.

Although there is no indication from the part of the file made available to the public that the FBI had a phone tap on Brecht, we have direct evidence that mail from him and those around him was being turned over to the Bureau. Here, for instance, is an excerpt from a report dated January 8, 1948 (after he had departed America and was living in Switzerland):

> On November 20, 1947, a copy sent by [name deleted, but certainly Ruth Berlau] to [name deleted] a film producer whose offices are located at [address deleted] was furnished by [name

---

* The myth was perpetuated and filled out in detail in subsequent reports; for example: "BRECHT is supposed to have escaped from a concentration camp in Germany disguised as a woman."

deleted]. From the content of this document it was apparently true that [Berlau] and BRECHT had been negotiating for months relative to the Galileo contract. [Berlau] was extremely up set [*sic*] that the contract had not yet been signed because she stated that she did not have any money and as a result was trying to sell her furniture, "my apartment, and everything." [Berlau] went on to say that BRECHT was writing to her from Paris, that he had often told [Berlau] how important it was for [Berlau] to get away and that [name deleted] should have money ready for her. [Berlau] implored [name deleted] to send her the promised $3,000.00 and stated that she had received BRECHT's power of attorney and could then sign the contract as soon as she received it.

That Brecht was of interest to the FBI at all after he had left the country is curious. Regular reports were issued on him from Los Angeles until 1952.

One item from a report of June 30, 1945, is of interest if only for gossip value and speculation. It tells of a meeting between Brecht and Billy Wilder at a gathering for the latter when he was selected by the Office of War Information "to handle American motion pictures in Germany after the war." According to the FBI's informant, the event was staged "principally so that BRECHT might talk to WILDER." Why did Brecht want his ear? "Brecht discussed with WILDER the names of various individuals in Germany affiliated with the stage and movie industry. BRECHT referred to these individuals as 'reliable' persons." This is interesting on a couple of counts. First of all, Wilder told me in an interview that he knew Brecht hardly at all and that he had met him "only at a couple of parties." (Well, this may have been one of the parties, and he may have attached no importance to the meeting, though the FBI certainly did.) Secondly, it was Wilder who wisecracked, "Of the unfriendly nineteen, only two are talented, the rest are just unfriendly." Did he consider Brecht one of the talented?

One of the areas of the FBI's keenest interest in Brecht was his activity in various émigré organizations. The Council for a Democratic Germany included, says the FBI file on Brecht, "the most important German anti-Fascist figures from the 'Catholic Center' to the 'far left' "—including, of course, Bertolt Brecht. Although he did his best to push this group to the Left, the only real conflict he had with them was in protesting the Allied demand for the unconditional surrender of Germany (he broke completely with Thomas Mann on this point), which he felt, as others also did, would prolong the war needlessly and result in the death of thousands on both sides.

Of far more interest was his supposed involvement with the Free German Movement, which was headquartered in Mexico City. Because the Mexican government was at least nominally revolutionary in its sympathies, it had admitted many confirmed Communists, including the writer Anna Seghers, the Comintern veteran Gerhard Eisler, and Spanish Civil War veterans of the Ernst Thälmann Brigade such as Gustav Regler (who later became an active anti-Communist) and Bodo Uhse. There is no mention of it in either the FBI documents I have seen or in Brecht's *Work Journal,* but he almost certainly had direct contact with Gerhard Eisler during his years in Hollywood. On at least one occasion Eisler came to visit his brother, the composer Hanns, who was a close associate of Brecht's, and he would certainly have been brought around to meet with Brecht. It seemed to be suspected that this hard-core group was, in effect, a German Communist government in exile and if Brecht was associated with the Free German Movement, then he, too, was slated for a political post of some kind in postwar Germany. In spite of his repeated denials that he was connected with the Movement to various FBI informants (he also declared, says the FBI report, that "he had no desire to obtain any governmental position in Germany after the war; all he wanted to do was to return to his work in Germany"), Brecht was nevertheless considered one with Gerhard Eisler and company.

Why? Except for the appearance of some of his work in the Free German Movement's magazine, *Freies Deutschland,* there was no evident reason to link him with them. The Bureau must have had some especially trusted source that indicated a close, perhaps clandestine, contact with the group. While it is generally useless to conjecture on the identities of the FBI's informants—in one long report on Brecht dated October 2, 1944, the sources number up to forty— it seems likely that one of them was Ruth Fischer. She was the sister of Gerhard and Hanns Eisler and a strident anti-Communist by the time she came to the United States. Yet she had sources in the Party—could one of them have been Gustav Regler?—and she kept close watch on the activities of her two estranged brothers all during the war and after. In her book, *Stalin and German Communism,* Ruth Fischer denounced Brecht as "the paid minstrel of the GPU," and, out of all proportion, devoted a whole chapter to him as the foremost apologist for Stalinism among German writers. To buttress her case, she cites Brecht's play *The Measures Taken* and certain poems that were synopsized and translated in the FBI reports and with which Brecht was subsequently confronted by the House Committee on Un-American Activities.

• • •

The FBI file on Brecht that has been made available to the public is notoriously incomplete. What is most interesting, however, is that there is a whole year missing. That year is 1947, the one in which Bertolt Brecht made his appearance in Washington before the HCUA. The nineteen who had received summonses knew, or at least strongly suspected, that they had long had the attention of government investigators. Those among them who were Communists were known to be Communists because the secretary of the Party in Los Angeles was a secret FBI informer. Since they had all been subpoenaed together and had already been labeled "unfriendly" by the press, they decided to pool their resources and plan their legal strategy together. A whole team of lawyers—eventually six in all—that included a former attorney general of the State of California, Robert Kenny, was put together to serve the nineteen. The plan they worked out was an extremely bold, not to say foolhardy, one. It was decided among them that they would volunteer to read prepared statements—and read them, if permitted—but that they would refuse to answer all questions put to them by the Committee. The grounds on which they would refuse would *not* be the customary Fifth Amendment to the Constitution (that to answer might tend to incriminate the witness), but rather the First (that the witness's right to free speech also included his right to keep silent). They guessed—quite rightly, as it turned out—that this would bring them all contempt citations but that such a case could be appealed up to the Supreme Court, and in that court, as it was then constituted (with the balance of liberal justices in their favor), they would win the case and set an important precedent. Only Bertolt Brecht held back from this position and plan. Because he was not an American citizen and had by that time made firm plans to leave for Europe as soon as he had testified before the Committee, he was afraid that a refusal to cooperate might lead to the revocation of the permit he had just received to travel to Switzerland. And so with appropriate expressions of regret, he declined to stand with the rest. They were sympathetic and allowed him to continue to share legal counsel with them; his was clearly a special case.

It should not be supposed that at least in the beginning the cause of the "unfriendly nineteen" was an unpopular one in Hollywood. Far from it. There were meetings; rallies were held; collections were organized. The attitude first taken by the movie industry when threatened by this attack by Congress was one of aggressive defense, almost defiance. Even some of the studio heads—Louis B. Mayer and Sam Goldwyn, for instance—felt that if there was any housecleaning to be done, then it was up to the industry to do it; the government should keep its nose out of their business. Of course there was and always had been a strong right-wing element in Hollywood. This was the faction that provided the House Committee on Un-American Activities with its "friendly" witnesses—among them one studio head, Jack Warner.

As it turned out, there was no difficulty in putting together a star-spangled deputation that far outshone the right-wing group that had been invited to testify before Congress. It represented an ad hoc organization called the Committee for the First Amendment and included such celebrities as Humphrey Bogart and Lauren Bacall, Danny Kaye, Gene Kelly, John Huston, and Sterling Hayden. They preceded the nineteen to Washington and, as the "friendlies" made their appearances in the Caucus Room bemoaning the nearly complete Communist takeover of Hollywood before the HCUA, the First Amendment supporters held press conferences in the halls outside, denouncing and disputing the testimony before the Committee. This went on until the first of the nineteen subpoenaed witnesses, John Howard Lawson, was called to testify on October 27, 1947. Although not openly a Communist, Lawson was in fact the senior Party member in the movie industry. If there was a Communist boss of Hollywood, it was John Howard Lawson. When he took the witness chair, he proved to be unruly and argumentative. Once he was denied the right to read the statement he had prepared, he began railing at the

Committee and its counsel Robert Stripling, yelling out his demand that he be allowed to enter the statement in the record. Questions were put to him. He ignored them, continuing to shout that his rights were being violated. In the end, when asked if he was a member of the Communist Party, he refused to answer altogether. It was quite a performance. All in all, it shocked and appalled the Hollywood liberals who had trekked across the country to give their support. They began drifting away until by the next day they were nowhere to be found.

On October 28, 1947, the next of the "unfriendlies," Dalton Trumbo, came before the Committee. He was nearly as uncooperative as Lawson had been, although not as loud or rude. He also argued his right to read his prepared statement but had it denied him. But when Stripling demanded that he answer questions with a simple yes or no, he declared, "I shall answer in my own words. Very many questions can be answered 'Yes' or 'No' only by a moron or a slave."[2] Trumbo won his point, and he did try to cooperate in his own way. It was just that the Committee wanted none of his explanations and fewer of his criticisms. In the end, he was forcibly led away from the witness chair as he shouted:

MR. TRUMBO: This is the beginning—
THE CHAIRMAN (pounding gavel): Just a minute—
MR. TRUMBO: Of an American concentration camp.
THE CHAIRMAN: This is typical Communists' tactics.[3]

Dalton Trumbo was immediately cited for contempt of Congress, as John Howard Lawson had been before him.

During the rest of that day and the two that followed, the subpoenaed "unfriendly" witnesses were brought before the Committee. Although there were differences in the treatment given some—a few of the more docile were allowed to enter their prepared statements into the *Congressional Record*, but none was permitted to read his aloud—the result was in the end the same: they refused to answer the Committee's questions, some of them specifically citing the First Amendment; and each in turn was noted "in contempt of the House of Representatives of the United States." Ring Lardner, Jr., did manage somehow to interrupt the routine with a bit of mordant humor.

When he was asked repeatedly by the Committee chairman J. Parnell Thomas if he was a Communist, he at last replied, "I could answer, but if I did, I would hate myself in the morning."[4] The rest of the ten came and went in fairly rapid order. In all, with screenwriter Lester Cole last on the list, there were ten* called before Bertolt Brecht was summoned on October 30.

He was the eleventh. Looking awkward in an ill-fitting suit that he seldom wore, Brecht took the oath, swearing to tell the truth, the whole truth, and nothing but the truth, so help him God (whatever that could have meant to a confirmed atheist). He took the witness chair and rather tensely dealt with a series of questions by Committee counsel Robert Stripling concerning details of his birth and his immigration to the United States. Stripling touched briefly on Brecht's American film career, asking him about *Hangmen Also Die.* Brecht deviated slightly from the truth, saying that it had been written "maybe around '43 or '44. I don't remember quite."[5] It was actually written in 1942, as he must certainly have remembered. Why he chose to hedge on this point one can only guess.

It was then, however, that counsel Stripling settled down to the business at hand:

MR. STRIPLING: Mr. Brecht, are you a member of the Communist Party or have you ever been a member of the Communist Party?

MR. BRECHT: May I read my statement? I will answer this question but may I read my statement?

MR. STRIPLING: Would you submit your statement to the chairman?

MR. BRECHT: Yes.

THE CHAIRMAN: All right, let's see the statement. (Mr. Brecht hands the statement to the chairman.)

THE CHAIRMAN: Mr. Brecht, the Committee has carefully gone over the statement. It is a very interesting story of German life but it is not at all pertinent to this inquiry. Therefore we do not care to have you read this statement.[6]

---

* They became the famous Hollywood Ten. They were Alvah Bessie, Herbert Biberman, Lester Cole, Edward Dmytryk, Ring Lardner, Jr., John Howard Lawson, Albert Maltz, Samuel Ornitz, Adrian Scott, and Dalton Trumbo. All eventually went to jail for contempt of Congress.

Stripling, after making the point that Brecht was appearing before them in answer to a subpoena, returned to his original question:

MR. STRIPLING: . . . Are you now or have you ever been a member of the Communist Party of any country?

MR. BRECHT: Mr. Chairman, I have heard my colleagues when they considered this question not as proper, but I am a guest in this country and do not want to enter into any legal arguments, so I will answer your question as well as I can.

I was not a member or am not a member of any Communist Party.[7]

After getting him to repeat this a couple of times, and then underscoring his association with Hanns Eisler, Stripling launched into a dialogue with Brecht on certain of the latter's works, a dialogue for which he, Stripling, was certainly ill-prepared. First he took up *The Measures Taken*, and, reading directly from a summary of the work given in an FBI report, he then put his finger accurately on the point made in the plot by the death of the young revolutionary at the end of the play:

MR. STRIPLING: Because he would not bow to discipline he was murdered by his comrades, isn't that true?

MR. BRECHT: No; it is not really in it. You will find when you read it carefully, like in the old Japanese play where other ideas were at stake, this young man who died was convinced that he had done damage to the mission be believed in and he agreed to that and he was about ready to die in order not to make greater damage. So, he asks his comrades to help him to die. He jumps into an abyss, and that is the story.[8]

This was pure double-talk, but Stripling had not sufficient knowledge of the play or of any of Brecht's other works to challenge him on this rather outlandish interpretation by the author. All he knew about *The Measures Taken* was what the FBI had told him.

Undiscouraged, Stripling went on to other works by Brecht—two songs, "In Praise of Learning" and "Forward, We've Not Forgotten," which were published in translation in the American Communist Party magazine *New Masses*. In both instances Brecht pleaded that he had been mistranslated, even getting the interpreter supplied by the Committee—a Mr. Baumgardt—to side with him on the specific meaning of certain key phrases. The entire nature of this phase of the questioning is well characterized by this frequently quoted exchange between Stripling and Brecht:

MR. STRIPLING: . . . . Did you write that, Mr. Brecht?

MR. BRECHT: No. I wrote a German poem, but that is very different from this. [Laughter.][9]

But once more the Committee counsel hit hard at Brecht's involvement with the Communist Party in Germany. After all, some of the FBI's informants had given it as a certainty that he was a Party member from about 1930 when he wrote *The Measures Taken*.

MR. STRIPLING: Mr. Brecht, did you ever make application to join the Communist Party?

MR. BRECHT: I do not understand the question. Did I make—

MR. STRIPLING: Have you ever made application to join the Communist Party?

MR. BRECHT: No, no, no, no, no, never.

MR. STRIPLING: Mr. Chairman, we have here—

MR. BRECHT: I was an independent writer and wanted to be an independent writer and I point that out and also theoretically, I think, it was best for me not to join any party whatever. And all these things you read here were also written for workers of any other kind; Social Democrat workers were in these performances; so were Catholic workers from Catholic unions, so were workers which never had been in a party or didn't want to go into a party.

THE CHAIRMAN: Mr. Brecht, did Gerhart [*sic*] Eisler ever ask you to join the Communist Party?

MR. BRECHT: No, no.

THE CHAIRMAN: Did Hanns Eisler ever ask you to join the Communist Party?

MR. BRECHT: No; he did not. I think they considered me just as a writer who wanted to write and as he saw it, but not as a political figure.[10]

The stress laid here on Gerhard and Hanns Eisler suggests, to me at least, that their estranged sister, the renegade Communist Ruth Fischer, was lurking somewhere in the background.

With this exchange, Chairman J. Parnell Thomas (who would later go to prison himself for payroll padding) seemed oddly to take Brecht under his wing. He even went so far to remark, evidently to Stripling, "He is doing all right. He is doing much better than many other witnesses you have brought here."[11] When Stripling then tried to bring the witness back to one of the songs he had written that had been published in *New Masses*, Thomas cut him short. He dismissed Brecht very politely: "Thank you very much, Mr. Brecht. You are a good example to the witnesses of Mr. Kenny and Mr. Crum."[12] (These were two of the attorneys representing the subpoenaed witnesses.)

We never do find out from the testimony, or indeed anywhere else, just what Robert Stripling meant when he said, "Mr. Chairman, we have here—" He had used a similar phrase when he introduced into evidence Dalton Trumbo's alleged "Communist Party Registration Card" made out to "Dalt T." That he had such "proof" of Brecht's membership in the Communist Party seems doubtful on a couple of counts: first, if it had been a document dating from the pre-Hitler period, it is unlikely that it would have survived the war; second, it is even more unlikely that Stripling could have come up with proof of Brecht's membership in CPUSA, for while Brecht was in this country he laid low politically and had contact with very few American Communists—notably only with John Howard Lawson.

Then, too, if the Committee and, presumably, the FBI had had such evidence, they would surely have made it public sometime after the hearings; at the very least it would have been included in that part of Brecht's FBI file that has been allowed out under the Freedom of Information Act.

It has become a tradition among Brecht scholars and biographers that their man made monkeys of the Committee. According to them, he was in command throughout, double-talking and obfuscating his way through his testimony, leading them by the nose precisely to the conclusions he wished them to draw. This, I believe, is far too flattering to Brecht. First of all, he was worried (for good reason, as it turned out) that the Committee would block his exit from the United States. He was, after all, under great pressure—an alien appearing before a Committee of Congress, he must have felt at their mercy, as indeed he was. And his testimony bears this out. He seems scared. Going from the *Congressional Record* to the taped transcription of his appearance (which is available from Pacifica Broadcasting), one is immediately aware from the tension in his voice and the frequent repetitions ("No, no, no, no, no, never") that he was nervous and apprehensive throughout. If he denied often and with great vehemence that he himself had ever been a member of the Communist Party, he was sufficiently rattled that he did give implicit confirmation in the exchange already quoted between himself and Chairman Thomas that both Gerhard and Hanns Eisler were Communists.

Was Brecht in command? Certainly not. Did he lead the Committee by its collective nose? Of course he didn't. When he came away from the witness chair he must have been quaking inside. For if he had managed to lie successfully to Stripling, Thomas, and company—that is, if at some time in his life he actually *had* been a member of the Communist Party—then Brecht would have been under considerable strain, wondering what the Committee had on him, whether it could be proven, and how the Government would deal with him if his lie were exposed. If, on the other hand, he had told the truth and had really never officially joined the Party, then he must have felt some sense of betrayal, of embarrassment at having denied something in which he believed, for from about 1929 or 1930 onward he had unfailingly behaved and written as though he *were* a Party member and not the liberal fellow traveler that he presented himself to the Committee to be.

In any case, he was emotionally spent by the time he left the Capitol. We have this on the authority of Lester Cole, one of the Hollywood Ten, who told me in an interview: "I was the tenth witness called up, and Brecht was the eleventh. I stayed through his testimony, and we drove back together to the hotel in a cab. Naturally we talked about the ordeal we had just been through, and he was in tears because, as he said, he had wanted to take the same position as the rest of us had and refuse to answer the Committee's questions. But he thought there was nothing he could do but cooperate with the

Committee and answer questions. But still, he felt he had betrayed us by taking a different position. He didn't want to stay in this country another minute."[13]

. • .

And indeed he didn't stay long. Brecht left that very afternoon by auto for New York and arrived that evening. The next day, October 31, he flew from New York to Paris. His account of his experience as a Congressional witness, perhaps written the next day on the plane, appears in his *Work Journal* under the date October 30, 1947. It is the only mention he makes of these events—nothing of receiving the subpoena and nothing of his intention to cooperate with the Committee—and in this entry he simply narrates his experience and gives no summary of the episode. Since this is Brecht's version of what happened, it is worth quoting in full:

Morning in Washington before the Un-American Activities Committee. According to two Hollywood writers (Lester Cole and Ring Lardner, Jr.) the question of whether they belonged to the Communist Party, only insofar as it had to be answered, as they said, may be unconstitutional. I was called to the witness stand followed by the lawyers for the 19, Bob Kenny and Bartley C. Crum, who in any case were not allowed to interfere. Approximately 80 representatives of the press, two radio stations, cameramen, and photographers [were there], along with theater people from Broadway as friendly observers. In agreement with the 18 and the lawyers, I answered the question, and indeed truthfully, with "no." The prosecutor Stripling recites a lot of *Measures Taken* and allows me to tell about the fable. I refer to the Japanese model and understate the idea of the substance and contradict the interpretation that it concerns a disciplinary murder with justification, [declaring that] it concerns a self-sacrifice. I testify that the foundation of the piece is Marxist and ascertain that works, especially those with historic contexts, cannot be written intelligently otherwise. The hearing is unfailingly polite and ends without accusation; it is to my advantage that I had practically nothing to do with Hollywood, that I never mixed in American politics, and that my predecessors on the witness stand had refused to reply to the

Congressmen. The 18 are very satisfied with my testimony, and also the lawyers. I leave Washington with Losey and Hambleton who had come along. In the evening I listen with Helli and the Budzislawskis to a part of my hearing.[14]

Losey was, of course, Joseph Losey, who directed the Brecht-Laughton production of *Galileo*; Hambleton was T. Edward Hambleton, who coproduced it. In New York Brecht and Helene Weigel stayed with the émigré German journalist Hermann Budzislawski and his wife.

There is nothing more to tell here, except to note an obscure item from an FBI report dated January 8, 1948, less than three months after Brecht's departure for Europe:

> [*Name and affiliation deleted*] advised that BRECHT had left New York City bound for Paris, France, on October 31, 1947, via AIR FRANCE AIRLINES and that a customs stop had been placed by New York City for the subject's return.

And so we see that it was not at all intended that Brecht be permitted to leave the country so easily. He simply slipped through due to the oversight of some customs official. Perhaps the House Committee on Un-American Activities intended to bring him back to testify again. Perhaps HCUA counsel Robert Stripling wished to finish that sentence: "Mr. Chairman, we have here—"

11

THE RETURN
OF THE EXILE

On October 31, 1947, the day after his appearance before the House Committee on Un-American Activities, Bertolt Brecht left America and flew to Europe after more than six years here. It was all planned out in advance, of course. He had had no real intention of returning to California; his house there had been sold; his manuscripts had been packed and were with him; he was ready to move again. In a sense, Brecht had gotten all he wanted, or even hoped for, out of America. It had provided him, his family, and his mistress with sanctuary during most of the war. He had been able to earn enough money from the movie industry and other sources to support himself and those who depended on him. He had even realized—or was about to realize—his express ambition to get a play on Broadway: the Laughton *Galileo* was already in rehearsal in New York for its December opening when Brecht passed through on his way to the airport. Laughton expressed his relief that Brecht's appearance before the Committee had brought no headlines (even so, the production closed after three weeks). The playwright was ready to try Europe again—even a Europe that had been in large part reduced to rubble—for it was there, and now only there, that he saw his future.

Brecht flew to Paris. He landed at Le Bourget, intending to push on immediately to Zurich, his ultimate destination. But there at the airport he met the American screenwriter Donald Ogden Stewart with his wife, Ella Winter. They urged him to stay a few days, and since he had heard that the German novelist Anna Seghers would soon be coming to the French capital from Berlin, he decided to do just that. Paris he described in his *Work Journal* on November 1, 1947, as "shabby, impoverished, one big black market."[1] Still, when he was invited out by the Stewarts to a "fabulous meal," he ate the black-market food without apparent qualms.

Anna Seghers had spent the war in Mexico. Her novels *The Fisherman's Revolt in Santa Barbara* and *The Seventh Cross* were among the strongest anti-Fascist statements in fiction by any German writer. She returned to Berlin in order to be part of the building of the "new Germany." But in spite of her Marxist sympathies, she chose prudently to live initially in the British sector. Brecht wanted a firsthand report on the situation there. What he heard from her— she called the city a "witches' sabbath" of spying and political maneuvering[2]—was enough to discourage him from moving on quickly to Berlin. Besides, as his biographer Klaus Völker put it, "Brecht wanted to go to Berlin as a claimant, not as a suppliant."[3] Brecht wanted a theater, and he knew his best chance for getting one was in the East Zone, but he did not want to sacrifice his chances of getting produced in the West. He saw that for now his best chance for maintaining his guise as an independent Marxist lay in first establishing himself outside Germany. And so he proceeded with his original plan and headed for Zurich.

Why Zurich? Because even while in exile he had managed to maintain considerable standing in the German theater there. In fact, three of his plays—*Galileo, Mother Courage and Her Children,* and *The Good Woman of Setzuan*—had their world premieres there. Munich actress Therese Giehse, who had emigrated to Switzerland during the Nazi period, appeared in the latter two of the three productions, playing the title role in *Mother Courage*. At that time Giehse was considered one of the foremost interpreters of Brecht — although from reports he had received he had already decided she must have been far too emotional in her performances. His wife, Helene Weigel, who had gone on with their daughter, Barbara, would be joining Brecht in Zurich, and he was determined to make her his interpreter, for she was schooled in his techniques. With regard to the theater, at least, she was his creature.

That being the case, it is curious that in preparing the way for her in Zurich he tried hard to find accommodations for himself apart from his wife and daughter. He may have had in mind arranging a place for him to live with his mistress, Ruth Berlau, who had stayed on in New York to prepare a photographic record of the New York production of *Galileo*. However, he found nothing suitable, and when Weigel and Barbara came, the three of them moved into a studio that had been lent to him by the dramaturge of the Zurich Schauspielhaus. When Berlau came she was left, as usual, to shift for herself; Brecht's final loyalty was always to Weigel. Less than three weeks after his arrival, he had agreed to prepare an adaptation of *Antigone* for the Stadttheater in Chur, and he had negotiated the title role for his wife.

Of all the records of Brecht's stay in Zurich, by far the most interesting is that of Max Frisch, the playwright and novelist. At the time they met — only days after Brecht's arrival — Frisch was still an architect, then just beginning to try his hand in the theater. Frisch found Brecht a little difficult to talk to: "Brecht looks for discussion everywhere. I myself get least from our conversations when Brecht checkmates me with his arguments: one feels beaten, but not convinced. Going home through the night, reflecting on his comments, I find myself not infrequently immersed in a reluctant monologue."[4] Then, later: "Ideological discussions, unavoidable in the early days, became less and less and less frequent: not because of my objections, but because I was not expert enough for him, and Brecht had better things to do than teach me."[5]

But Frisch discovered that Brecht was always willing to play the student. He took Brecht around the construction site of one of the buildings he had designed and found the playwright was delighted to learn how problems were solved and things were done: "Technical know-how, especially when seen in practice, filled him with respect."

Although obviously uneasy up on the scaffolding, Brecht went up with him to the observation platform, then came down and pronounced his blessing. "You have a good honest profession," he told Frisch.[6]

Such anecdotes aside, Frisch, as the sure artist he became, is at his best in describing Brecht, the man. First, physically:

> He was wearing his convict's face again: little beady bird's eyes sticking out from a flat face above a too-bare neck. A frightening face, perhaps even off-putting if you didn't know him already. . . . A prisoner with a cigar. One felt like giving him a muffler for his neck. Hardly any lips. He was washed, but unshaven. No *clochard*, no Villon. Simply gray. His haircut at such times looked like a treatment for lice or an attempt to humiliate him. His walk lacked shoulders. His head was too small.[7]

And then his manner:

> Certainly warmheartedness was by no means the prime characteristic of this man who did not like giving raw material, and feelings are raw material. Nor in his presence could one display warmth: his habit of using the same vocabulary to express toleration or respect or affection in his personal relations gave him an almost judgelike air. His gestures (I am always coming back to his gestures, though they were never flamboyant, but at times almost automatic and stereotyped) conveyed above all a sense of parody—and how many things there were to be parodied! Brecht must have been conscious of a sentimental streak in his nature, and anything that showed the slightest tendency in this direction he clamped down on. . . . Familiarity he shot down at once, when necessary with considerable harshness. It clearly made him uncomfortable.[8]

With such an individual it would obviously have been difficult to maintain any sort of normal give-and-take relationship—yet Frisch managed one as long as Brecht was in Switzerland. He was helpful and supportive. He attended one of the matinee-only performances of Brecht's *Antigone*—hardly more than a workshop production— and was at the Zurich premiere of *Herr Puntila and His Man Matti,* which was not very well received. (Brecht himself directed both productions, although without credit because he had no Swiss work permit.) The playwright shrugged off the relative failure of both productions, commenting to Frisch: "One must put on plays like this over and over again until people get accustomed to them . . . as they've grown accustomed to Schiller. That will take some years."⁹ However, Max Frisch found that when Brecht moved on to Berlin, and as Frisch himself gradually achieved some degree of fame as a writer, the friendship, such as it was, gradually withered.

Brecht traveled first to Berlin by way of Prague on October 30, 1948, precisely one year after he had appeared before the House Committee on Un-American Activities. He had failed to establish himself either on Broadway with *Galileo* or even in Zurich, as he had hoped to do. The bait that brought him back to Berlin, however, was a promised production of *Mother Courage and Her Children* at the Deutsches Theater in the Russian sector, which he was to direct and which was to feature Helene Weigel in the title role. Upon his arrival, he wandered through all four sections of the divided city, remarking in his *Work Journal* on the "gray color of the faces" of the people there, listening to the "drone in the night of the freight planes of the airlift," and noting that, "On the Berlin blockade question one is clearly on the defensive."¹⁰ It was a strange time to be in the city. Coming when he did, he was given a front seat to the first battle of the Cold War. And as he readied his production, he found himself in the midst of a battle of another sort: the culture arbiters of the Soviet Union had launched their attack on formalism. Brecht, of course, with his theories on Epic Theater, was at least potentially a prime target. He ruminated on the problem, and on his play's likely reception under the circumstances, as rehearsals on it proceeded.

As it happened, things went quite well. Brecht was proud of Weigel's performance: "Helli's interpretation of Courage beautiful, of great daring."¹¹ The selected audiences of students and workers who saw the production responded to it warmly. It looked as though the two of them were well established there in the Soviet sector of Berlin. In fact, on January 6, 1949, only days before the production opened, Brecht and Weigel had sat down with the mayor of East Berlin and officials of the city's operating theaters to discuss the possibility of providing them with rehearsal facilities and theater for a permanent company. He came out of these discussions, which were to lead to the founding of the Berliner Ensemble, with an agreement in principle and many details to be ironed out. These he left to Helene Weigel and went back to Zurich with Ruth Berlau—ostensibly to recruit talent for the new company.

Even before arriving there, he got news that he must have taken as an omen of censorship difficulties to come. He was to have had an edition of his poems from exile published in East Berlin by Aufbau, a state-owned publisher; but once the galleys of the new collection were seen by officials of the crypto-Communist government, many of the poems were judged unacceptable either politically or because they showed evidence of "formalism." Brecht learned in Zurich that the entire edition had been dropped. The evaluation was probably that of Johannes R. Becher, the onetime poet who was to become Minister of Culture in the government of the German Democratic Republic. Yet the final decision to withdraw the book must have rested with Walter Ulbricht himself, the secretary of the East German Communist Party.

While in Zurich Brecht made certain cautionary "preparations" for his return to the East. He had been asked to do a play for the Salzburg Festival and indicated his willingness, planning a kind of Marxist version of *Everyman*, which he was calling *The Salzburg Dance of Death*. However, in lieu of immediate payment, he requested Austrian passports for himself, Weigel, and their daughter, Barbara. The passports were issued, as he requested, without publicity. Not long after he got them, he dropped the Salzburg project.

It may also have been on that trip to Zurich that Brecht opened a numbered account at one of the many banks there. Even in his lifetime he was persistently rumored to have one. Why would he have needed such a "secret" account? He had made arrangements very early on with Peter Suhrkamp to have the West German publisher look after rights and permissions to his plays and literary works. Suhrkamp had written to Brecht in California immediately after the war—his was, in fact, the first letter to reach the playwright from Germany in 1945—offering to serve as his German-language publisher, and specifically to resume the *Versuche* ("Experiments") series of new works in gray-paper format. Brecht was personally in his debt: he had been hidden by Suhrkamp during the roundup of Leftists that followed the burning of the Reichstag. He gladly gave permission, happy to have a publisher in Germany once again. Suhrkamp may at times later have come to consider this association less a blessing than a curse, for he soon found that since leaving Germany in 1933, Brecht had made similar arrangements with other firms— two exile houses and another in Switzerland. It took years to untangle rights and establish Suhrkamp's control over Brecht's work, and, as it turned out, that control was never total. One of his publishers in exile, Wieland Herzfelde, sold out to Aufbau in East Germany (thus the planned edition of Brecht's poems that was killed in galleys by the political authorities), and Brecht decided, finally, that he wished Suhrkamp to oversee permissions only in *West* Germany, Austria, and the German-speaking portion of Switzerland, as well as translations and performances throughout the political West. But these, of course, were to prove essential. Suhrkamp gave him a direct connection to the West. As long as he had it, Brecht would never be totally under the domination of the East German authorities.

When at last Brecht did return to East Berlin in June 1949, he had an Austrian passport, a publishing contract with the West, and very likely a Swiss bank account into which royalties might be paid. If he was planning the establishment of a theater company, he was also making preparations for an easy exit from the Soviet sector if and when those plans should go awry. When he arrived in East Berlin with commitments from Therese Giehse and other luminaries of the Zurich stage, he found that Weigel had done her part and more in arranging things for the new company. The Berliner Ensemble was, in fact, a reality by that summer. Organized in large part by Weigel, who served until her death as executive head, the company was headquartered at the old Theater am Schiffbauerdamm, where Brecht had enjoyed his greatest triumph with *The Threepenny Opera* in 1928. Rehearsals began. Inevitably, they became classes in Brecht's methods of Epic Theater acting and production, for he was not only determined to do his plays but also to do them *his* way. The first season of the Berliner Ensemble opened November 12, 1949, with *Herr Puntila and His Man Matti*; it was followed at last by his adaptation of the old Lenz classic *Der Hofmeister* in April 1950. With only two attractions, it was a thin year at best, but one that met with great popular and (initially) great critical success there in the East. At least as an artistic entity, the Ensemble was very firmly established.

Politically, however, the continued life of the company was anything but certain. Although in its first year the Berliner Ensemble became a cultural showpiece of the East German regime, Brecht had enough enemies in the German Democratic Republic and even in Russia to assure that whatever gains were made on the stage would have to be rigorously defended in the conference room. As the Cold War heated up, Brecht and Weigel found themselves suspect simply for having spent most of World War II in America—never mind that he had been hauled before the House Committee on Un-American Activities and had immediately left the country fearing further persecution. Brecht, who had formulated his Epic Theater methods in direct opposition to the Stanislavski approach (which was the official Communist theater aesthetic), was wide open to attack by the culture commissars for his putative formalism. The growing popularity of his plays in the West was held by his enemies as proof that he was both aesthetically in error and politically unreliable. While the Berliner Ensemble productions were popular in East Germany, they were not emulated in any of the Soviet-bloc countries; and although Brecht himself was officially honored in the socialist camp (he was awarded the Stalin Peace Prize in 1955), he had little influence as a writer and less as a theoretician of the drama.

Brecht did have some political misgivings. Although he had fought hard for his favored position, he was a little uncomfortable in it, even at the start. Also the practical and human problems inherent in the forging of a socialist state caused him some personal difficulties. Some of these misgivings and difficulties found expression in poems written by him during these last years. One poem especially, entitled "Changing the Wheel," was widely accepted by his friends in the West as clear evidence of Brecht's uneasiness with socialism in the German Democratic Republic:

> I sit by the roadside
> The driver changes the wheel.
> I do not like the place I have come from.
> I do not like the place I am going to
> Why with impatience do I
> Watch him changing the wheel?[12]

The poem, dated 1953, was one of a number published in a memorial issue of *Sinn und Form*, the East German literary magazine, in 1957, one year after the playwright's death. It certainly indicates an attitude of moral discomfort—perhaps more than that. But by the time it appeared in print, Brecht's political reputation had been so blackened in the West that admirers of his, such as Martin Esslin, seized upon it to "prove" his disaffection from the GDR's Communist regime.

At issue was Brecht's response to the East German workers' uprising that took place on June 17, 1953. Rising prices and increased government work demands led to protests in East Berlin and other cities in the GDR—protests that exploded into angry riots. The government sent out the paramilitary Volkspolizei to put down the disturbances, and the Russians supplied tanks. The lid was back on in a day's time, though not without a few deaths, some property damage, and considerable embarrassment to the Communist government. Only days afterward the official Party newspaper, *Neues Deutschland,* printed a direct and simple declaration of loyalty from Brecht to Walter Ulbricht, head of the East German Communist Party (S.E.D.): "I feel it necessary at this moment to write to you and express my association with the S.E.D. Yours, Bertolt Brecht." The statement caused such consternation in West Germany, where feelings ran strong in support of the workers, that theaters there joined in a general ban of his plays that lasted until his death.

In 1959, however, Martin Esslin published two provocative articles in the magazine *Encounter* in which he sought to rehabilitate the playwright's political reputation. In one of them Esslin presented the poem already quoted and some others that he suggested expressed dissatisfaction with the regime. But in the other article Esslin went so far as to declare that "it is now possible to state with absolute certainty" that Brecht's loyalty statement to Ulbricht "was in fact *the last sentence of a long and critical letter* to Ulbricht, which the latter had suppressed." Esslin also quoted a short poem, entitled "The Solution," which he said had been written by Brecht and was privately circulated by him:

> After the uprising of the 17th June
> The Secretary of the Writers' Union
> Had leaflets distributed in the Stalinallee
> Stating that the people
> Had forfeited the confidence of the government
> And could win it back only

By redoubled efforts. Would it not be easier
In that case for the government
To dissolve the people
And elect another?[13]

Unmistakably Brechtian in style and tone, this poem actually
appeared in the 1964 collected edition of his poems in *both* East and
West—which was less a sign of how the GDR had grown more liberal
in the decade following the workers' uprising than of the advantage
to any Communist-bloc writer of having a Western publisher admin-
ister his copyrights. As for Esslin's claim that Brecht's statement of
loyalty to Ulbricht was simply the final, positive note in a long, negative letter, this has been generally supported by other writers—
although, to my knowledge, the complete letter has never seen print.

Yes, Brecht did have his difficulties. They were not, however, so
great that he was seriously tempted to pick up and leave East Germany and his Berliner Ensemble behind; as they say in the Catholic
Church, a thousand difficulties don't make a doubt. Although there
is no entry in Brecht's *Work Journal* for two months after June 17,
1953 (if not an indication of censorship then certainly of self-censor-
ship), the first one following the event, August 20, 1953, does deal
at length with his response. "The 17th of June has alienated my
entire existence," he begins. "In all its directionlessness and miser-
able helplessness the demonstrations show over and over again that
here the rising class is not the acting middle class, but rather the
workers." He goes on with a rather farfetched class analysis of the
worker's revolt:

It all hinges on fully exploiting this first encounter [between
the workers and the government]. That was the contact. It
came not in the form of an embrace but rather in the form of
a blow of the fist. —The Party should take alarm but not
despair. Considering the complete historical background, it
couldn't hope for the spontaneous assent of the working
class. . . . But now, by way of a most unfavorable circumstance
came the great opportunity to win the workers. For this reason,
I found the alarms of the 17th of June to be not simply
negative.[14]

From this it would not be unfair to conclude that no matter how critical that long letter to Ulbricht was, Brecht's strongest sympathies indeed lay with the Party.

Except for *Turandot, or The Congress of Whitewashers* (which was based on a novel he had worked on intermittently for two decades but never completed), Brecht did no new plays for the Berliner Ensemble. He satisfied himself with productions of his own works written in exile and with adaptations of the work of other playwrights. Among the latter were *The Days of the Commune* (after Nordahl Grieg's *The Defeat*), *Drums and Trumpets* (based on Richard Brinsley Sheridan's *The Recruiting Officer*), *The Trial of Joan of Arc in Rouen, 1431* (a staging of Anna Seghers's radio play of the same title), and Gerhart Hauptmann's *The Beaver Coat*. Some of these adaptations were sufficiently free that they could rightly be counted among his own works. Some of them were not. The Ensemble continued to attract audiences but came to be given indifferent treatment by the East German press. It became clear that the official attitude toward Brecht's theatrical experiments was to permit them but ignore them. But if he and the Berliner Ensemble were without much honor in their own land, they received a considerable amount of it abroad. Critics visited from the West and came away ecstatic. Even though there was an informal ban on performances of his plays in West Germany for three years, his works continued to be published there by Suhrkamp; and they were performed in other West European countries and in America as well. In 1954 the Berliner Ensemble and Helene Weigel enjoyed a great triumph in Paris with performances of *Mother Courage and Her Children*. It was all that was needed to establish Brecht, his wife, and his company firmly in the international postwar world of the theater. He, however, was not present in Paris. He was too ill to make the trip.

His health was not good, but he worked to the end. During rehearsals of *The Caucasian Chalk Circle* in the summer of 1956 he was so weak that he could not yell at the actors onstage as he usually did from the orchestra seats, and so he had a microphone set up so that he could register his muted criticisms. As his voice came— tinny, amplified, and disembodied—one of the actresses remarked prophetically that he sounded as though he were speaking from a coffin. Suffering from severe aftereffects of a bout with influenza, he had arranged to go off to a private hospital in Munich to effect a complete cure, but when he was set to leave—on August 14, 1956—he had a heart attack. He died that very day. He had chosen his gravesite in a cemetery practically under the window of the apartment that he kept in Berlin, and had specified that he be buried in a zinc coffin. He had even written an epitaph for himself:

> Here, in this zinc box
> Lies a dead person
> Or his legs and his head
> Or even less of him
> Or nothing, for he was
> A trouble-maker.[15]

· · ·

As he was to the FBI during his stay in America, Bertolt Brecht was of considerable interest to the CIA once he had returned to Europe. In fact, the Agency's wartime predecessor, the OSS, had begun keeping tabs on him as a member of German émigré political groups while he was still in America. Nearly all the early items in his CIA file (which I obtained under the Freedom of Information Act) have to do with this aspect of his activities and for the most part are duplicated in his FBI file with the same sort of silly errors: his name is often misspelled; he is listed as a "composer" and as "unmarried." It is interesting to keep in mind that Herbert Marcuse, who was an acquaintance, if not a friend, of Brecht's, would almost certainly have been a reader and evaluator of this and later information; it is curious that he did not feel called upon to correct the errors in it.

If anything, in Europe Brecht was of even greater interest to the American intelligence community. He had barely arrived when, on December 19, 1947, a CIA station chief sent a memo by pouch to Washington—subject, "Berthold Brecht":

> We are reluctant to ask [*name deleted but obviously an agent in the field*] to report to us on subject's movements inasmuch as we are trying to drop all contacts with him. Since subject's movements will probably be reported in the press, we feel that it is unnecessary to try to obtain information clandestinely.

One month later to the day, CIA Washington responded by wire: "In view possibility Brecht's movements not overt knowledge, and due great interest, request you implement Paragraph 2." Whatever "Paragraph 2" might be, this is obviously an order to continue clandestine observation of Bertolt Brecht.

Giving the Agency the benefit of the doubt, it is nevertheless true that most of what was subsequently sent back to Washington from the field *could* have been gathered from a careful reading of the press. One long report dated April 30, 1949, for instance, is headed, "Some Indications of Communist Penetration of the Bavarian Theater," and it details the success of the first Munich production of *Herr Puntila and His Man Matti* and the interest taken in Brecht and his work by the local press and radio. The unstated fear seems to be that Brecht will make a permanent move to Munich and from there manage somehow to infect all of Western Europe with his brand of Marxist poison—thus the urgent wire sent from CIA headquarters in Washington over a year later on September 11, 1950: "Rumor circulating Brln claims Bert Brecht in Munich to stay. Pls question [name deleted] and advise."

Apart from periodic updates on Brecht's activities and position in East Berlin, there is little else of note in the file until after his death.* What is missing is any sort of comment or advisory on Brecht's overt or covert attitude toward the events of June 17, 1953. If he was important enough to be given clandestine attention, there should have been some interest in whether he did or didn't support the government of the GDR against the workers—especially since this very question was mooted so earnestly in a magazine later revealed to be subsidized by the CIA. Of course it may be that the pertinent documents were among those (eighteen in all) that the CIA has deemed unreleasable for various reasons. It may also be that information on Brecht's position with regard to June 17, 1953, was communicated from the CIA to somebody associated with the magazine *Encounter* (which had ties to the Agency). That may be how Martin Esslin came to "state with absolute certainty" that Brecht's "message of loyalty"

---

* For some reason the CIA seems to have taken quite an interest in Brecht's son, Stefan (who is and was then an American citizen), and a couple of documents in the file have more to do with him than with his father.

to Ulbricht was only the last sentence of a critical letter. The Agency certainly seems to have been aware of the existence of this letter and other such material. On December 14, 1960—four years after Brecht's death—a CIA station chief sent the following cable to Washington:

> 1. In Aug 1960 Helene Weigel widow of Berthold [*sic*] Brecht announced in East German cultural circles her intention to allow publication of Brecht works on 17 June 1953 revolt which are unpublished and damaging to S.E.D. regime. Weigel was finally dissuaded by senior East German culture officials in exchange for promise of extensive financial support for Brecht archives in East Berlin. Unpublished works allegedly still remain in Weigel's possession in spite of repeated efforts East German culture functionaries to obtain full control of Brecht estate.
>
> 2. REF [*presumably a CIA informant*] describes developing contact between [name deleted] and Weigel. In view planned termination, [name deleted] request approval for him discuss this Brecht material with Weigel. He would state that he acting in behalf of West German publishing agent wishing to review material for publication in West. . . .

The rest of the communication is so patched with deletions that it is largely incomprehensible—as is the Agency's reply, dated January 31, 1961:

> 1. [*Paragraph deleted.*]
> 2. [*Paragraph deleted.*]
> 3. [*First part of sentence deleted*], since the East German authorities are anxious to assume full control over the Brecht estate [presumably to preclude publication of anything that might detract from the symbol that their propaganda has made of Brecht].

This *seems* like a go-ahead from CIA headquarters to make the proposed visit to Helene Weigel—but then, your guess is as good as mine. In any case, the only material by Brecht dealing directly with the East German workers' revolt that has so far seen print was published both in the East and West through the normal channels.

. • .

If, in 1960, Helene Weigel bargained with officials of the German Democratic Republic for the establishment of a Brecht archive, it must have been evident even then to those on both sides of the table that his influence as a writer and a man of the theater would last well into the future. It has lasted, of course, and there is certainly some evidence that it will continue. In fact, Max Frisch may well have been right when, as early as 1964, he said that Brecht had achieved "the penetrating ineffectiveness of a classic." What he meant was that Brecht had become so widely accepted on stages around the world that his works had lost the power to shock, annoy, anger—and, therefore, also the power to instruct.

Brecht's influence in America has been profound. Yet it should be understood that he has never enjoyed real popular success here. In spite of the years in America trying, he never managed a hit on Broadway—nor did he have better luck in absentia or posthumously. Broadway has always been beyond him, or beneath—or someplace, anyway, other than where he was. This is not to say that he has not had success in New York. A production of *The Threepenny Opera*, starring Lotte Lenya in the Pirate Jenny role she had created in Berlin, opened Off Broadway at the Theatre de Lys in Greenwich Village on March 10, 1954. It received a rave review from Brooks Atkinson, theater critic for *The New York Times*,* played the twelve weeks that had been allotted for it at the de Lys, then left to make room for the next booking. Atkinson agitated for its return. Finally, on September 20, 1955, it did come back and did not close until December 17, 1961. At 2,611 performances it was the longest-running musical in the history of the American theater up to that time. The only other unqualified success Brecht has had in New York came again with *The Threepenny Opera*—the New York Shakespeare Festival's production at Lincoln Center, which was presented in limited run as part of the regular 1975–1976 season. Whether it was the new translation of the play by Ralph Manheim and John Willett, or

---

* Remember that he had roundly panned the 1947 production of Brecht's *Galileo*, starring Charles Laughton.

whether it was the free hand in cutting exercised by director John Foreman, or whether it was simply Raul Julia's riveting performance as Mack the Knife—no matter what it was, this Brecht production connected with critics and audiences alike, as many before it and a few since have not.

For the most part, Brecht's influence in this country has been achieved through regional theaters and university stages. He has been, and still is, very popular with actors, directors, and drama-department people in this country—if sometimes for what Brecht himself might have judged to be the wrong reasons. To them, and to the German scholars who give them strategic support, Brecht has become the modern classic author *par excellence*—one whose most casual effort deserves classic status and treatment simply because he, whose greatness has been accepted, happened to write the thing. (According to this attitude it is possible to take inferior work such as *Baal* and *The Resistible Rise of Arturo Ui* with the same seriousness you might *Mother Courage* or *The Good Woman of Setzuan*.) A vast Brecht industry has been built up, mass-producing monographs and papers, banging out books, even bringing branch managers together with research and development personnel at the annual Congress of the International Brecht Society. The Brecht industry, self-activating and self-sustaining, is a kind of intellectual equivalent of the old perpetual-motion machines of the nineteenth century, whose sole function was to maintain their own movement.

In Germany, both East and West, Brecht's fate has been much different. Following his death in 1956, Helene Weigel held the Berliner Ensemble together with a tight hand, keeping standards of performance high without altering the essentially experimental nature of their work. When she died in 1971 the company was soon riven by strife. Its leading director, Manfred Wekwerth, left, and Ruth Berghaus, whose training was in opera, took over management of the company. Also out were Ekkehard Schall, the Ensemble's leading actor, and his wife, Barbara, Brecht's daughter. And so, for a time at least, the family chain was broken. Never mind that that rift was eventually patched over; the Berliner Ensemble has never been the same since.

In the West, Brecht has always had a greater following. On the seventieth anniversary of Brecht's birth, his publisher, Suhrkamp Verlag, announced that since 1950 there had been 15,920 performances of his plays in West Germany, Austria, and German Switzerland that had drawn audiences of no less than 7.9 million—third only to Schiller and Shakespeare! That, however, was in 1968. Since then, although Brecht's plays continue to be popular with German-speaking audiences in the West, they no longer draw the critical response they once did, nor do they seem to have the importance they previously did to the theatrical community. Brecht's Epic Theater theories had won many adherents in the West; for a while he was both a "classic" and, antithetically, the chief avant-garde influence upon the German stage. Now, no more. He is acknowledged by many directors, actors, and playwrights as an important influence, but one that they have now superseded. The Austrian playwright Peter Handke, for example, has dismissed Brecht's theatrical parables as political "fairy tales" and in general has attacked him as a reactionary force in the German theater. (To Handke, whose antidramatic monologue plays are so dependent upon the audience's indulgence, even Brecht's works might indeed seem to be old-fashioned and excessively accommodating.) But some critics agree with him; and, even more important, the attitude of the best and most active of the young directors in the German-speaking West (a couple of whom are Berliner Ensemble-trained) is one of polite indifference—at best—toward Brecht. *They* are tired of Brecht, even if as yet the audiences are not.

Bertolt Brecht, always the political artist, was first persecuted and later rewarded because of his politics. Due to his outspoken advocacy of Marxism in his works, he was forced to leave Germany in 1933 and go into exile for the duration of the Nazi domination. He left America in 1947, fearing that the whole scenario was about to be repeated, after he had been called before the House Committee on Un-American Activities and questioned closely on the extent of his involvement with the Communist Party and its influence on his work. It was, after all, because of his involvement with the Communist Party and the influence it had had on his work since 1930 that he was invited to East Berlin and given a theater company of his own. Even after he was thus established, his reputation was affected by the Cold War: during his lifetime there was an unofficial boycott of his work in the West because of his published expression of loyalty to the East German Communist Party at the time of the workers' revolt of 1953. After his death, too—at the time of the building of the Berlin Wall in 1961, and of the Russian invasion of Czechoslovakia—performances and productions of Brecht's plays were canceled in West Germany and Austria as an expression of protest against Communist oppression.

By and large, however, Brecht's reputation has benefited from his political identification. Even in the German Democratic Republic, where in his lifetime his works were widely regarded as "Formalist," he is now officially exalted as a "Classic of Socialist Realism" (which, of course, is pure doublethink). In America, especially during the sixties and early seventies, when Brecht was firmly established here, an enthusiasm for his work became a kind of badge of radicalism, a sign that you favored free speech, opposed the war in Vietnam and the Nixon administration. He was at least part of the package—and at the most, to some, a touchstone of radical authenticity.

In West Germany, which went through a briefer radical cycle, though one that was in some ways just as intense, there is some evidence that interest in his work is declining. That is a healthy sign, because for the first time attitudes toward his work by critics and theater people seem not to be motivated by political considerations. Instead, Brecht is falling victim to the age-old antagonism of the younger generation and to the neglect of those who feel he is just one playwright among many to learn from, one theatrical theorist of several whose ideas must be considered. And so, at least for a time, Brecht's reputation may go into decline in Germany—perhaps in America and all over the West as well. Let it. For it is only when that reputation has been depoliticized that his work can be properly considered and evaluated for what it is. Only then will we know how great a playwright he really was, or wasn't.

Notes

PROLOGUE:
FIVE DIFFICULTIES IN WRITING ABOUT BRECHT

1 Bertolt Brecht, *Gesammelte Werke* [*Collected Works*] (Frankfurt am Main: Suhrkamp, 1967), vol. 3, p. 222. (Unless otherwise indicated, all citations from Brecht's published works are taken from this German edition, translation by the author.)

2 Martin Esslin, *Reflections: Essays on Modern Theatre* (Garden City, New York: Doubleday, 1969), p. 61.

3 Bertolt Brecht, *Poems 1913–1956*, ed. John Willett, Ralph Manheim et al. (New York: Methuen, 1976), p. 152.

4 Ronald Gray, *Brecht: The Dramatist* (Cambridge: Cambridge University Press, 1976), p. 53.

5 U.S. Congress, House of Representatives, Committee on Un-American Activities, *Hearings Regarding the Communist Infiltration of the Motion Picture Industry*, 80th Congress, 1st sess., October 30, 1947, pp. 496–97.

6 Bernhard Reich, "Erinnerungen an den Jungen Brecht," *Sinn und Form* (Berlin: Rutten and Loening, 1957), pp. 434–35.

7 Siegfried Unseld, *The Author and His Publisher*, trans. Hunter and Hildegarde Hannum (Chicago: University of Chicago Press, 1978), p. 102.

8 Martin Esslin, *Brecht: The Man and His Work* (Garden City, New York: Doubleday, 1960), p. 200.

9 Klaus Völker, *Brecht: A Biography*, trans. John Nowell (New York: Seabury, 1978), pp. 239–40.

10 Ruth Fischer, *Stalin and German Communism* (Cambridge, Mass.: Harvard University Press, 1948), p. 615.

11 Gerhard Szczesny, *The Case Against Bertolt Brecht*, trans. Alexander Gode (New York: Frederick Ungar, 1969), p. 44.

12 Bertolt Brecht, *Schriften zum Theater* (Frankfurt am Main: Suhrkamp, 1957), pp. 285–86.

13 Eric Bentley, *Theatre of War* (New York: Viking, 1972), p. 114.

14 Esslin, *Brecht: The Man and His Work*, p. 86.

1: ARRIVALS AND DEPARTURES

1 Interview with Gina Kaus, February 1977.

2 According to Christopher Isherwood, interviewed February 1977.

3 Bertolt Brecht, *Gesammelte Werke [Collected Works]* (Frankfurt am Main: Suhrkamp, 1967), vol. 9, p. 539.

4 John Lehmann, *The Whispering Gallery.*

5 According to Albert Maltz, interviewed July 1973.

6 Ibid.

7 Hy Kraft, *On My Way to the Theater* (New York: Macmillan, 1971), p. 147.

8 Bertolt Brecht, *Poems 1913–1956*, ed. John Willett, Ralph Manheim et al. (New York: Methuen, 1976), p. 260.

9 Walter Benjamin, *Understanding Brecht*, trans. Anna Bostock (London: New Left Books, 1976), p. 116.

10 Ibid., pp. 117–18.

11 Ibid., p. 120.

12 Ibid., p. 121.

13 Bertolt Brecht, *Arbeitsjournal [Work Journal], 1938 bis 1955* (Frankfurt am Main: Suhrkamp, 1973), January 1, 1940, p. 59. (All translations from the *Arbeitsjournal* are by the author.)

14 Ibid., June 11, 1940, p. 79.

15 Ibid., September 16, 1940, p. 134.

16 The following story is related again, with other details, on pages 152–53.

17 Brecht, *Poems 1913–1956*, p. 363.

2: WHY HOLLYWOOD?

1 Bertolt Brecht, *Arbeitsjournal [Work Journal], 1938 bis 1955* (Frankfurt am Main: Suhrkamp, 1973), August 1, 1941, p. 210.

2 Ibid., November 1, 1941, p. 224.

3 Ibid., July 22, 1941, p. 209.

4 James K. Lyon, *Bertolt Brecht in America* (Princeton, N.J.: Princeton University Press, 1980).

5 Brecht, *Arbeitsjournal*, October 4, 1941, p. 214.

6 Werner Hecht, ed., "Brecht und der Film," in *Brecht 73* (Berlin: Henschelverlag, 1973), p. 262.

7 Margot Resch, "Brecht's Concerns in Early Film" (Paper delivered at Brecht Congress, Austin, Texas, 1976).

8 Bertolt Brecht, *Diaries 1920–1922*, trans. John Willett, ed. Herta Ramthun (New York: St. Martin's, 1979), p. 7.

9 Ibid., p. 18.

10 Ibid., p. 13.

11 Wolfgang Gersch, *Film bei Brecht* (Berlin: Henschelverlag, 1975), p. 27.

12 Arnolt Bronnen, *Arnolt Bronnen gibt zu Protokoll* (Hamburg: Rowohlt, 1954).

13 Gersch, *Film bei Brecht*, p. 13.

14 Bertolt Brecht, *Texte für Filme* (Frankfurt am Main: Suhrkamp, 1969), p. 343.

15 Bertolt Brecht, *Kuhle Wampe* (Frankfurt am Main: Suhrkamp, 1969), pp. 93–94.

16 Gersch, *Film bei Brecht*, p. 184.

3: WHICH WAY TO DOHENY?

1 Katia Mann, *Unwritten Memories*, trans. Hunter and Hildegarde Hannum, ed. Elizabeth Plessen and Michael Mann (New York: Knopf, 1975), p. 126.

2 Hanns Eisler, *Brecht: As They Knew Him* (New York: International Publishers, 1974), p. 94.

3 Ibid.

4 H. Stuart Hughes, *The Sea Change* (New York: Harper & Row, 1975), p. 151.

5 Lion Feuchtwanger, *Success*, trans. Willa and Edwin Muir (New York: Viking, 1930), p. 66.

6 Bertolt Brecht, *Arbeitsjournal [Work Journal], 1938 bis 1955* (Frankfurt am Main: Suhrkamp, 1973), July 22, 1941, p. 209.

7 Katia Mann, *Unwritten Memories*, p. 94.

8 Interview with Marthe Feuchtwanger, February 1977.

9 Katia Mann, *Unwritten Memories*, p. 128.

10 Hughes, *The Sea Change*, p. 169.

4: BRECHT AND FRITZ LANG

1 Bertolt Brecht, *Poems 1913–1956*, ed. John Willett, Ralph Manheim et al. (New York: Methuen, 1976), p. 382.

2 Bertolt Brecht, *Arbeitsjournal [Work Journal], 1938 bis 1955* (Frankfurt am Main: Suhrkamp, 1973), March 15, 1942, p. 285.

3 Interview with Arch Oboler, March 1977.

4 Brecht, *Arbeitsjournal*, March 29, 1942, p. 281.

5 Brecht, *Arbeitsjournal*, April 11, 1942, p. 285.
6 Brecht, *Arbeitsjournal*, June 5, 1942.
7 Lotte H. Eisner, *Fritz Lang* (New York: Oxford University Press, 1977), p. 131.
8 Gavin Lambert, "Fritz Lang's America," *Sight and Sound*, Summer 1955, p. 16.
9 Quoted in Eisner, *Fritz Lang*, p. 116.
10 Peter Bogdanovich, *Fritz Lang in America* (New York: Praeger, 1967), p. 38.
11 Eisner, *Fritz Lang*, p. 194.
12 Interview with Lily Laté, February 1977.
13 Wolfgang Gersch, *Film bei Brecht* (Berlin: Henschelverlag, 1975), p. 200.
14 Brecht, *Arbeitsjournal*, June 29, 1942, p. 319.
15 Bogdanovich, *Fritz Lang in America*, p. 60.
16 Brecht, *Arbeitsjournal*, August 5, 1942, p. 331.
17 Ibid., September 14, 1942, p. 342.
18 Ibid., October 16, 1942, pp. 344–45.
19 Ibid., November 15, 1942, p. 354.
20 Bogdanovich, *Fritz Lang in America*, p. 60.
21 Interview with John Wexley, November 1977.
22 Bogdanovich, *Fritz Lang in America*, p. 83.
23 Interview with John Wexley, November 1977.

5: SUNDAYS IN MABERY ROAD

1 Salka Viertel, *The Kindness of Strangers* (New York: Holt, Rinehart and Winston, 1969), p. 132.
2 Christopher Isherwood, *Prater Violet* (New York: Random House, 1945), pp. 16–17.
3 Christopher Isherwood, *Christopher and His Kind, 1929–1939* (New York: Farrar, Straus & Giroux, 1976), p. 155.
4 Sybille Bedford, *Aldous Huxley: A Biography* (New York: Knopf/Harper & Row), p. 402.
5 Ibid., p. 406.
6 Interview with Peter Viertel, February 1977.
7 Bertolt Brecht, *Poems 1913–1956*, ed. John Willett, Ralph Manheim et al. (New York: Methuen, 1976), p. 392.
8 Interview with Mel Frank, February 1977.
9 Interview with Hans Viertel, March 1977.
10 Ibid.
11 Vladimir Pozner, "bb," in *Sinn und Form* (Berlin: Rutten and Loening, 1957), p. 448.

6: BRECHT AND THE BROTHERS MANN

1 Nigel Hamilton, *The Brothers Mann* (New Haven: Yale University Press, 1979), p. 23.

2 Kurt Pinthus, "Leipzig and Early Expressionism," in Paul Raabe, ed., *The Era of German Expressionism* (Woodstock, N.Y.: Overlook, 1974), p. 73.

3 Bertolt Brecht, *Gesammelte Werke* [*Collected Works*] (Frankfurt am Main: Suhrkamp, 1967), vol. 19, p. 470.

4 Thomas Mann, "German Letter," *The Dial*, November 1924, pp. 417–18.

5 Brecht, *Gesammelte Werke*, vol. 18, p. 49.

6 Katia Mann, *Unwritten Memories*, trans. Hunter and Hildegarde Hannum, ed. Elizabeth Plessen and Michael Mann (New York: Knopf, 1975), pp. 127–28.

7 Bertolt Brecht, *Poems 1913–1956*, ed. John Willett, Ralph Manheim et al. (New York: Methuen, 1976), p. 198.

8 Thomas Mann, *Order of the Day: Political Speeches of Two Decades*, trans. H. T. Lowe-Porter, Agnes E. Meyer, and Eric Sutton (New York: Knopf, 1943), p. 178.

9 David Caute, *The Fellow-Travellers* (New York: Macmillan, 1973), p. 151.

10 Brecht, *Gesammelte Werke*, vol. 19, pp. 476–77.

11 Katia Mann, *Unwritten Memories*, pp. 89–90.

12 Hamilton, *The Brothers Mann*, p. 273.

13 Hermann Kesten, *Deutsche Literatur im Exil* (Vienna: Desch, 1964), p. 193.

14 Salka Viertel, *The Kindness of Strangers* (New York: Holt, Rinehart and Winston, 1969), p. 251.

15 Brecht, *Arbeitsjournal*, December 12, 1941, pp. 231–32.

16 James K. Lyon, *Bertolt Brecht in America* (Princeton, N.J.: Princeton University Press, 1980), p. 264.

17 Interview with Marthe Feuchtwanger, February 1977.

18 Brecht, *Gesammelte Werke*, vol. 19, pp. 479–80.

19 Thomas Mann, *The Story of a Novel* (New York: Knopf, 1961), p. 65.

7: BRECHT AND KURT WEILL

1 Bertolt Brecht, *Arbeitsjournal* [*Work Journal*], *1938 bis 1955* (Frankfurt am Main: Suhrkamp, 1973), February 12, 1943, p. 368.

2 Ibid., October 20, 1941, p. 218.

3 James K. Lyon, *Bertolt Brecht in America* (Princeton, N.J.: Princeton University Press, 1980), p. 23.

4 Brecht, *Arbeitsjournal*, March, April, May 1943 (Summary), p. 370.

5 Ronald Sanders, *The Days Grow Short* (New York: Holt, Rinehart and Winston, 1980), p. 146.

6 Ibid., p. 148.

7 Brecht, *Arbeitsjournal*, April 15, 1942, p. 286.

8 Quoted in Sanders, *The Days Grow Short*, p. 219.

9 Brecht, *Arbeitsjournal*, March, April, May 1943 (Summary), p. 370.

10 Ibid., June 28, 1943, p. 376.

11 Allan Kozinn, "Kurt Weill, A Composer for Our Times," *Ovation*, July 1981, p. 22.

12 Brecht, *Arbeitsjournal*, Mid-November 1943 to Mid-March 1944 (Summary), pp. 410–11.

13 Ibid., June 6, 1944, p. 420.

8: BRECHT AND HIS WOMEN

1 John Houseman, *Front and Center* (New York: Simon and Schuster, 1979), p. 237.

2 Interview with Albert Maltz, July 1973.

3 James K. Lyon, *Bertolt Brecht in America* (Princeton, N.J.: Princeton University Press, 1980), p. 225.

4 Bertolt Brecht, *Poems 1913–1956*, ed. John Willett, Ralph Manheim et al. (New York: Methuen, 1976), p. 35.

5 Ibid., p. 41.

6 Bertolt Brecht, *Diaries 1920–1922*, trans. John Willett, ed. Herta Ramthun (New York: St. Martin's, 1979), p. 43.

7 Bertolt Brecht, *Collected Plays*, ed. Ralph Manheim and John Willett, vol. 1 (New York: Pantheon, 1960), p. 4.

8 Ibid., p. 11.

9 Klaus Völker, *Brecht: A Biography*, trans. John Nowell (New York: Seabury, 1978), p. 88.

10 Interview with Gina Kaus, February 1977.

11 Ibid.

12 Brecht, *Poems 1913–1956*, p. 277.

13 Ibid.

14 Bertolt Brecht, *Arbeitsjournal* [*Work Journal*], *1938 bis 1955* (Frankfurt am Main: Suhrkamp, 1973), July 13, 1941, p. 205.

15 Houseman, *Front and Center*, p. 238.

16 Ibid., pp. 238–39.

17 Interview with Hans Viertel, March 1977.

18 Houseman, *Front and Center*, p. 238.

19 "Brecht in Hollywood," Radio Broadcast by Pacifica Foundation radio station KPFK, Los Angeles, May 1963.

20 Interview with Marthe Feuchtwanger, February 1977.

21 Bertolt Brecht, *Collected Plays*, ed. Ralph Manheim and John Willett, vol. 6 (New York: Random House, 1976), p. 23.

22 Ibid., pp. 96–97.

23 Ibid., p. 100.
24 Ibid., p. 102.
25 Ibid., p. 103.
26 Bertolt Brecht, *Collected Plays*, ed. Ralph Manheim and John Willett, vol. 7 (New York: Random House, 1976), p. 227.
27 Völker, *Brecht: A Biography*, p. 349.
28 Interview with Hans Viertel, March 1977.

9: GALILEO IN HOLLYWOOD

1 Quoted in Igor Stravinsky and Robert Kraft, *Themes and Episodes* (New York: Knopf, 1966), p. 75.
2 Bertolt Brecht, *Poems 1913–1956*, ed. John Willett, Ralph Manheim et al. (New York: Methuen, 1976), p. 397.
3 James K. Lyon, *Bertolt Brecht in America* (Princeton, N.J.: Princeton University Press, 1980), p. 168.
4 Bertolt Brecht, *Brecht on Theatre*, trans. John Willett (New York: Hill and Wang, 1964), p. 166.
5 Ibid., pp. 165–66.
6 John Houseman, *Front and Center* (New York: Simon and Schuster, 1979), p. 232.
7 Interview with John Houseman, June 1977.
8 Ibid.
9 Ibid.
10 Interview with Frances Heflin, September 1976.
11 Interview with John Houseman, June 1977.
12 Brecht, *Brecht on Theatre*, p. 168.
13 Interview with Frances Heflin, September 1976.
14 *Los Angeles Examiner*, July 31, 1947.
15 *Los Angeles Times*, July 31, 1947.
16 *Los Angeles Daily News*, July 31, 1947.
17 Eric Bentley, "The Science Fiction of Bertolt Brecht," Introduction to Bertolt Brecht, *Galileo* (New York: Grove, 1966), pp. 9–42.
18 Quoted in Frederic Ewen, *Bertolt Brecht: His Life, His Art, and His Times* (New York: Citadel, 1967), p. 332.
19 Bertolt Brecht, *Gesammelte Werke* [*Collected Works*] (Frankfurt am Main: Suhrkamp, 1967), vol. 17, pp. 1106–09.
20 Brecht, *Galileo*, p. 115.
21 Ibid., p. 121.
22 Ibid., p. 122.
23 Ibid., p. 124.
24 Interview with John Houseman, June 1977.
25 Interview with Sol Kaplan, September 1976.

10: THE HOLLYWOOD ELEVENTH

1 Interview with Sol Kaplan, September 1976.

2 U.S. Congress, House of Representatives, Committee on Un-American Activities, *Hearings Regarding the Communist Infiltration of the Motion Picture Industry*, 80th Congress, 1st sess., October 30, 1947, p. 331.

3 Ibid., p. 334.

4 Ibid., p. 482.

5 Ibid., p. 493.

6 Ibid.

7 Ibid., p. 494.

8 Ibid., p. 497.

9 Ibid., p. 504.

10 Ibid., pp. 502–03

11 Ibid., p. 503.

12 Ibid., p. 504.

13 Interview with Lester Cole, September 1974.

14 Bertolt Brecht, *Arbeitsjournal* [*Work Journal*], *1938 bis 1955* (Frankfurt am Main: Suhrkamp, 1973), October 30, 1947, p. 491.

11: THE RETURN OF THE EXILE

1 Bertolt Brecht, *Arbeitsjournal* [*Work Journal*], *1938 bis 1955* (Frankfurt am Main: Suhrkamp, 1973), November 1, 1947, p. 492.

2 Ibid., November 4, 1947, p. 492.

3 Klaus Völker, *Brecht: A Biography*, trans. John Nowell (New York; Seabury, 1978), p. 327.

4 Max Frisch, *Sketchbook 1946–1949* (New York: Harcourt Brace Jovanovich, 1977), p. 200.

5 Max Frisch, *Sketchbook 1966–1971* (New York: Harcourt Brace Jovanovich, 1974), p. 23.

6 Ibid., p. 24.

7 Ibid., p. 22.

8 Ibid., pp. 26–27.

9 Ibid., p. 23.

10 Brecht, *Arbeitsjournal*, November 6, 1948, p. 530.

11 Ibid., January 11, 1949.

12 Bertolt Brecht, *Poems 1913–1956*, ed. John Willett, Ralph Manheim et al. (New York: Methuen, 1976), p. 439.

13 Ibid., p. 440.

14 Brecht, *Arbeitsjournal*, August 20, 1953, p. 597.

15 Brecht, *Poems 1913–1956*, p. 216.

INDEX